## DEDICATION

*To the "Home Office" — who made our Japan assignment possible.*

*To Wife Sarah and the kids — who made it bearable.*

*And to the Japanese people — who have given us the most fascinating years of our lives.*

Don Maloney

# Japan:  It's Not All Raw Fish

The **Japan Times**, Ltd.

First edition:    April 1975
12th printing:    April 1980

Library of Congress Catalog Card Number: 75-319087

Cover and art work:    Koji Detake

Published by

**The Japan Times, Ltd.**

5-4, Shibaura 4-chome, Minato-ku,
Tokyo, 108, Japan

Printed in Japan

# CONTENTS

FOREWORD by John Roderick ........................ 8
PREFACE ............................................ 10

I. THE LANGUAGE................................. 12
DO YOU UNDERSTAND? ........................... 14
A RIDDLE RANGUAGE GOES A WRONG WAY........ 15
TAKE MY WORD FOR IT........................... 17
OUT OF GAS..................................... 19
OUT OF GAS — AGAIN............................ 22
MAYBE WE'RE GETTING A NEW CAR............... 23
YES, WE HAVE NO BANANAS...................... 25
WHAT YOU SHOULD KNOW ABOUT "NO"........... 27

II. TRAVEL ....................................... 30
GETTING THERE IS *ALL* THE FUN ................. 32
OBENTOS, CUCUMBERS AND ALL.................... 34
SO *THAT'S* WHAT HE'S TALKING ABOUT............ 36
AN INVITATION TO BREAKFAST .................... 38
FASTEN SEAT BELTS ............................. 40
IT'S OFFICIAL: TOKYO TAXI DRIVERS ARE "CHOOSY" . . 42
YOU'VE BEEN WRONG ABOUT TAXIS................ 44
I FELT BETTER WITH THE PAPER .................. 46
NEVER THE PLANE, EITHER........................ 48
THE QUAINT CUSTOMS OF JAPAN .................. 51
WHO'S SORRY NOW? .............................. 53
THERE'S SOMEPLACE LIKE HOME................... 55
SOME SECOND THOUGHTS ......................... 57

III. HOME LIFE ................................... 60
THEY SPELL IT ALL OUT — OR DO THEY?........... 62
OPEN HOUSE ..................................... 64
EVERYBODY, IT TURNS OUT, HAS A GATE .......... 66
THE DAY THE TOILET PAPER RAN OUT.............. 67
YOU MAY HAVE ALREADY WON — OR LOST ......... 69
SAYONARA, KAMIKITAZAWA........................ 71
I HOPE NOTHING HAPPENED TO YAMAMOTO SAN..... 73
ALL GAIJINS HAVE FUNNY NAMES.................. 75
TO SLURP OR NOT TO SLURP? ..................... 77
COOL IT, YOU "IRATE FOREIGNERS".................. 79
LOVE IT OR LEAVE IT............................. 81

IV.  SOCIAL LIFE. . . . . . . . . . . . . . . . . . . . . . . . . . . . . . 84
   NOTHING TO DO . . . . . . . . . . . . . . . . . . . . . . . . . . 86
   THE PLEASURE OF YOUR COMPANY . . . . . . . . . . . . . 87
   OH, HOW THE TOKYO SOCIAL WHIRL GOES ON! . . . . . . . 89
   VISITING FIREMEN. . . . . . . . . . . . . . . . . . . . . . . . . 91
   ALL THAT FOR ¥100 . . . . . . . . . . . . . . . . . . . . . 93
   IT'S ALL THERE IN BLACK AND WHITE. . . . . . . . . . . . 95
   IT REALLY *WAS* A BASEBALL GAME! . . . . . . . . . . . . 97
   FIRST DOWN, 10,000 MILES TO GO . . . . . . . . . . . . 100
   PARLOR GAME, AZABU STYLE . . . . . . . . . . . . . . . . . 101

V.  COST OF LIVING — AND LEAVING . . . . . . . . . . 104
   CALL ME A TAXI. . . . . . . . . . . . . . . . . . . . . . . . . . 106
   A PERFECT DAY, MITI STYLE . . . . . . . . . . . . . . . . . 107
   THE BIG BARGAIN SALE. . . . . . . . . . . . . . . . . . . . 109
   EAT 'EM AND BEAT 'EM . . . . . . . . . . . . . . . . . . . 111
   SOUR GRAPES. . . . . . . . . . . . . . . . . . . . . . . . . . . 113
   NOT EVEN HONORABLE MENTION. . . . . . . . . . . . . . 115
   ALL THIS, PLUS:  IT'S OK TO DRINK THE WATER . . . . . . 118
   *THAT'S* WHAT I'VE BEEN TRYING TO TELL THEM . . . . . 120
   THE HIGH COST OF LEAVING . . . . . . . . . . . . . . . . . 122
   BACK TO THE $5,000 ELECTRIC FRYING PAN . . . . . . . . . 123

VI.  ECOLOGY . . . . . . . . . . . . . . . . . . . . . . . . . . . . . 126
   GINZA GOMI . . . . . . . . . . . . . . . . . . . . . . . . . . . 128
   THE GROSSEST NATIONAL PRODUCT. . . . . . . . . . . . 129
   RANCID TRANSIT . . . . . . . . . . . . . . . . . . . . . . . . 131
   RULES ARE RULES . . . . . . . . . . . . . . . . . . . . . . . 133
   IT SOUNDS FISHY TO ME . . . . . . . . . . . . . . . . . . . 135
   NOW HEAR THIS. . . . . . . . . . . . . . . . . . . . . . . . . 138
   IT WAS ONLY AN EARTHQUAKE . . . . . . . . . . . . . . . 140
   NOBODY WILL BE HERE TOMORROW. . . . . . . . . . . . 142
   YOUR LIFE JACKET IS UNDER YOUR SEAT . . . . . . . . . 144

VII.  HOME LEAVE. . . . . . . . . . . . . . . . . . . . . . . . . . 148
   THE HOMECOMING. . . . . . . . . . . . . . . . . . . . . . . 150
   IT'S STILL PARADISE. . . . . . . . . . . . . . . . . . . . . . . 152
   SET YOUR WATCHES BACK . . . . . . . . . . . . . . . . . . 154
   HOME SWEET HOME — OFFICE. . . . . . . . . . . . . . . . 155
   RETURN TO THE WOMB. . . . . . . . . . . . . . . . . . . . 157
   STRANGER IN PARADISE. . . . . . . . . . . . . . . . . . . . 159
   PLEASE PASS THE SUSHI. . . . . . . . . . . . . . . . . . . . 161

**VIII. THE HOLIDAYS**............................ 164
  CHRISTMAS, IT WASN'T ......................... 166
  THE SIPPING O' THE GREEN .................... 167
  MERRY CHRISTMAS................................. 169
  'TWAS THE PLIGHT BEFORE CHRISTMAS ........... 172
  SLOW BURN....................................... 173
  OVER THE RIVER AND THROUGH·THE WOODS...... 175
  JUST MENTION MY NAME IN HOSOYA ............. 178
  SWEET AND SOUR CHRISTMAS .................... 180
  'TIS THE SEASON TO GOMENNASAI................. 182
  FUN CITY — FOR FIVE DAYS...................... 184
  SLOW TRAIN TO AKITA .......................... 186

**IX. THE REAL JAPAN**........................... 190
  THE INN THING TO DO .......................... 192
  SAKURA, SAKURA — OUR VERY OWN SAKURA....... 194
  THE *REAL* REAL JAPAN ......................... 196
  THESE INSCRUTABLE ORIENTALS ................... 198
  TV OR NOT TV... ............................... 200
  CRIME IN THE STREETS.......................... 202
  IT JUST AIN'T FAIR............................. 205
  WHEN IN ROME................................... 206
  A LAMB IN THE YEAR OF THE TIGER.............. 209
  THEY'RE GOING TO THROW THE BOOK AT ME..... 211
  WHAT *DO* CANADIANS EAT? ...................... 213
  FIGURES OF SPEECH ............................. 215
  THINGS HAVE CHANGED .......................... 217
  AMERICAN FAIR ................................. 218
  OCCIDENTAL ORIENTATION ....................... 220
  I JUST DON'T KNOW HOW TO TELL HIM........... 222
  HE COULDN'T PICK A BETTER TIME................ 224
  WHAT EVERY VISITING PRESIDENT SHOULD KNOW.... 227
  THE ELECTION'S OVER — I THINK .................. 229
  OVER THERE, THE PEOPLE ROB THE SUPERMARKETS .. 230
  PLEASE, TANAKA SAN, SEND BACK THE KEY ...... 232
  THERE *MUST* BE A WAY.......................... 234
  THIS TIME NEXT YEAR, YOU COULD BE IN THE U.S. ..... 236
  GOMEN NASAI — IN TRIPLICATE.................... 239
  TWO STORIES DOWN, 10,999,998 TO GO ............ 241

**X. NO MORE LITTLE WHITE —
                 OR YELLOW — LIES**............ 244

# FOREWORD

It was Flaubert, I think, who said: "Human language is like a cracked kettle on which we beat out tunes for bears to dance to, when all the time we are longing to move the stars to pity."

For writers of any kind, journalistic or literary, this sentence has a peculiar relevance. We spend our lives trying to make language move the stars to pity, or at the very least, to make them laugh. More often we end beating out tunes which no one, not even bears, find interesting or amusing.

We have all been told that anyone can write, and indeed, in one way or another, to some degree or other, nearly everyone can. But it is quite another thing to use language so well and skillfully that it provokes tears or laughter. A comparative few ever achieve that level of perfection.

Perfection, come to think of it, probably is not the word. Most of us, as writers, have acquired after years of painstaking work a passable ability to communicate our ideas. All of us, without exception, believe we are witty or humorous; to accuse anyone, particularly a writer, of lacking humor is akin to denying his or her virility. Americans, especially, take umbrage at such a slight.

But the plain and unassailable truth is that real wit or humor are reserved for a minority. Try as we will, our attempts at being funny, satiric or epigrammatic, hilarious though they may seem to us, generally fall flatter than a pancake. Don Maloney is an exception, one of that special and rare breed we call humorists.

There was a German baron who died in the first third of the 19th century, Wilhelm von Humboldt by name, who advanced the quite plausible idea that the character and structure of a language reflect the inner life and knowledge of its speakers. This theory, it seems to me, can be applied to the individuals who use that language. Certainly just as we are what we eat, we also are perceived as John Jones or Yoshihiro Tanaka by what we say and how we say it.

And that brings us down to Don Maloney. Early in life, he dreamt of being a journalist and actually went to journalism school. In the event, he ended up as a business executive and, in the course of things, came to Japan with Wife Sarah and a brood of articulate children.

In his first book, "Japan: It's Not *ALL* Raw Fish," he puts down his wildly humorous reactions to life in these inscrutable islands. In doing so he demonstrates that the years of journalism training were not wasted; he has an unerring eye for the vagaries and curiosities of Japan and the Japanese which, in many ways, is more acute than that of the trained foreign correspondent. In our first days in Japan we noted all the little things, the frustrations and absurdities, of which he writes. But like everyone else we succumbed to familiarity; the curious and the unusual faded into the subconscious. It is Don's gift that his vision never stales. Years after his first wide-eyed encounter with Japan and the Japanese he continues to see them with the gaze of innocence. Part of the pleasure we get from reading his columns in the *Japan Times* derives from a feeling of deja vue. "Yes," we say with a smile. "That's right. The same thing happened to me."

Of course it is not enough simply to point out the incongruities of life in Japan as seen by an outsider. A simple narration would drive us into deepest boredom. Much depends on how the anecdotes are written and the twist they are given. Don has a winning way with words and a special ability to create suspense, holding our attention until the final, mirth-provoking climax.

Some people have failed to see the real Don Maloney behind all this. They complain that he is a well-heeled foreigner living in a foreign ghetto poking superior fun at the Japanese. Why doesn't he go home if he doesn't like it? Well-heeled he may be. (He was wise not to get into foreign correspondence.) But to say that he stands aloof from Japanese life and the Japanese is to miss the point. No one who dislikes Japan would become so minutely involved in the minutiae of existence here. Nor would he bother to make so valiant — if losing — an assault on the complex Japanese language.

The fact is that it is not the Japanese who are the butt of his humor. It is Don Maloney, a large, shambling, middle-aged American businessman caught up in the toils of an unfamiliar culture and losing every battle in a never-ended mini war. He is victim, not victor. And we smile because he reflects our own experiences.

In the end, though, he is the wiser. For the Japanese have a proverb which says: "Man learns little from victory but much from defeat."

John Roderick

Kamakura
March 10 1975

9

# PREFACE

Certainly everyone has heard or read Rudyard Kipling's "East is East and West is West and never the twain shall meet."

Well, it's not true.

For the thousands of foreigners from the West — businessmen, educators, diplomats, etc., and their families — who make a temporary home in Japan, that twain meets countless times every single day.

Sometimes the meeting is humorous. Sometimes it's serious. It's *always* confusing. But the twain meets. In the house, in the office, on the streets and sometimes even in the coed public bathrooms out on the countryside or in the sushi shops. And, believe me, it's not *all* raw fish.

People who have never witnessed this meeting of the twain often ask: "What's it like living in Japan?"

Oh, how I wish I had ten yen for each time somebody has hit me with that question. Better yet, I wish I had ten yen for every hour I've spent trying to come up with a suitable one-sentence answer for that question.

During my first "Home Leave" back in Cleveland — and even before that when I was answering letters that asked the same question — I tried to come up with a sensible reply that accurately represented my personal feelings about the life (or the plight) of the Westerner — or "Gaijin", as the Japanese call him — living in Japan.

But soon I found that almost nobody really wanted to know *that* much about it. "What's it like living in Japan?", I discovered, is merely a polite question much like the automatic "How are you doing?" people ask each time you meet back home.

They really aren't looking for a "Life in Japan" report with the former question anymore than they expect the results of your latest physical check-up when they spring the "How are you doing?"

I could never be sure, however, who *really* wanted an answer and who didn't. So, I began thinking up supposedly zippy replies that would hopefully satisfy everybody. You know, clever comebacks like:

"If you're Japanese, it's just like home."

Or: "Not much different than living in Okinawa."

Or: "It's very Oriental."

Or even: "The Chinese restaurants there are not as good as the ones in New York."

But, smart-aleck answers like those didn't satisfy anybody. The askers who didn't really give a damn didn't hear them. The ones who really wanted to know were turned off.

There are, as I see it, only two alternatives to that smart-aleck approach. One is to ignore the question altogether. Like the guy who answers "How are you doing?" with "How are *you* doing?", you could snap back with "What's it like living in Des Moines?"

That approach, however, very closely resembles the smart-aleck answers.

The other approach is to *really* and *honestly* tell *exactly* what it's like. And that's precisely what I've tried to do in this book.

The stories you are about to read are true. None of the names have been changed, because nobody is innocent.

Don Maloney

Tokyo
April 1975

# I. THE LANGUAGE

When I first started to travel for Harris Corporation, I remember standing on a street corner in Detroit and thinking how it reminded me of Cincinnatti.

I used to feel that Chicago and New York were a lot alike. London reminded me of New York, too. And there were times when Milano seemed very much like Pittsburgh.

Then, I landed at Haneda Airport in Tokyo. I think the last intelligible sentence I heard for the next ninety days was the Northwest stewardess telling us what a pleasure it was having us that day.

The ride from Haneda to downtown Tokyo could not possibly remind any foreigner of any city anywhere — except, maybe, of Osaka.

Oh, there are a couple of signs along the way that blink "WELCOME TO TOKYO" in understandable Roman letters. But the rest are all Kanji, the name given to the Oriental hieroglyphics that the Japanese unfortunately copied from China a few thousand years ago.

And the language everybody speaks in Tokyo is slightly less intelligible to the foreigner than the blinking neon signs.

By the time you arrive at your hotel — or even-up chances are at the *wrong* hotel — and the fact sinks in that you're here to stay for a while, you realize that you're just going to *have* to learn the language. If it is, indeed, a language.

The hotel bookstores have plenty of books that promise even *you* can learn it in a matter of hours. One clever little language school ad shows a four-year-old Japanese girl saying: "She can speak Japanese. Why can't you?"

And, you say to yourself, "Why not, indeed."

Then all too soon, you find out *exactly* why not. Oh, not that you don't *try*. And, Lord knows, there are all kinds of ways to go about it. I think I've *tried* all of them. Does it work? Read on . . .

# DO YOU UNDERSTAND?

Because I'm an "Old Japan Hand," foreign newcomers frequently ask me "What's the best way to learn the Japanese language?"

If any of these people had ever heard me try to tell the girl in our office building's snack bar that I *don't* want cucumbers on my chocolate sundae, they'd know that I'm not the best source of advice in matters Japanese. But, in my "Old Japan Hand" role, I feel required to make some comments.

First of all, you must realize that the *only* sure-fire method of learning to speak fluent Japanese is to be born a Japanese of Japanese parents in a Japanese town. Obviously, the advice-seekers have missed this once-in-a-lifetime opportunity and so we'll discuss only the alternate possibilities.

You can, of course, attend one of the famous Japanese language schools with courses designed especially for English-speaking foreigners. I've done it. The only problem is that I can now only carry on a somewhat sensible Japanese conversation with other foreigners who have attended the same school. No one else knows what the hell I'm talking about.

Or, you can enroll in one of those all-the-way courses where — for thirty days or so — you pair off with a genuine Japanese linguist for eight hours a day, six days a week. You speak only Japanese with him, and he with you. The idea sounds great. But, when it's all over, you're dying to speak English again just to see if you still know how. And, because these all-the-way lessons cost so much, you have to stay home for the next few months because you can't afford to go out. So, after a month of genuine Japanese, you speak only English for a month with your family and you're right back where you started.

One workable solution to the language problem is to live in one of those big apartments in Roppongi or Aoyama where the other foreigners live, spend all your free time at the American Club, shop only at Kinokuniya Supermarket or the American Pharmacy, and vacation in Karuizawa. This combination will prevent you from ever being exposed to people who speak Japanese, so you won't need it.

Or, you can go the opposite way and arrange to surround yourself with Japanese friends and so force yourself to speak Japanese. The problem here, of course, is that all the Japanese want to learn English. Even if you do manage to ask a question in perfect Japanese, they'll answer you in English. Or — worse than that — you may find one who will answer you in Japanese. Then what?

And one more way to go is to hire a Japanese-speaking maid. This will end your frustration caused by that parade of people at your door looking for whatever it is they're looking for. In any event, not being able to understand them is the problem. With the Japanese maid, *she* can answer the door and talk to these people in their very own Japanese. The problem now, however, is that you don't know what the maid is talking about.

The more I think about all this, the more I think I've found the final solution. It works like this: All foreigners in Japan should total up the amount of money they are spending each month for Japanese language lessons. Then, drop out of language school and send a check each month for that amount to the "Maloney Final Solution to the Language Problem Fund." The fund will see that all the money is used to teach English to all the Japanese.

And you'll have free time because you're not spending hours in Japanese school. So, you can hire yourself out to the "Fund", and earn extra yen teaching English to those same Japanese.

I tried this idea out the other night on an American friend of mine. He said he had a better idea, and that his idea succeeded so well that he and his whole family learned fluent Japanese in a matter of two months. He told me that he would explain the whole thing to me over lunch this week. But, alas, we'll never know his secret. When I called his office yesterday to make a luncheon appointment, he wasn't there.

His company had transferred him to Spain.


# A RIDDLE RANGUAGE GOES A WRONG WAY


It was a few years ago, so I may be off a minute or two, but my recollection is that I was only in Japan about seven minutes when I made a firm resolution to learn the language.

I bought a clever little phrase book at the airport store and started my studies immediately on the taxi ride in from the airport.

It was frustrating, I remember, trying to read during the ride. But it wasn't nearly as terrifying as looking out the taxi window on our first Kamikaze trip into downtown Tokyo.

That first book promised I'd be a native speaker in 30 hours — or less, maybe.

Actually, I did get pretty good at some of the phrases listed in the book. The problem is that I have yet to give or point out a book to some Japanese person, so finely-honed phrases like "Kore wa hon desu (This is a book.)" haven't been much help.

In retrospect, those first days in Japan — as aggravating as they seemed, language-wise — were really the easiest. Certainly, I couldn't speak or understand one legitimate Japanese word. And, of course, I knew it.

Because I knew I was stupid, I only pointed at things I wanted. I didn't even try to speak. Just sign language.

And, when it came time to pay for anything, I gave everybody more than what I was buying could possibly cost. The major drawback to that system was the fact that I always had my pockets filled with about five kilos of the coins I'd received in change.

As time went by, just plain exposure to Japanese all day long, plus my miracle 30 hour phrase book, plus the seemingly never-ending language classes, I began to pick up a little Japanese here and a little Japanese there. And, as a result, I felt that I was ready to go.

No more pointing. No more holding up fingers. No more sign language of any kind. I was going to *speak* Japanese. The linguistic tragedy that began at that point still continues.

Oh, how I remember my first try. I was at Yotsuya Railroad Station in Tokyo. I knew that three train lines were there, the subway, the yellow-cars JNR line and Chuo Rapid Service line. I wanted the subway.

I practiced my questions for five minutes over in a corner. Then, I boldly approached the first Japanese that went by and, in perfect vernacular, asked, ''Which way do I go for the Marunouchi Subway Line?''

In equally perfect English, he answered, ''Down those stairs over there and to the right.''

Soon after that, undaunted, I asked in Japanese for needed directions up in the Shinjuku area. This time, the answer came back in Japanese. I was thrilled that he understood my question. But, I was still lost because I didn't understand a single word of his answer.

One of my most embarrassing moments centered around the tin ear I have for Japanese pronunciations.

One day, I was to take an overnight train down to Mihara in Southern Japan. I was in a sleeping car and, since the train arrives at Mihara just before six in the morning, I had to get up about five o'clock.

My secretary told me I could arrange this simply by telling the conductor, before I went to bed, ''Ashita no asa goji ni, oko shite kudasai.'' That simply means, ''At five o'clock tomorrow morning, please wake me up.''

Once on the train, I said it. It worked and I got off at Mihara on schedule.

A couple of weeks later, back in Tokyo, I had to catch a 6:45 a.m. Bullet train for Nagoya. That meant I'd have to get up at 5 o'clock again. I recalled the phrase I used earlier on the conductor — so I thought — and casually asked our maid, Machiko San, to ''Ashita no asa goji ni, Oka shite kudasai.''

She turned chalk white. Son Donald and Daughter Barbara — both of whom have a firm handle on the language as most kids do — roared with laughter. When I finally calmed them down, I discovered that instead of wake me up — *okoshite* — I had asked Machiko San to violate me — *okashite* — at five o'clock in the morning.

I decided then and there that I would probably never be able to *speak* Japanese, so I turned all my efforts to learning how to read and write it.

My troubles, by no means, ended there.

Just last week, the new car was delivered. All of the windows were practically covered with stickers. You know the ones: "Love your car; Love your family" (in exactly that order), "Power Steering," "New Model Crown," plus a series of "OK" stickers and a little green and white one on the front left side window.

Well, I can't take stickers on the window anymore than I can take the plastic covering the seats. So, razor blade in hand, I cleared them all.

All of these stickers were in English except the little green and white one on the left front window. Fortunately — I thought *fortunately,* anyway — the Japanese on this sticker happened to include some of the Japanese characters I'd been studying.

It was obviously an advertisement for some kind of gasoline, so I scraped it off with the rest. It was by far the toughest one to remove.

Since then, a Japanese friend has pointed out that the green and white sticker was the only thing that testified that my car conforms to the new exhaust gas emission control law in Japan.

Without it, I'm subject to a stiff fine. The law — for some typically Japanese reason, I suppose — requires not only that you have the device but the sticker that says you have the device. Getting another sticker — I don't have it yet — has become one of those Japanese federal cases.

What I'm trying to say is that if I didn't understand *any* writing, I wouldn't have removed the sticker at all. If I couldn't speak *any* Japanese, I'd never utter an incorrect word.

My whole point is that I've decided the only times a foreigner is certain of survival here in Japan is in the beginning when he understands *nothing,* or when he finally understands *everything.*

The 38 years in between can bring stark terror.


## TAKE MY WORD FOR IT

Just recently, I was trying to warn newcomers to Tokyo to be especially careful when talking to English-understanding natives because they are quite apt to take what we say very literally.

Anyway, as I was later thinking over that advice, I decided that the warning wasn't stern enough. So, I've got two more stories that should further underscore my point.

The first has to do with a recent Gala Bank Opening in Tokyo. This particular party ushered in the National Bank of Paris. And, as you might expect, the Frenchmen did everything right.

Although the French invited a larger number of people than were involved in the activities on the original Bastille Day, everything was adequate. The food was superb and the wine — all of it direct from France — was fantastic. I decided to settle on Mumm's Champagne as my beverage of the evening.

As is typical of first-class affairs like Gala Bank Openings, supplied along with the food and drink were scores of pretty native girls all done up in flowery kimonos. All during the evening, one or the other of these girls was at my side offering to fetch another stick of yakitori or another plate of raw fish or another glass of spirits.

I've always thought it a shame that, during all this revelry, nobody ever mentions *any* bank — including the host of the evening.

The girl that was standing next to me on this particular occasion, marveling at my attempt to dislodge a raw oyster from its shell with chopsticks, finally spoke. "Is the food all right?" she wanted to know.

I assured her that it was perfect.

"And," she asked, "how is the wine?"

Holding my fourth or fifth glass of Mumm's on high in a sort of "Bottoms Up" salute, I said — for some smart-aleck reason I'll never understand — "It's definitely **not** Mercian."

Of course, she took this flip remark very seriously. "You have to understand," she said, "that this is a *French* bank opening. So, we have only French wine. Since Mercian wine is a Japanese brand, there is not one bottle in this ballroom."

And, with that, she disappeared.

Why, oh why, I thought, do I keep making remarks like that when they only give these people an absolutely inaccurate impression of what I'm trying to say. Then, I turned to a Japanese man standing next to me and struck up one of those elementary "Have you ever been to Mt. Fuji?" conversations.

Minutes later, I felt a tug at my arm. My kimono girl was back. As I turned to face her, she plucked the glass of Mumm's from my right hand and replaced it with an empty one. From a little towel-wrapped bottle she was carrying, she filled my new glass with a red liquid. Smiling broadly, she announced, "Since there was no Mercian here, we sent out to a local bar for this bottle especially for you. Enjoy it, please."

And she wouldn't leave my side until I finished it.

As I stood there sipping my Mercian among hundreds downing their Mumm's, I had to laugh right out loud. Because, the situation reminded so much of a similar laugh I'd had a couple of weeks before at the expense of another quick-mouthed foreigner who, like me, should have known better.

That occasion was "Navy Day," the day on which the United States Navy celebrates their birthday. A big ball was set for Yokosuka, the U.S. Navy base near Yokohama.

Both of us were to attend this ball. His job there was to present some engraved trophy-style plaques to sailors who were selected as "Sailor of the Year Ashore" and "Sailor of the Year Afloat."

My friend decided to order these plaques here in Tokyo. And, so, he called a man who knew a Japanese plaque engraver who would give him a "good deal."

He explained that the citation would be the same on all plaques (there were four of them) and, under the citation, would appear the name of the sailor chosen. Since time was running out and the Navy had not yet selected the names, his telephone instructions were "Do the citation engraving now (he gave them all the wording) and under the citation will later be engraved the names."

Of course, the engraver asked what the names were.

"The names," he was told, "will come later."

Well, the engraver kept his word. The plaques were delivered on time. The citations were engraved word-for-word just as they were given to him. And, under each citation was engraved: "THE NAMES WILL COME LATER."

What I'm trying to get across in all this is that you never have to say to a Japanese: "Take my word for it."

He *always* does.


# OUT OF GAS

Maybe it was midnight, maybe it was more like one a.m. I'm not sure which, but I know it was late. I had a couple of those home office people we affectionately refer to as "visiting firemen" out to the house for dinner.

After dinner, and after my visitors had solved all of the current problems of doing business in the Orient — and, of course, after the last train of the evening had left for downtown — they offered (as *all* home office people offer) to have me forget about them and let them take a taxi back to the hotel.

Since I don't have a driver (an earlier home office visitor solved *that* problem), and since I decided our Japan operation was far enough over the year's profit objective (despite home office help) to assert myself just slightly, I agreed that they should, indeed, take a taxi. Now no Tokyo taxi driver in his right mind (if there *is* such a Tokyo taxi driver) is going to cruise down my street. So, I explained, the least I could do was to run them up the few blocks to the main highway in my car. I did. And, I flagged a taxi and bowed them off in the direction of the Hilton Hotel.

I jumped back in my car, turned the key, and listened while the starter groaned. Nothing. I turned the key again. Again, nothing. I looked at the gas gauge. The little white needle was resting between "EMPTY" and positively. My heart sank. But, then, I remembered the JAF. That's the Japan Auto Federation, a sort of Asian version of the American Automobile Association. When I gave them ¥ 2500 for my membership card, bringing gas to dummies like me was among their promises.

A coffee shop across the street from my predicament was still open. Using better than average judgement, I decided to have our maid phone JAF for help. I called home, gave her my JAF membership number and told her where I was and what the problem was. I strolled back to the car and waited. And waited. And waited. No JAF.

Back to the coffee shop and a call to home for a progress report. JAF, the maid advised, will *not* come if the maid calls. The member himself must call. She hated to keep me waiting, but she didn't know the number of the coffee shop to relay the bad news.

Now, the fury within me was building — both at myself for letting the gas run out, and for the JAF "members only" rule. I got their number from my membership card and dialed them, "Mushy, mushy" — the Japanese telephone "Hello" — finally came after about seven rings. In the interest of ever getting them out to where I was stranded, I asked — in my best school book Japanese — if the man who answered spoke Englich. In Oxford-perfect tones came a "Yes, sir. Very well."

I thanked God and got down to the business at hand. "My name is Maloney," I said, "and I'm out of gas on the Koshu Kaido Highway in the town of Kamikitazawa. Please get some gas to me very soon."

"Where are you?, he wanted to know.

"Right on the Koshu Kaido, just east of Kampachi at Kamikitazawa. I'm the only car on the highway and you should have no trouble finding it or me," I said and described the car and exact location in further detail.

"Aren't there any gas stations open around there?" he asked.

The gist of my reply was "If there were, I wouldn't call you, sir." Actually, the language was much more vivid.

He went on: "I've never been up where you are. If I can find you, how will I get the gas in your car? Do you have a siphon hose?"

Well, my tightening grip nearly destroyed the telephone handset, but I

20

kept most of my cool, after all, I *needed* the gas. So, I explained that his gas can probably had a long spout and that spout would make a siphon hose unnecessary. I'd show him how to get it into the tank.

"OK," he said, "except I don't *have* a gas can."

That almost did it. But, instead of really widening his English vocabulary, I found out that he was now in Kaminoge, a town on the Kampachi Highway. That, I explained to him, was the highway he would take to get from where he was to where my problem was. I told him — while gritting most of the enamel from my few remaining molars — that I knew of a few all-night gas stations on that road and that surely one would lend him a gas can.

I detected some reluctance in his "OK, I'll try and see you in a few minutes" answer. Far more reluctance, at least, than JAF showed when it grabbed my ¥ 2500. I could no longer resist telling him what I thought of his attitude and offered to read him my JAF number which the rules wouldn't let my maid give him earlier.

"What telephone number are you calling?" he asked. I read him the one in my JAF card.

"I'm sorry," he apologized "but this is one number away from that. I'm not JAF. I'm Mr. Tsuyuki, a biology teacher at St. Mary's International School."

"I'll never really remember exactly what I said then, but I'll never forget how I felt. I tried desperately to somehow make up for the verbal lashing I'd dealt him — only the highlights of which are outlined above. I tried to tell him why I lost patience, who I thought I was calling, and how really sorry I was. The words sounded hollow then and still do now as I think back.

I hung up the phone and — trying to avoid the stares of interested bystanders in the coffee shop I got up another ¥ 10 and slowly — ever so slowly — dialed the JAF number again. This time it was the real JAF. I made certain of that. And he spoke no English. I finally got across my problem. In less than five minutes, help arrived. He put ten liters in the tank, had me sign the road service slip and disappeared after he was certain my car had started.

Next morning over breakfast in the Hilton, my visitors bragged that the taxi got them back to town in 20 minutes and were happy that I was able to go right to bed.

I just smiled and ordered another coffee. What the hell. They already wonder who decided that I should represent our company in Japan. If I told them my story, I would have been on the afternoon flight back to Cleveland.

# OUT OF GAS — AGAIN

I have already told of running out of gas on the Koshu Kaido Highway in the middle of the night and of the nightmare that followed when I called the JAF (Japan Auto Federation) for help.

Well, I did it again. Only this time, it was right in front of my own house. Here's what happened:

Wife Sarah and I were returning home from a party down in Roppongi. Just as I was backing my car into our driveway, the engine quit. There was enough momentum for my car to roll back to where my rear bumper just kissed the front bumper of Sarah's car, which was already parked there.

It was after one a.m. and I had no intention of tangling with JAF again, so we just went to bed.

In the morning, I asked our maid — Machiko San — to walk up to the corner gas station and get them to bring me a can of gas. Simple enough request, right?

Wrong. That simple request kicked off my very first *daytime* Japanese nightmare.

Machiko was back at the house in a few minutes and said the gas would be here shortly. Soon after that, the doorbell rang. I answered it and found two service station boys standing near my car. After a conversation comprising 10% English, 5% Japanese (really over my level at the time) and 85% sign language, I got their message: My battery was dead.

Unbelieving that I understood the message, I got in the car and tried it myself. The battery was, indeed, very dead. I decided to check under the hood to see if the cables were disconnected. After all, it was a new car and the battery should have been OK.

To get around to the front of the car, I had to move the gas can. I could hardly lift it. More sign language to determine how much gas they had put in the car. Their answer was an unmistakable wave of the hands indicating none.

They led me around to the rear of my car to show me that my gas cap was located right in the middle of the back of the car under the license plate. And, they pointed out — because I backed my car right up against Sarah's — they couldn't possibly pour the gas in.

They really didn't have to tell me the rest. I guessed that when they couldn't get at the gas cap, they tried to start my car so that they could move it forward a bit. Because there was no gas, it wouldn't start and, eventually, the battery died. Preposterous, I thought; It couldn't have happened that way.

Oh, no? The next round of English-Japanese-Sign Language

confirmed beyond doubt that's *exactly* how it happened. Most of the English used in that round, of course, was mine. And all of it was unprintable.

I used up the full head of steam I'd generated to push my car forward a few feet. In one hand, I picked up the full gas can I could hardly move minutes before and emptied it into the tank.

Now, I signalled, please charge my battery. I stormed into the house, traded my morning coffee for a Bloody Mary, and fumed. As the second Bloody Mary began to take hold, my occidental anger calmed down and I began to see the traces of humor in one more of a seemingly endless chain of Tokyo-manufactured frustrations.

Machiko came in to tell me that the service station boys had returned and that my car was running fine. I ran outside and apologized — in 100% Japanese — for losing my temper.

Just to show them how serious my apology was, I decided to tip them for their efforts. They presented no bill, but I figured that the emergency gas can held about 10 liters. At about ¥65 a liter (then, not now), that should come to ¥650. I was nowhere near sorry enough to offer any payment for the battery charge. What the hell, I reasoned, that was their fault. Anyway, to the ¥650 for the gas, I added a ¥350 tip for them and offered a ¥1000 bill to the older boy.

He sign-languaged that they couldn't accept any of it. I insisted. They bowed, and continued to decline. I really insisted now, shoved the ¥1000 in his shirt pocket, returned their bowing, and whistled my way back into the house — glad that the whole incident was over.

Once inside, I laughed as I explained the whole thing to Sarah and kids — right down to where they were reluctant to accept my ¥1000 peace offering. Donald Jr., our 11-year-old son and resident translator, relayed my story in Japanese to Machiko. She laughed, too, and said something to Donald as she handed him a slip of paper.

"No wonder they didn't want to take your money," Donald said as he handed me the paper. "This is your receipt. Machiko had already paid them ¥2100 when they came back with the battery."


## MAYBE WE'RE GETTING A NEW CAR

My son just bought a new car.

Big deal, you say. Lots of people's sons buy cars in this affluent age. What's so special, you say, about *your* son buying a car?

I'll tell you: He's only eleven years old — *that's* what's so special.

This is one of those "It could only happen in Japan" stories; so let

23

me start from the beginning.

I've been driving my own car in Tokyo for almost two years now. When I purchased my first car in Japan, I wasn't really convinced of my chances for survival so I bought a used car, one that was already two years old.

The way that I am forced to drive in Tokyo, my car — and me, too, I'm afraid — ages one full year each and every month.

Anyway, the old car started making a funny noise a couple of weeks ago and so I brought it in for repairs. All I could get out of them was that "something fall off." I assume that during the two days they kept the car they put the something back on. In any event, that particular funny noise has stopped.

Now, however, I hear new funny noises and I picture many somethings falling off.

That, plus the fact that the mysterious every-two-year Japanese vehicle inspection was almost due, made me think I had better get a new car.

I call that every-two-year inspection "mysterious" because nobody has ever really explained what you get for all the yen it costs other than that piece of paper they paste on your windshield.

So, I looked around. I narrowed it down rather quickly to two cars — the rotary engine job or another one like the one I have now.

I test drove both and really couldn't make up my mind. The rotary engine car was jazzy but the other one was bigger. If you have ever seen me in the flesh, you know that the size of any car I own would be more than somewhat important.

While I was thinking over my choice, more and more funny noises appeared in the old car and I decided to buy the bigger new one if I could make a good deal.

The only time the salesman was free last week was on a Thursday night. I would have preferred to talk to him during the day at the office where a reliable translator is always available, but that would have taken another week and the funny noises were getting funnier and oftener.

The man who came on Thursday night spoke no English. My Japanese turned out to be woefully inadequate for car buying. Thursday is the maid's day off, so she was out. Our 16 year old — Barbara — wasn't home from school basketball practice yet.

And so, everything fell to Son Donald, who is 11 years old. Why I — after ¥ 6 million worth of language lessons (most of them, thank God, at the old rate of ¥ 360 = $1) — why I still need one of the kids to translate is a subject to be discussed some other day.

Back to my story: I told Donald what I wanted, and he told the car salesman. The car salesman told Donald what it would cost and Donald told me.

Going back and forth like this, we established model, color, accessories, delivery, warranty, price, trade-in, etc. Donald did a masterful job. He even arranged for the family to go for a test drive in the car the salesman brought over to the house.

Ah, what an experience this was. There I was with the automobile pamphlets. The pictures were clear enough — but not a single word was understandable.

Donald and the car salesman would have long conversations back and forth in Japanese and then Donald would turn to me with a simple "Yes" or "No" or "Not on this model" or "It's extra."

Only if you've been through this yourself could you possibly imagine what a leveler it is for the big, know-it-all, American hot-shot businessman to be in the hands of an 11-year-old. You'll certainly never know how much Donald enjoyed it.

Now I've used Donald before in some language squeezes. But the usual squeeze involves no more than finding out that the guy at the door is collecting money for the priviledge of watching the national television network.

Once, I remember, we used Donald in a semi-serious situation. A home office visiting fireman came down with a rather terminal looking boil on his cheek. We took him to a local skin doctor in Kamikitazawa.

The doctor speaks no English, so we brought Donald along (it must have been a Thursday night again). After listening to Donald's translations, the doctor handed out some medicine and the fireman got the schedule of doses. I still feel traces of the glow I enjoyed watching my visitor in the hands of my then 10-year-old. Beautiful.

Anyhow Donald obviously understood because the boil went away two days before the visiting fireman did.

But, I digress.

The fact is we're getting a new Toyota Crown. It will be a four-door, beige-colored sedan with power steering and air conditioning. They gave me a good price for my own car and should deliver the new one this coming week.

At least that's what Donald says.


## YES, WE HAVE NO BANANAS

It was early during my first trip ever to Japan, back in 1969, that I realized how differently the Japanese take almost everything we say. And, it was then that I received my first lesson on how to speak Japanese-English rather than my native American-English.

We were in the United States Trade Center in Tokyo setting up a display of our American-made printing machinery. Our Japanese partner had kindly furnished a couple of local mechanics — both spoke some English — to help us with the assembly.

I noticed that all of the crates were carried from the receiving dock at the Center into the showroom, except for one small cardboard box. I tapped one of the Japanese helpers on the shoulder and asked, ''Don't we need that cardboard box?''

''Yes,'' he said, but didn't make any move to go get it.

So, I asked him again: ''Don't we need that one last box out there.''

And, again, he assured me: ''Yes.'' But, he obviously wasn't going after it.

Well, I decided, he's probably figured that he's carried enough crates and boxes today and feels it's my turn to bring in the one that was left. So, I went over to the dock and picked up the box.

As I started into the showroom with it, a Trade Center guard who had witnessed the whole exchange asked me where I was going with that box. And, I told him I was taking it inside to our display.

''Why?'' he asked.

''Because my friend in there — who certainly can read Japanese labels — says we need it.''

''No, he didn't,'' said the obviously Japan-born guard. ''He specifically said that you *didn't* need it. Besides, it's not even yours.''

''I beg your pardon,'' I interrupted, ''but I specifically asked him 'Don't we need that box?' and he specifically answered 'Yes.' ''

''Exactly,'' smirked the guard. ''So please put the box back where you got it. You see,'' he elucidated, ''you asked him 'do *not* we need that box?' and his reply was, in total, 'Yes, we do *not* need that box.' Now I ask you again, please put it back.''

Since my face was already red from the strain of lifting the box, I'm certain the guard didn't notice how red it became from the embarrassment of having my own language explained to me by a Japanese.

I put the box back and never again asked another negative question. But that hasn't stopped the confusion.

For instance, the first Sunday morning we spent in our Tokyo home after moving in from Kamikitazawa, I was awakened just after six in the morning by noises coming from the upstairs hall closet. As they grew louder, I realized that somebody was in there.

Prepared for the worst, I picked up one of Donald Jr's baseball bats, tiptoed out into the hall and whipped open the closet door. There was Maid Machiko pinned against the back wall of the tiny closet by a half-opened ironing board. She couldn't move.

I dropped the baseball bat, and — after a 10-minute struggle — extracted her and the ironing board.

"Machiko," I asked, "what the hell are you doing in the closet with the ironing board?"

Machiko, surprised at my shocked look, answered calmly, "Mrs. Maloney told me that, in this new house, I'd have to do the ironing in the closet." With that, she started to go back in there.

"Get out here," I told her, "and wait until I talk to Mrs. Maloney."

Wife Sarah, never too thrilled about being yanked out of bed at such an early hour, eventually became coherent enough to offer this explanation: It seems she told Maid Machiko that — out in Kamikitazawa — it was OK to do the laundry on Sunday and hang the clothes out in the yard. After all, our Japanese neighbors there did the same.

But, Wife Sarah recalled, she told Maid Machiko that we were living near other foreigners now who might frown on such servile works being performed among them on Sunday. "But," she added, "it's OK to do the ironing on Sunday if you want."

Then, remembering that we used to store the ironing board in the kitchen in Kamikitazawa, Wife Sarah decided to mention, "Here, Machiko, we keep the ironing board in the upstairs closet."

Maid Machiko thought *that* meant — well, you already *know* what she thought.

That Sunday morning Oriental crisis was second only to a Tuesday evening one we once had. On that day, Wife Sarah mentioned to Maid Machiko that, because of one school or the other's Mothers' Club Meeting that afternoon, she would be home too late to start dinner.

When Maid Machiko asked what she could do to get dinner ready for us, Wife Sarah yelled over her shoulder as she went out the door, "At about six o'clock, Machiko, heat up those leftovers in the refrigerator."

I'll spare you the details of *that* disaster.

The idea of all of this is to warn you newcomers, especially, to be very careful how you phrase things — even in your very own native language. The Japanese will answer your questions *precisely* as you ask them and will carry out your orders *precisely* as you give them.

You'll excuse me now, please, while I form a search party to look for a Japanese co-worker of mine. I just realized that yesterday, in order to express beyond a reasonable doubt my complete and utter disapproval of a suggestion he made, I told him to "Go jump in the lake."


## WHAT YOU SHOULD KNOW ABOUT "NO"

Right after they finish reading "Japanese in 21 Hours" and finish three or four lessons at their local language school, most newcomer Gaijins

27

think they are ready for a verbal duel with the natives.

Poor things.

It isn't that the ''Japanese in 21 Hours'' book is no good. Or that the schools are useless. Quite the contrary — I've been reading the book and taking the lessons for over three years now.

It's just that even after months of both, you're not *really* ready. Knowing all the words and phrases isn't enough. You've got to learn how to put them all together in the illogical order that Japanese understand.

And, you not only have to learn when to *use* all the words; You've got to learn which ones not to use — *ever*.

One of these never, never words — for instance — is ''*No*.'' There is no sense even learning it, because you'll probably never hear it from any self-respecting Japanese. He or she would rather die first.

For months, that gave me fits in the office. Every sentence I ever spoke to a Japanese was acknowledged by a nod of the head, the likes of which meant ''Yes'' back in Cleveland. This is fantastic, I thought. They agree with *everything*.

But, as time slipped by, I couldn't help but notice that projects they welcomed with that repeated yes-type nodding never ever got underway. Jobs I though they agreed to do went undone.

Finally, I discovered that the nods and the out-loud ''Hais'' — translated in my ''21 Hours'' book as ''Yes'' — meant only ''Yes, I hear you,'' not ''Yes, I agree with you'' or even ''Yes, *I understand* you.'' Just ''Yes, I heard you.''

So, I decided to introduce the English word *''No''* to everyone at the office. I told everyone to please say this ''No'' when they meant ''No.'' And, to use it anytime they didn't absolutely mean ''Yes.'' I told them I wanted to know immediately when there was no hope.

But, that was a mistake. Notice that when a Japanese says ''No,'' it usually comes off as a nasty nasty word. It sounds exactly the same as my father's *''No''* did when I used to ask him to borrow the car back in my high school days.

Anyway, we don't use it in the office anymore. Now, we all signify ''No'' by just bringing our right hand up in front of our nose and waving it rapidly back and forth, windshield wiper style, in front of — and very close to — our noses.

Or, we tilt our heads 45 degrees to the left, close our eyes, open one side of our mouth, and draw in as much air as possible through clenched teeth for exactly four seconds. Now, we *all* understand ''No.''

''Yes'' is accepted *only* in writing.

But, newcomers, don't think you can have this ''No'' problem only in the office. It's all around you. Let me tell you how it happens in the store, for example.

In the stores in Japan, the sales-girls *never* say "No." They make *you* say it. Here's what I mean:

First, I'll give away the whole plot of my example story. Unless you know the ending ahead of time, you really won't understand the story as it unfolds.

The plot is that you have decided you want to buy a few pads of simple blue-lined paper. And, the store you have decided to buy it in doesn't *have* blue-lined paper. They never *did* have blue-lined paper.

OK, that's the plot. Now, the dialog:

You walk in and ask, "Do you have blue-lined paper pads?"

The girl asks, *"Blue*-lined pads?"

You: "Yes, *blue*-lined pads."

She: "How many?"

You: "Oh, three or four."

She: "Three or four?"

You: "Yes, three or four."

She: "What size?"

You: "Regular size. Legal size. I don't really care."

She: "How many sheets to the pad?"

You: "Makes no difference, really. Thirty or 40 or 50 sheets — any number is OK."

She: "You want them now? Today?"

And, on and on it can go. I'll spare you the rest. But the point is, *she's* not going to *say* she doesn't have blue-lined paper. *You* are. Because after about 45 minutes of conversation like this — less time as you're here longer — the light will finally dawn on you and you'll say to her, "You mean you don't *have* blue-lined paper?"

And then, she'll smile broadly and, with a sign of relief, say, *"Yes."* Meaning, of course: "Yes, we *don't* have any."

Now, if you think all this is slightly exaggerated, stop into your local shoe store this afternoon and ask for some pads of blue-lined paper. Then, sit down.

And don't be fooled by those girls in the department stores over on Ginza who wear those buttons saying "I Speak English."

Notice that the buttons *don't* say "I *Understand* English." To the newcomer, there doesn't seem to be any difference. But that's not usually the newcomer's *first* mistake.

He already made *that* first mistake out in the bookstore at Haneda Airport when he bought that "Japanese in 21 Hours" book.

# II. TRAVEL

Years ago, I remember, some steamship company ran a series of ads each of which carried a headline that read: "Getting There is Half the Fun." I don't remember the name of the steamship company, but I'm certain now that they didn't sail to Japan.

If they did, the ads surely would have said: "Getting There is *All* the Fun." I say this because once you *do* get here, getting *around* here is hardly any fun at all. Not until you fully develop your sense of humor, anyway. And the simplest reason is that there are just too many people in Japan who want to move around at the same time you do — and, invariably, to the same places. After all, there are very many people and very few places to go.

In order to understand what I mean, you first have to get Japan in its proper geographical focus: The whole country is about the size of the state of California. Got that in mind? OK, now remove 80 per cent of *that* because that's how much room the craggy mountains take up.

Still with it? OK, *now* remove about half of *that* for farms and rice paddies. Next, in that little area you have left — about 10% of the size of California — deposit half of the total population of the United States.

Now, put the people who want to go to work, or go shopping, or go on a vacation or business trip and put them on a train, bus or subway. Next, *you* get on that train, bus or subway with them. *That's* what I'm talking about.

It's impossible to accurately describe what travel — by any means — is really like in Japan. When I try, it always sounds like a gross exaggeration. Believe me, it isn't.

For example, you've no doubt heard or read about how crowded the commuter trains and subways are in Tokyo. Let me relate a small story that will tell you just *how* crowded they are.

Until just recently, some Japanese rail commuter lines had special cars on morning rush hour trains that were reserved for women and children only. The papers reported recently that these special cars would be discontinued and that the women and children would be on their own. And, the newspaper report concluded, women were unhappy about it because they enjoyed the special cars since they were rarely filled "to more than 230 per cent of capacity."

How could you exaggerate a number like *that*?

Foreigners involved in this transportation crush do have one good thing going for them. If you're an average sized foreigner, you're a head taller, at least, than the average Japanese and so your head is up where you can breathe.

I've tried to sum up the whole problem of getting around Japan in the following:

# GETTING THERE IS *ALL* THE FUN

Probably the most often-heard lament when you're talking to another foreigner here goes something like: "If I could only master the Japanese language. . ." Actually, I'm not too sure that its a good idea to learn one single word of Nihongo. *Really.* I'll tell you why I feel that way.

When we first arrived here, and couldn't utter a single recognizable word, I honestly think we had more fun. We certainly saw plenty of Japan that we would never had seen if we understood.

For instance, getting to our house out in Kamikitazawa by taxi from downtown Tokyo in those days when we didn't know our "migi" from our "hidari" was always an adventure. Only the ticking meter subtracted some measure of joy from those occasions.

I used to get in the cab and say — ever so slowly — Ka-mi-ki-ta-za-wa. Invariably, the driver would answer with an "Uh?" So, I'd repeat: Ka-mi-ki-ta-za-wa. Second time around was almost never an "Uh?," but only that familiar hissing sound as he drew most of the air in the taxi through the space between his left eye tooth and incisor (if that's where the incisor is.)

Eventually, after maybe three or four times, he'd finally smile and signal understanding with "Hai, hai" and we'd be off. But, almost never to Ka-mi-ki-ta-za-wa. Oh, it would be some za-wa or other, but not the Ka-mi-ki-ta one.

That's how I first got to see Shimokitazawa, a great little shopping town out on the Odakyu Railroad Line out of Shinjuku. There's a lot of discount shops out there (30% off on Seiko watches with no arguing), a big supermarket, plenty of French — well, close to French — bakeries and even, for old times' sake, a giant McDonald's and a Kentucky Fried Chicken shop.

There always seemed to be a new Pachinko Parlor opening up in Shimokitazawa, so you could always catch one of those three- or four-man (or are they women?) Japanese bands marching down the street. They're always playing the same song, it seems, and are always dressed the same — like Asian Emmet Kellys. Even if you don't buy a watch, the band alone is worth an on-purpose trip to Shimokitazawa.

I also got introduced to a place called Komazawa this way and another spot named just plain Kitazawa — no Shimo in front. I'm sort of neutral about Komazawa. I didn't see a French bakery or a grand opening of a Pachinko Parlor there. I didn't feel one way or the other about just plain Kitazawa at first, but later I found out that's where my local tax office was and I've never cared much for it since.

Going out to Kamikitazawa by train opened new vistas, too. From the Keio Line station at Shinjuku, there are three kinds of trains.

There's a local that stops everywhere, including Kamikitazawa (It's the eighth stop if you're counting. And you'd better count, 'cause even the Japanese passengers couldn't possibly understand the announcements on those trains.)

Then, there's sort of an express. 'Sort of', because it stops almost *everywhere,* but skips Kamikitazawa. So does the third kind of train, an honest-to God super-duper express. Usually, these three kinds of trains pose no problem. Usually, the cars on the local are painted green and the ones on the sort of and super expresses are painted yellow.

*Usually.*

Keio mixes them up just often enough for the non-Kanji reading Gaijin to go off on a mystery train ride. That's how both Wife Sarah and I got to know Chofu — it's the first super express stop after you streak through Kamikitazawa. Chofu impressed me as kind of like Chinatown in New York. Because there's a U.S. military base near there, you see almost as many Gaijins on the street as you see natives.

At least I imagined the Gaijins were there because of the base; but now that I think of it, maybe they came out on the express, too.

Riding busses can *really* widen your world. I don't know if you've ever noticed, but Tokyo bus companies are definitely anti-Gaijin.

I mean there's *nothing* in English on any bus in town with the exception of a sometimes Pepsi-Cola ad on the side. At least most railroad stations have signs with their names written in our favorite alphabet.

And you can't figure where buses are likely to go. I think the law requires them to turn either left or right every three or four blocks. You won't get much help from the driver, either, because I'm sure that if drivers learn English, they are immediately replaced.

Driving around town in your own car can be broadening, too. I used to plan my trips around town very carefully. Japanese people don't seem to like street names anymore than they would like being caught out without shopping bags hanging on both arms.

So, I used to get out my map and count streets. You know, I'd figure three streets straight, then turn left for four streets, right to the railroad track, then left for four streets and that's where I want to go.

Simple.

Simple, my compass. Sure as hell, the place where I'm supposed to turn right after four streets is one way to the left. When I turn right on the street after that, it never *does* go to the railroad tracks.

Naturally, then, you ask the first policeman you see. Usually, he's on a bicycle going the other way. But, if you wave furiously enough, he'll pedal over. You ask him; he understands. Then he answers you; you don't understand. And you're off to another new world.

You get my point? If you ever *do* learn this language, your Japanese world will really shrink to almost nothing. You'll end up going to only those places where you *really* want to go.

You might never see Shimo or any other Ki-ta-za-wa, and you could miss Chofu, too.

And, you'd never hear a classic like the time Wife Sarah called from Shinjuku and said she'd be home in fifteen minutes. An hour and a half later, she walked in the door.

"My God," I said, "*Where* have you been?"

"I have no idea," she said. "It was wherever you wind up when the green trains go where only the yellow trains are supposed to go."


## OBENTOS, CUCUMBERS AND ALL


Railroading is sort of a family affair with the Maloneys. In fact, the first job I ever had was with the New York Central Railroad back in New Jersey.

My Dad, Mother, Sister and Brother all spent some time working for the New York Central, too. My Dad, over fifty years. Wife Sarah herself is part of all this, too. It was while she was working for the New York Central back in White Plains, N.Y. that we met each other for the first time. We were both still working together on the railroad when we got married.

Now I tell you all this because I want you to know that it's with more than a passing interest that I ride around Japan via train. Oh, I'm not one of those dyed-in-the-wool railroad buffs you frequently read about in Japan who line up somewhere all night to catch the last ride ever behind a steam locomotive from Someplace-yama to Someplace-zaki. I'd just rather ride the train around Japan than fly or drive.

Anyway, because of this Maloney family history, I am frequently asked by some old New York Central colleagues to write and tell them how railroads in Japan differ from railroads back in the United States.

I haven't answered any of those letters because I don't really know where to begin. It's not that there isn't a big difference — it's that the difference is as *big* as it is.

Let's start with the subways, for instance. New Yorkers, especially, are used to crowded subways. They accept the idea of having to stand up on the subway.

But would they believe that Tokyo Subways are so crowded during rush hours that pushers have to be hired to pack in all the people *and* their shopping bags? Would they believe the shopping bags? Would they believe that, on more than one occasion, the packing-in job was so efficient that I had to ride right by my stop?

As a result, would they believe people here not only push to get *on* the subway (New Yorkers do that, too) but that they push to *get off*?

And, what are the chances of them believing that we get a little ticket here on the subway that has to be punched on the way in and surrendered on the way off? And that, more times than not, after I arrive at my destination I spend more time looking through my pockets for that damn ticket than I did riding the subway?

Would they believe that all Japanese sleep during their subway rides — even the ones who are standing up?

What would their reaction be if I told them that no policemen ride the subway in Tokyo? (Mainly, I guess, because there's no *room* for policemen on the subway here. Besides, the danger of having your pocket picked on a Tokyo subway is practically nil. You're lucky if you can get your *own* hand in your *own* pocket.)

Where would I start my comparison about the long distance trains? I suppose I could explain that in American, as they know, train travellers either look out the window or read their way through a trip.

In Japan, travellers *eat* their way through a trip. But, no explanation of this eating would be complete without giving an accurate idea of the odor given off by the things native people eat from those box lunches called "Obentos." How could you do that?

I thought of mailing them an Obento — you know, the one with raw octopus, raw herring, raw ginger and cold cooked rice with a cherry on top — but then they would get only the smell of *that* particular Obento. And, you know, it's the collection of *all* the different odors of *all* the different Obentos that *makes* the train ride here.

And, since each station the train stops at has an Obento all its very own — both in ingredients and odor — all this winds up *quite* a collection.

The famous "Bullet Trains" are another story. They don't stop often enough or long enough at any station for people to jump out and buy an Obento. They don't have to. All through the trip, girls run up and down the aisles of the train selling all sorts of goodies.

The other day, on a trip I made via the Bullet Train from Tokyo to Osaka, they offered — among other things — a "mixed sandwich" (that means 90% bread, 1% ham, 9% cucumbers), a "hamburger obento" (not to be confused with American hamburgers that contain beef), dried squid (no comment) and peach nectar.

I decided on that trip, since it was only 8:30 in the morning, that I'd go back to the buffet car for breakfast.

Now, I completely lost my head and forgot that breakfast on the Bullet Train stops at 8:30 exactly. The menu handed me had three main choices: Beef Stew, Curry Rice, or Mixed Pizza (all included green tea). There was also a seasonal special of Barbecued Eel.

I almost decided on the Mixed Pizza — 8:30 or not — but then remembered that, in Japan, ''Mixed'' is a translation of ''cucumber'' and decided to simply have a peach nectar and wait for Osaka.

Oh, there are a lot of other differences about that train I could write home about — *if* they'd believe me.

Like the telephone from which you can theoretically call all around Japan. But that would take pages. (Try it sometime.)

Or the announcements over the train's public address system. What always bothers me here is that the announcement in Japanese goes on and on for ten minutes. The English translation that follows merely says ''The next stop is Nagoya.'' What is it that they are not telling me?

On last week's round trip, the train was seven minutes late coming back to Tokyo. An announcement — this one in Japanese only — dutifully apologized for the seven minutes.

How do I explain such an apology? Or that — as a result of the seven minute delay — the president of the Japanese National Railways probably had to resign the next day?

Anyway, I've decided to hell with it. I'll just write and tell them that the only difference between railroads here and railroads in the United States is that Japan *still* has railroads.

Obentos, cucumbers and all.

## SO *THAT'S* WHAT HE'S TALKING ABOUT

Surely, at one time or another — no matter how brief your stay in Japan — you've taken a ride on the Shinkansen (Bullet Train) down to Nagoya, Kyoto or Osaka. And just as surely, you've heard those long announcements the conductor makes in Japanese over the train's public address system.

And — like me, I bet — you've often wondered how come each announcement lasts about fifteen minutes in Japanese, but the English translation that follows is usually only a single sentence like ''The next stop is Nagoya.'' Like I've mentioned here before, I constantly worry about what's going on that they aren't telling me about.

That's no exaggeration about the in-Japanese announcement being long, either. And they come often, too. I even heard a rumor sometime ago that the Japanese National Railroad's engineering department had come up with a simple little improvement that would allow the Shinkansen to make the Tokyo-Osaka run in an hour's less time than they do now.

They never installed the improvement, however, and they don't plan to. Because, if the trip is an hour shorter, there won't be enough time to make all the announcements.

Anyway, what I'm trying to get at is the fact that I hope you didn't miss the article in the Japan Times sometime ago that said the English translation of Shinkansen announcements will soon be liberalized. They're going to tell us *more,* but not *all.*

Specifically, a member of the Japanese Diet has asked the railroad's President to translate — besides the name of the next station — the announcement that explains that passengers are entitled to a partial refund on their tickets when the Bullet Trains are more than an hour late. You see, you pay extra for Shinkansen's speed (the announcements are free) and you get that extra back if the speed isn't delivered as promised.

In a way, I'm glad to hear that. I've had a Japanese friend explain that refund to me before, but since that recorded litttle girl never mentioned it in English on the train, I assumed the refund was only paid to the natives.

Now, obviously, there's still more in those long announcements besides the names of the stations and the promise of your-money-back-if-not-delivered-on-time. So, there remains plenty they're not letting us Gaijins in on.

I decided to find out exactly what that in-Japanese-only portion is, and so I looked up the friend who tipped me off earlier about the refund system.

The first thing he mentioned was that the announcements usually tell you what other lines you can change to at the next stop. And, he added, they even tell you what track at the next station each connecting train will leave from.

Personally, I don't care if they *ever* translate that part about changing trains. The few times I have changed trains in Japan, the results have been disastrous. Now, if I can't get there on one single train from Tokyo, I stay home.

Another thing the Japanese announcements tell everybody is not to forget anything. On rainy days, for instance, they specifically warn not to forget umbrellas. Now *that* part ought to be translated. I'm not sure how much you get back when the train is over an hour late, but I'm sure it's less than I've paid to replace the umbrellas our family is constantly leaving on trains.

They also announce which side of the train the doors will open on at the next stop. Now, why can't they tell us *that*? Bullet Trains stop for such a short time at each station that a simple wrong guess about whether you'll get out the left side or the right side could cause you to spend your next Kyoto weekend in Osaka.

Besides that, they also tell you how long the train's doors will be open

37

at the next stop. That's a translation *must.* More than once, I've seen some unsuspecting Gaijin jump off at, say, Nagoya to grab a newspaper and then watch his train pull out while the newsstand girl is trying to explain to him how much he owes for the paper.

Another thing we ought to be told in English is that the girls are about to come through pushing those aisle-wide carts with the cold box lunches and warm beer. That's usually announced by a female voice in Japanese only. That's important information to have, because more than once — as a result of my warm-beer intake — I've chosen the wrong moment to use the Shinkansen's ''Western Style'' you-know-what and was trapped behind one of those carts for the duration of my trip.

And, my friend said, the last announcement on each trip tells the Japanese that the train is approaching the end of the line and that the railroad — like all the U.S. airlines — ''enjoyed having you today,'' plus the fact that this announcement is the last.

I asked my friend who gives the money back for non-performance. I mean, for example, if we're an hour late because of one of the monthly labor-protest slowdowns, does the union pay us or does the management? And, what if we're behind schedule because too many honeymoon couples stand too long on the platform taking too many ''Banzais'' from the groups who come to see them off? Who pays then, the fathers of the brides?

He wasn't sure, and suggested I listen for the new announcements.

Anyway, I'm not complaining about the lack of English announcements — and certainly shouldn't.

I don't recall ever hearing a single Japanese word on the Super Chief or the 20th Century Limited.


# AN INVITATION TO BREAKFAST


As a result of a special last-minute invitation I received, I got to have breakfast aboard one of those brand-new king-size dining cars on the Bullet Train to Osaka last week. It's only fair to tell you that it was the maiden voyage of this latest Western-style phenomenon adopted by the Japanese, so things may be different by the time you try it out for yourself. But I'll tell you what it was like that day.

First of all, let me remind you that — up to the time of this innovation — there were only four ways to have breakfast on the Bullet. For instance, you could brown-bag it by bringing a couple of hard-boiled eggs from home and buying one of those cute little plastic bottles of green tea at the station to wash the eggs down. (Fortunately, there are water fountains on the Bullet to wash the green tea down.)

Or, you could buy those box lunch "Obentos" right on the station platform. (Sometimes pondering the choice between cold recycled chicken and raw eel on dried seaweed for breakfast can cause you to miss your train.) With these Obentos, green tea isn't necessary — nor does it help.

Still a third choice was to just get on the train, sit down, and wait for the parade of push carts offering every type of food that has made this country so famous and McDonald's alternative so profitable.

Last was the possibility of eating in one of the "buffet cars". There were two on every Bullet — half a car length each. With a counter on one side where about ten people could stand and eat, plus seats on the other side where about twelve people could sit. In this space for 44 people — counting both cars — about 1500 tried to have breakfast each morning.

Every time I got involved in those buffer cars, I found myself wishing I'd been a little more open-minded about the recycled chicken or the raw eel.

But, all that's changed now with the addition of these super dining cars to the super expresses. The diners seat 42 people. That's not many, but the Japanese National Railroads have come up with a great idea to control the crowds. They charge about 50% more than the buffet cars, 100% more than the platform box lunches, and triple the average brown bag cost.

On my invitational trip, breakfast was ¥700. For this you had a choice of either tomato juice or orange juice, fried eggs or omelet, and ham, toast, butter, jam, plus coffee or tea.

And, they really tried to do it Western-style. For instance, there were no ice cubes in my tomato juice, and ice cubes always came as standard equipment in the old buffet car. To tell the truth, though, I missed the ice cubes. They used to give me a Bloody Mary feeling in the morning.

Second attempt at Westernization was the offering of eggs either fried or in an omelet and serving them on a real dish. In the buffet cars, eggs are normally served in the same soup bowl in which they are cooked in a microwave oven. Or scared by the oven, anyway.

Breakfast in the new dining car also included a piece of ham no matter how you chose to have your eggs. The only reason I know it was ham is because that's what the menu said — in English. Perhaps a little was lost in the translation. A lot was lost in the cooking.

And, instead of the normal roll dipped in shellac that comes with buffet car breakfasts, the dining car morning meal includes toast. It's only one piece of toast, but — as you might imagine — that one piece is sliced as thick as a hard cover version of "Gone With the Wind".

So, all this might help to explain why on the new diners you pay ¥700 for what is a ¥500 meal in the buffet car next door.

While I was having my morning tea after breakfast, I noticed some other things about the new diners that bear mentioning. Things besides the food and the fact that you do get a napkin.

For instance, there are windows down only one side of the car. The other side is a non-transparent Formica wall. The side with the window is the non-Mt. Fuji side. I think that's a great idea.

The buffet cars have windows down only one side, too — but they are right on the Mt. Fuji side. It always tore at my heart in the old buffet cars when — about an hour out of Tokyo — all the natives would gaze out the window in vain for a glimpse at a mountain that appears only on picture post cards.

On that non-Mt. Fuji side, you can see the "real Japan" all the way to Osaka. On those occasions when it's not in one tunnel or another, anyway.

Incidentally, the new diners serve only the one breakfast I described. If you prefer traditional Japanese breakfasts like Curry Rice, Beef Stew, Pizza or a Cucumber Sandwich, you can still get those in the buffet cars.     Now, I know you're wondering how I managed to get a personal invitation to the maiden voyage breakfast. Well, it came just the night before — late — when I told Wife Sarah that, because I had a 9:30 a.m. appointment in Osaka the next morning, I had to get the 6:00 a.m. Bullet Train from Tokyo. And that meant I would have to leave our house about 5:15 a.m.

"Please," Wife Sarah invited, "have breakfast on the train. Don't wake me up."


## FASTEN SEAT BELTS

If you're one of those foreigners who is more than somewhat terrified at the idea of driving your own car in Japan, I understand.

When we first arrived in this country — on our way downtown from Haneda Airport — I made a solemn pledge never to let anyone put me in a Tokyo driver's seat. For nine months, I lived up to that pledge.

During that time, I moved around Japan by taxi in spite of the terror associated with being a passenger with no control over your survival, much less over your destination.

In those periods when I dared open my eyes in those back seats, I observed the traffic around us. And — when I felt that I had figured out the rules of Tokyo traffic clearly enough — I took the big step and bought my own car.

That was a year and a half ago. Now that I'm driving myself, the terror continues — believe me. But, I rest a little easier as a driver than I ever did as a passenger. Even though I still don't know really what the other drivers are going to do next, at least I have a vague idea of what I might do in my own car. That's a feeling you cannot experience as a taxi passenger here.

The secret of my survival — at least up to this writing — is the understanding of the Tokyo rules of the road. Please remember that this understanding comes only from observation. Here's how I see those rules:

First of all, *never* observe the posted speed limits. The numbers on those signs are obviously put there by the same people who put the numbers on the "Suggested List Price" tags in discount stores back in Cleveland. The only difference is that you *divide* the list prices by two; you *multiply* the speed limit numbers by two.

Do observe very carefully the "No Right Turn" and "One Way" signs. But, never miss an opportunity to make a U-turn, no matter what the signs say.

At an intersection, never stop for a red light unless it has been red for at least five seconds. And never, *NEVER* stop for a yellow light. Once you have stopped for a red light, don't wait for it to turn green before you take off. As soon as you spot the light turning yellow for the cars crossing in front of you, go.

If you are planning to turn right at the next intersection, be certain to get into the far left lane. Once securely all the way over to the left, turn on your right turn directional signal and cut across the traffic.

You can almost never find a curb-side parking area on "No Parking" streets like Roppongi. There are always other cars already parked there. Simply double park.

If you are trying to pull out from a side street into a busy thoroughfare, don't wait for a break in the traffic. Simply put up your hand, the back of it facing the side window of your car. Wave it back and forth — doing a slight bow at the same time — and pull out. Answer any horn-blowing by blowing your own.

When you are fortunate enough to find a street with two lanes or more — like Aoyama Dori — don't ever stay in one of those lanes for more than half a block. Keep switching.

Every time you do stop in traffic, pull on your emergency brake. If it's night time, turn off your headlights. Everybody else thinks you've parked there, and you catch them well off guard when you speed away.

Remember that trucks, busses and taxis in Japan always have the right of way. If you don't believe this, try to take it away from one of them.

Pedestrians have the right of way in Tokyo only if they are already in front of your car. If they're not already in front, you must do everything you can to prevent them from getting there — even if their hands are up or they are carrying that little yellow flag. (It really should be a white flag.)

No matter why the car in front of you has stopped, blow your horn at him. And keep blowing it until he moves. Do not exhibit patience under any circumstances.

Move your eyes around all you want, but always keep your head pointing straight to the front. If you turn your head, the drivers on either side may think you see them edging in on you and keep coming. If they don't think you see them, they might not.

During rush hours, especially, always block intersections. After all, if you let the cars enter from side streets, your street will become even more crowded.

Those general rules above apparently apply to everyone. There is one rule for foreigners only:   In the event a policeman takes issue with you over any infraction of the traffic rules, you must never admit to him that you speak one word of Japanese no matter how much you've spent for language lessons. You might try just repeating "Gomen nasai,"(I'm sorry) but *never* any other Japanese. And, if he speaks some English, don't answer except by telling him over and over that his English is magnificent.

One last observation:   If you think driving in Tokyo is dangerous to your health, try changing trains at Shinjuku station in Tokyo at about 8:30 some morning.


# IT'S OFFICIAL: TOKYO TAXI DRIVERS
# ARE "CHOOSY"

Well, you can relax now. It's official:   Some taxi drivers in Tokyo *are* "choosy" and some of them *do* "discriminate."

And, I mean that about being *official*. Because "choosy" and "discriminate" are the exact words used in a newspaper story last week about survey results released by the Tokyo District Land Transport Bureau.

The Bureau even went further than that and actually named the ten worst taxi companies in town — companies that the report says, in what has to be an all-time masterpiece of Oriental understatement, "whose guidance to drivers was found inadequate."

Starting last April 1, the Bureau says, they conducted this survey for a period of three months in all the 23 wards in Tokyo as well as in Musashino and Mitaka. During this 90-day period, they discovered 2,100 drivers who were "found to discriminate."

Why, the report says, they *even* found drivers who demanded "extra fees" or "refused to carry passengers." Indeed, "In many cases, drivers demanded four or five times the normal fare."

You know I'd be the last one in town to take exception to *any* Bureau's findings. But that's *exactly* what I'm going to do.

Please, however, don't get me wrong. It's not that I don't believe that the Bureau came up with 2,100 discriminating drivers. It's not that at all.

It's just that I find it next to impossible to believe that it took them anywhere like three months to do it.

Good Lord, I've been passed up by 2,100 taxis in a single hour in Shibuya at night. I just figured out now that, if I stood in front of Shibuya Station for one hour at midnight every night for three months, I could be passed up by 189,000 of these "choosy" guys — at least.

But I don't mean to pick on Shibuya. Neither does the Tokyo District Land Transport Bureau. In fact, they said things taxi-wise were at their worst in Shinjuku, only slightly better in Shinbashi. Then, on their list, comes Shibuya.

The "discrimination" begins to ease up even more in Ueno and Ikebukuro, the Bureau says.

But, back to Shibuya.

One night — it was in February, I remember, some seven months after we first arrived in Tokyo — Wife Sarah and I were at a party near the American Club. Because we had to make the usual overland safari back to our Kamikitazawa home, we were — at about midnight — among the first to leave the party. We stood out on Roppongi waving at all the empty taxis going by.

One thing I'll say for them, they *all* waved back. But, they were *not* waving with the whole hand, just with two or three or four fingers (meaning they would take us for the meter fare plus a few thousand yen). Now my taxi language at the time was the mandatory "masugu"-(straight), "migi"(right) and "hidari"(left) and included no finger-type sign language.

So they just kept going by. And we just kept waving.

After standing there about an hour, another couple from the party — in their own car — stopped and asked us what we were doing standing out there on the corner an hour after we left the party.

I answered as civilly as I could under the circumstances, and they offered us a ride to Shibuya — about 1/5 of the way to Kamikitazawa — where, they told us, there are always a lot of taxis.

Well, we joined the line of people waiting for taxis in front of Shibuya Station. And our friends were certainly right. There were many, *many* more taxis there.

And they, too, just drove by the line holding up fingers. Soon, I understood the game and started answering by giving them a finger sign of my own — one which I learned back in High School in Teaneck, New Jersey.

The discriminating taxi drivers did not, I'm certain, know what it meant. But *I* did, and that eased my aggravation somewhat. Wife Sarah did, too, and made me stop.

Eventually — it was shortly after 3 a.m. — a taxi stopped. No fingers; he just opened the door and let us in. And, we beat the sunrise to Kamikitazawa. Furthermore, we only paid the fare on the meter.

That driver must be the one that the Land Transport Bureau people were riding around with for 89 1/2 days of their 90 day survey.

Anyway, next morning, I went against a firm resolution I'd made earlier after spending my first five minutes in Tokyo traffic. I bought a car of my own.

Of course, my trials with Tokyo taxi drivers didn't end there. I'd only had the car about a week when one of them backed into the side of it. But, that's a whole other story.

I don't tell you about our night in Shibuya because it's an isolated incident. I could tell you at least 2,100 stories (I like that number) about our family's taxi-related tribulations here. And, if you've been in Tokyo more than one midnight, you probably have 2,100 stories of your own to tell.

And I don't mean it to be a funny story, either. It's really one of the only *sad* Tokyo stories I know. What makes it worse is that everybody else here is so damn nice.

On a typical day on the town, you can go to a department store here where there are sometimes more salegirls to help you than there are customers. Hell, one of them wipes the escalator hand rail for you. Another bows you into the elevator.

Then, you go out for dinner and a horde of waiters see to your every need. You even get a hot towel to start off.

If you get lost between the department store and the restaurant, anybody you ask — citizen or policeman — will go out of their way to set you straight.

Even the girl at the supermarket smiles and says "thank you" while she's ringing up $8 for that melon you bought.

Then, the day is over and you're ready to go home. You walk over to the corner and hail a taxi.

Now, even the Tokyo District Land Transport Bureau knows what happens — or *doesn't* happen — next.


## YOU'VE BEEN WRONG ABOUT TAXIS

One of those "other" newspapers in town recently published the results of a survey taken among taxi drivers here to determine why they rated certain prospective passengers as "Personae non gratae" (sic) and passed them by.

The survey report first established that Tokyo taxi drivers are not permitted to choose their customers, but — and I quote the report — "they are only human; they nevertheless cannot help becoming choosy."

I have ample reason to believe that statement is probably true. Not the part about taxi drivers being "human", but the part about them being "choosy". I've even suggested that here before, I'm sure.

But now, thanks to the survey, we know *why* they pass us up.

In the first case, the survey showed they don't like to pick up drunks. Drunks, one surveyed driver said, "are quite rude and often fail to tell the driver exactly where they want to go."

That observation on the part of a taxi driver shocked me, because just the other day I was talking to a friend of mine who was drunk the night before. He had, he said, managed to get a taxi to stop for him. But, he went on, the taxi driver was — and I quote my friend — "quite rude and failed to take me exactly where I wanted to go." What made my friend so mad was that a few days later when he was quite sober and on nothing but Pepsi, he had the same exact taxi experience.

Another reason a taxi driver told the survey people why he didn't want to pick up drunks was that those drunks "sometimes try to catch taxis near intersections or a pedestrian crosswalk. And," he went on, "it's quite dangerous to stop at such places."

Now that observation *didn't* shock me one bit. As an all-too-frequent pedestrian in Tokyo, I *know* how taxi drivers hate to stop for pedestrian crosswalks. I will admit, however, that up to the time I read the report I thought the *pedestrian* was the one in danger. I never realized that the *taxi* was threatened.

Another thing, it turns out, is that Tokyo taxi drivers don't like to pick up people who have animals with them. Mainly because dogs, especially, do you-know-what in the back seat when the driver isn't looking.

I, for one, never thought about that. Because, I guess, what annoys Wife Sarah and our girls so much is that taxi drivers don't mind stopping their cabs anywhere, stepping out, and doing that very same you-know-what in plain sight — no matter *who* is looking.

They also object, these drivers, to picking up parties of more than four people. When they do pick up a group of five, they say, the cab is too crowded, they can't see in the rearview mirror, and it's difficult to drive.

Not only do I agree with them there, but I'm especially relieved to see in writing that any Tokyo taxi driver has an intention, at least, to look in his rearview mirror. They fooled me about that up to now.

And, of all the "professions" — that's a quote, too — guess who they hate most to pick up? Sumo wrestlers! Not because it's a lot like picking up a group of five ordinary people (which they already established as a "dame"), but because, in a taxi driver's very own words, "They lack common sense."

As an example of what he meant, this same driver remembered that one Sumo San he picked up once "rudely asked him for a cigaret." Another driver said Sumo wrestlers "are, on the whole, rough speakers." None of the drivers in the survey, I should point out, complained that any Sumo wrestler threw salt around the back of the cab or tried to push the driver out with a "hidari yotsu" or whatever hold they use in the Sumo ring.

And that was about all the survey report had to say.

Please remember all this the next time a taxi ignores you on Roppongi some night.

Take a look at your reflection in one of the nearby store windows. You'll find that you either look drunk or appear to have a dog or cat hidden away in one of your shopping bags. Maybe, it's just because the other four people looking for taxis seem to be all together with you. Or, don't forget, it might be because you look like a Sumo wrestler who has just run out of cigarettes.

And all this time, you thought the Tokyo taxis were ignoring your frantic waves because you were a Gaijin! Well, not a single surveyed driver gave that as a reason for a fly-by.

Seems to me you should really "gomen nasai" to all taxi drivers for what you've been thinking up to now.

If, that is, you can get one to stop.


## I FELT BETTER WITH THE PAPER

Because the home office visitors who were in town a couple of weeks ago brought in a fresh supply of duty-free Old Grandad, we hosted a small gathering at our place last Saturday night.

Since there was only one other couple, in fact, it was classified by Tokyo social standards as a very small gathering indeed.

Anyway this other couple has been in Tokyo about four or five months now. And, they're doing all the "in" things. You know, she's taking Ikebana flower arranging lessons, studying Judo and learning Chinese Cooking; he's studying Japanese, reading all the "how-to" books about Japanese business, and jogging around the palace grounds every second morning.

As they were ready to leave, the wife asked the husband, "Do you have that little paper with our address for the taxi driver? You know, the one the maid wrote out for us?"

Who needs it?" he said. "You forget that I can speak some Japanese now."

On the other hand," she replied, "I've *heard* you speak your Japanese. That's why I ask you if you have that little paper."

"Look," he snapped, "I can certainly say 'Roppongi San Chome,

46

onegaishimasu' (Please take us to Roppongi three chome) can't I?''

She admitted that it did certainly sound like ''Roppongi San Chome, onegaishimasu'', but she quickly pointed out that *she* wouldn't be driving the taxi.

With that, we said our final ''goodnights'' and they were off into the night.

Wife Sarah noticed me snickering as I locked the door behind them. ''What's funny?'' She wanted to know.

''It's *not* funny,'' I assured her. ''In fact, it will border very close to tragedy if he doesn't come up with the maid's slip of paper.''

Don't get me wrong. It wasn't that you couldn't understand his Japanese. Even discounting the fact that he's going to the same Japanese school I did, his pronunciation was quite clear to me.

But there's more involved than clear, authentic pronunciation for a Gaijin to get a taxi driver to haul him to some specific place. I guess I was *really* chuckling at my departing friend because I remember back quite vividly to the day when I first thought I could throw away the cards and papers and manage Japanese taxi voyages with oral instructions.

On that first occasion, I was going to the big post office in front of Tokyo Station to pick up a package on which I owed some customs duty.

Now I was smart enough to know that I couldn't manage that customs operation inside the post office, so I took along my Japanese secretary. But, I was naive enough to think I could tell the taxi driver where we were going. So, I told my secretary to keep quiet, that I'd handle it myself.

We got in the cab and I said — with tones that would make Naganuma (the Japanese language school) proud: ''Chu-o yu-bin-kyo-ku''.

The driver put that ''What-the-hell-are-you-talking-about?'' look on his face and said, ''Eh?''

I repeated: ''Chu-o yu-bin-kyo-ku''

And he repeated: ''Eh?''

I gave my secretary a defeated nod and she said, not one bit better than I'd said it, ''Chuo yubikyoku''.

The driver shot back a ''Hai'', and we were off to the post office. The same sort of dialog, with the same sort of result, was repeated on the way back to the office.

Secretary Sumiko could see that I was crushed. ''Please understand,'' she soothed. ''Your Japanese is fine. It's just that taxi drivers — and many other Japanese, too — make up their minds when they see you that you speak a foreign language, *not* Japanese. So, even when you *speak* Japanese, they're all tuned to hear a foreign language and that's what it sounds like.

''Try warming them up first,'' she advised, ''with an ''Ano ne'' or with a ''Sumimasen'' (Japanese attention getters) repeated a couple of times. *That* will tune them back to Japanese and you'll be OK.''

47

I decided to try it that very night on the way home to Kamikitazawa. To get to our house, we had to turn left off the Koshukaido Highway at a certain traffic light. I had memorized the Japanese necessary to get taxi drivers to do that.

Trouble was, night after night we sailed past that light while the drivers were answering my Japanese instructions with the aforementioned "Eh?"

Anyway, that night came the test of Secretary Sumiko's theory. We were rolling along at the usual 80 KPH, and about five or six blocks from the traffic light. I leaned forward and gave him my opening "Ano ne".

Completely shocked, he hit the brake with both feet. As the tires squealed like a mailman's bicycle, I went over the back of the front seat and was standing on my head next to the driver.

Cars zooming by to the left and right of us blasted their horns while I climbed back where I belonged. Determined, I gave him another "Ano ne" and recited my thing about turning left at the light.

Still glassy-eyed, he started up again and followed the instructions to the letter.

Now, I warm up the drivers for my Nihongo by saying great tuners-in like "Konichi wa" or by humming songs like "Sakura, Sakura", even before the "Ano ne". And it's working. At least I manage to stay in the back seat now.

But, I'll tell you the truth: I felt a lot better with the little cards and pieces of paper.


## NEVER THE PLANE, EITHER

I read the other day about a Japanese association called the Sanrizuka-Shibayama Anti-International Airport League. From what I can tell, their main objective is, has been, and apparently will be to stop the opening of the new Tokyo Airport out in Chiba.

Whether you are aware of it or not, there *is* a new Tokyo Airport going up out in Chiba. As far as I can determine, it's about twenty minutes from Ginza by telephone and will be only slightly more convenient for us than the airport at Osaka. In fact, I'll bet if you take the Bullet Train, you can get to the Tokyo Hilton faster from Osaka airport than you can from the new Chiba one.

Anyway, the aforementioned S-SA-IAL is doing their best to keep Chiba from opening. I give you all this background because I don't want you to confuse this Japanese Anti-Airport group with the new association *I'm* starting.

I really haven't yet fixed on an official name for my new group, but —

until I do — the following will do the job: "The I'll-Never-Meet-Anyone-at-the-Tokyo-Airport-Again (either where it is now or where it's supposed to move to in Chiba) Association."

Now if you've ever met *anyone* — friend, relative or home office person — at Tokyo's Haneda, you will know what I'm about to talk about.

However, if you've been here more than ten days, you surely will have to go out to the International Arrival Building sooner or later at least once. And that means you'd better know *exactly* what I'm going to talk about. So, read on.

In the first place, I don't even know who started that hallowed Tokyo tradition of I'll-Meet-You-At-The-Airport. But, as of last week when I had to go out there three times, it's still going strong.

I remember vividly the night I first arrived in Tokyo. Of course, a group of my Japanese business associates met me at the airport. I remember how at the time I thought, "My God, they don't even think I can find my way from here to the hotel."

Actually, it's not fair for me to think that. After all, *most* of the people arriving at Tokyo Airport are Japanese. Certainly, it's fair to assume that any one of them can find his or her way from the Airport to home or wherever they're going. Still, some unwritten Japanese law obviously requires that at least six people meet each arriving passenger.

The other night, standing there waiting for my home office persons to come through the sliding doors, I suddenly realized why. It's because *every* returning Japanese — even the ones coming from Korea, I'm convinced — stops over at Hawaii. And, while in Hawaii, he buys two cases of pineapples, two of papaya, three bottles of duty-free Johnnie Walker Black, one carton of non-Hi-Lite cigarettes and a set of golf clubs. He couldn't possibly manage all that alone on the mono-rail into town — especially since he also has the two shopping bags and three furoshikis he left here with plus the handwoven palm tree leaf hat.

The tour director can't help him, because he has pineapples, papayas, Scotch, cigarettes, golf clubs, shopping bags, and furoshikis of his own. Plus, he's the one that has to carry the flag.

So, six of his friends and neighbors — minimum — have to meet him. Now let me tell you what all this does to the International Arrival Building at Haneda.

Each of the nights I was there, six Jumbos landed at exactly the same time. Each carried about 300 passengers. With the six-to-one ratio, that means 10,800 people were squashed into that waiting room ready to help with the pineapples.

To make matters worse, they "wait" with exactly the same zest they employ when changing trains at Shinjuku in the morning. If there are still those among you who feel flying can be dangerous to your health, meet somebody at Haneda. It will make future "Fasten Seat Belt" rides seem like a Sunday in Church.

And it's not just the crush *inside* the building that makes me say "Never again." It's just another item on a long list of aggravations that go with airport meeting.

High on that list is the parking lot at the airport. Thanks to the six-jumbos-all-at-once scheduling out there, there's always a long line of cars waiting to get in the lot.

First-timers heave a sigh of relief when they finally get through the parking lot gate. All too soon, however, they find out that's the easy part. While your visitor is circling high about Haneda in one of those six jumbos waiting for a runway, you'll — believe me — match him circle for circle around that parking lot.

Invariably — when you *do* finally park and get in with the huddling masses of fellow greeters — one glance at the big arrival board tells an entirely different story about what time the plane will *really* land compared to the "on time" they promised you on the phone.

And, besides just the six-meeters-to-one-passenger group in that arrival terminal, you'll find another group — usually about 130 to 150 — who just go out there to watch one of the two television sets. Especially when Sumo is on.

There's more, too. For instance, there's always somebody who forgot to add the day for crossing the International Date Line and has been in since yesterday. Fortunately, they are usually still out there 24 hours later hemmed in by shopping bags and papayas.

And the home office *loves* to send a guy over every once in awhile that you've never laid eyes on and vice-versa. That makes the meeting bit especially interesting. You have two choices: One, you can stand there holding up a sign with his name on. Or, you can go over to every Gaijin and ask him if he's yours. Either way, you feel like the idiot you look like to everybody else.

In any event, I've had it. Never, never again. Not to Haneda or Chiba or Osaka. Not even if they promise to give me all their pineapples, papayas, Scotch, golf clubs, palm leaf hats or anything else.

From now on, I'm mailing them one of those idiot cards they can hand to the Tokyo Airport taxi driver to get them to the hotel. On the back, I'll write my home phone number for them to call and tell me they're safely in their room. Then, I'll meet them one-to-one in the hotel lobby bar.

What the hell, I've decided, they can manage the first 10,000 miles of the trip without me. That's exactly what they're going to do from now on for the last 10 kilometers.

# THE QUAINT CUSTOMS OF JAPAN

A fair summary of what friends and neighbors back in Cleveland had to say when they heard we were moving to Japan would go something like this: "We really envy you your exciting opportunity to learn the quaint customs of Japan."

Well, that was about four years ago, and I'm still not sure I have learned anything about Japanese customs.

Now I know that, in Japan, you have to take your shoes off inside the house. Not in the houses of any of my Japanese friends, mind you — only in *our* Tokyo house where Wife Sarah insists on it.

"After all," Wife Sarah says, "if the Tokyo American Club can put little jars of toothpicks right on the table between the salt and pepper, *you* can be Japanese enough to take off your shoes."

Those sort of quaint customs I'm quite familiar with. The customs that I'll never understand is the one with the Capital "C" — the Customs that decides what you can and cannot bring into Japan.

My first tangle with Japanese Customs came right after I first arrived here. We came by plane and shipped our household goods separately. One day, a notice arrived saying they were here and would I please pick them up.

My Japanese business partner volunteered to do that chore for me and asked for the notice, my passport, and my copy of the "Declaration of Unaccompanied Goods."

I had the notice in my hand and the passport in my pocket. But, I asked, "What is a Declaration of Unaccompanied Goods?"

"You didn't fill out a form on the airplane saying your household goods weren't with you and give it to the Customs man when you arrived?" My partner wanted to know.

"No," I said. "Nobody ever gave me any such form."

The air he hissed through his teeth would have blown up half the balloons in Macy's Thanksgiving Day Parade. I already knew about *that* custom, too, and smelled big trouble.

"You'd better come to see the Customs Officer with me," he advised. And so I did.

My partner told the Customs man my story and they hissed together. This time, two parades worth.

"You must write a letter," the Customs man said, "to the man in charge here apologizing for breaking Japanese Law and promising never again to cause such trouble." He wouldn't guarantee, however, that such an apology and promise would be accepted. But, he'd try his best.

"What do I say?" I asked him.

"I'll tell you what to write," he told me and dictated my first "Gomen

Nasai'' letter ever. I wrote it word for dictated word and signed it.

"Now, where is the man in charge who gets this letter?" I inquired.

"*I'm* the man in charge," the dictator announced. "Please give me the letter."

He took it back to his desk and, right where I could watch him, read every word very carefully. He finished it, stared out the window for a minute, then opened his drawer, pulled out a little round-oblong gadget, hit a stamp pad with it a couple of times, and stamped my letter.

He came back over to the counter and proudly announced that my "Gomen Nasai" had been accepted. But, *only* because I promised *never* to break such a law again.

So, next time I came back to Japan unaccompanied by my goods, I filled out that form — in duplicate — and made sure the customs man at the airport stamped it for me.

When the goods arrived — an Oriental carpet from Taiwan — I gave the man my arrival notice, my passport and — very proudly, indeed — my Declaration of Unaccompanied Goods. They asked me to have a seat. From that seat, I could see that all my documents were the subject of one of the biggest meetings ever held in the Customs office. The gathering generated more paradefuls of hissing. The man who took the papers came back to the counter.

"No good," he said, pointing to the Declaration. "This form only lasts six months. You returned two days more than six months ago, and so you . . . . . . . ."

"Have to write a letter," I interrupted.

"That's right," he agreed. And, he dictated and I wrote — now doing a little hissing of my own and thanking heaven that this wasn't the same Customs man to whom I'd promised earlier that I wouldn't be bad again.

He took the letter, read it, but didn't stamp it. "Your letter OK, but you still have to pay the duty."

"Why?" I hissed. "I apologized. I promised never again."

"Yes," he said, "but the carpet is valued at more than ¥100,000 and unaccompanied, form or no form, letter or no letter, promise or no promise — duty must be paid."

So, I did. And — I thought to myself — now I know all there is to know about the quaint Customs of Japan.

But then we came back from home leave last month — unaccompanied by some more goods. I'll tell you about that some other time. That is if they don't match up my two "never again" letters by then.

# WHO'S SORRY NOW?

This is that other story about "Unaccompanied Goods" that could not accompany the previous story about the quaint Customs of Japan.

There are a whole lot of reasons why we always seem to return to Tokyo from home leave unaccompanied by some goods that have to be shipped separately. On our first couple of trips, the will-arrive-later boxes used to contain cake mixes, Alka-Seltzer, Milky Ways, and other vital necessities of Cleveland life that we couldn't get in Japan.

Eventually, however, we learned to do without these things just like we learned to do without New York pizza and bagels in Cleveland. We learned to live without the cake mixes and Milky Ways. And *that* doing without cut down the demand for the Alka-Seltzer, too.

But the most important items in those early boxes of unaccompanied goods were our size clothes and shoes. Since our own size hasn't changed much since we first arrived here, since the old shoes and clothes are wearing out, and since the Japanese stores don't seem especially interested yet in supplying the necessary jumbo sizes, we're still stocking up on wearing apparel when we get to the U.S.A.

Normally, we send it back here 'Unaccompanied.' And it was no different on our last Home Leave.

Wife Sarah wanted slacks proportioned so that she could put something in the pockets in case an emergency arose.

Son Donald wanted some T-shirts that didn't say "Love Young" across the chest like Japanese ones do.

Daughter Frances wanted some T-shirts that assumed you *had* a chest. And yours truly wanted shoes that allowed for the fact that the distance from my heels to my arches was not necessarily the same as the distance from my arches to my toes.

So, all of that — plus the items Son Sean and Daughter Barbara collected — were sent along separately. There was no room in our suitcases, I must confess, because we packed just a few cake mixes, Milky Ways, and a couple of boxes of Alka-Seltzer — just for old time's sake.

Anyway, having learned my lesson on previous trips and being aware of my "Gomen Nasai" letters promises never to do wrong again, I made certain that I filled out my two copies of the Declaration of Unaccompanied Goods .

Now anyone who had ever flown to Tokyo can imagine the scene at the Customs counter at the airport. There were six of us with two suitcases each. Each also had a flight bag. And we wouldn't think of coming back from Hawaii without our pineapples and papayas. Plus, of course, the legal limit of duty-free Old Grandad.

So, picture the Customs man looking at the six Gaijins with 24 pieces of luggage boxes and see-thru shopping bags, *and* the Declaration indicating there was *still* more to come. "Go ahead," he said, without opening one of them.

Now, understand, you fill out *two* copies of the Unaccompanied Goods forms in order that he can keep one, and stamp and give the other one back to you so you'll have it when the goods arrive.

By the time I got out front with the second cart-full of luggage, Wife Sarah already had the taxis lined up. I suddenly realized I didn't have my copy of the form. "Do *you* have it?" I asked Wife Sarah.

"No, he didn't give me anything back but the passports."

I ran back inside, found the same Customs man, and asked for the form. "Your wife has it," he assured me.

By the time I got back outside, Wife Sarah had left with the first load in the first taxi. When we got home, *nobody* had the form.

When the goods arrived about a week later, I went out to Haneda and simply told them that I didn't have the Declaration of Unaccompanied Goods because the Customs man never gave it back to me like he should have.

Well, we went through another long discussion which ended up with me having to write another "Gomen Nasai." The Customs man read it and pronounced it unacceptable. "If it happened as you said," he decided, "the letter isn't necessary. The duplicate copy will be on file. If it *didn't* happen like you said, well. . . . ."

He didn't have to finish; I knew what he was thinking. Following his directions — along with a map, of course — I found the building where the files are kept. And, they eventually found the un-returned copy. With the most satisfied smile I'd worn since I first came to Japan, I handed it to the Customs man who was holding my shipment. He read it, tore up my rejected "Gomen Nasai" letter, and said, "Go ahead, take the boxes. That's all there is to do."

"Oh, no," I said. "There's *one* more thing."

"No, that's all that's necessary.'

"Look," I pointed out, "this time *I* did everything right. I filled out the forms and I turned them in. This time *you* Customs people were wrong not to give me back the form. So this time I want *you* to write the Gomen Nasai letter to *me.*"

Well, all activity in the room stopped.

"It was just an error," the Customs man answered, "caused by the busy times at the airport these days."

"Put it in your letter."

"We don't write letters," he announced. "And besides, *you* were the

54

one who forgot to ask for your copy back. Maybe because of that, you should
. . . "

I didn't wait around to hear the end of his sentence.


## THERE'S SOMEPLACE LIKE HOME


I used to get more than mildly worked up over the fact that the international schools in Tokyo (including St. Mary's, which is *legally* "in Tokyo") make the kids go to school on Japanese National Holidays when I was off from work.

After all, I reasoned, we spend little enough time together as a family in this foreign land and here were togetherness opportunities we were blowing.

But, notice that I say "used to get." There are two reasons why it doesn't really bother me anymore. First, I guess, is that all of our kids are now past that age where they might look forward to spending a day off with the old man. Now, it's just plain "spending" that they enjoy.

So, even if we *were* off on the same days, their idea of which branch of Oriental culture to take in is remarkably at odds with the desires of Wife Sarah and me.

The second reason I don't excite anymore is the fact that I seem to have to attend some business convention or other someplace around this archipelago on every single Holiday.

A recent one — the "Coming of Spring" Holiday — was no exception. We showed some of our equipment at an exhibition in Hokkaido — Japan's northern-most island. And that's what I want to tell you about.

Hokkaido, *not* the exhibition.

Maybe, as I keep telling myself, I've been here too long. But, Hokkaido really and truly reminded me of Ohio. More than once over the weekend, I had to pinch my Alien Registration to convince myself I hadn't gone home.

If you fly to Sapporo the way we did — that "we" includes Wife Sarah, who is *not* attending one of the international schools and who was due for a little R & R anyway — you get a chance to see plenty of the Hokkaido countryside. And, I *mean* "plenty."

The flight itself on Japan Air Lines from Tokyo is only about an hour and a half. But the airport is nowhere near the city. In fact, I think the Sapporo airport also serves Seoul, Korea. And I bet Seoul is closer.

There's a bus into Sapporo city. And while it rolled through the Hokkaido countryside — and rolled and rolled and rolled — I really got the feeling that we were on Interstate 71 from Dayton to Cleveland. Even though that's a shorter trip.

Actually, the bus ride maybe isn't as bad as I make it sound —

although Wife Sarah was disappointed they didn't serve meals — but there's no place for your baggage and you have to hold it on your lap. For the rest of the passengers — all were Japanese — this presented no problem since it meant that the men only had to hold one of those little black zipper bags and the women little Tokyo ''departo'' shopping bags.

For Wife Sarah and I, however, it meant balancing our two-suiters all the way. I was glad I brought the extra suits. The one I was wearing died during the bus ride.

Anyhow, the countryside is amazingly Ohio-like. The barns on the farms look just like barns. You know, they have those octagonal or hexagonal, or whatever it is, shaped roofs. And behind each of them is a regular silo. Many of them are even painted red.

About the only thing missing were hex signs over the barn doors. And the farmland itself was not underwater the way it is most everyplace else around here.

Once you get in town — and you *do,* eventually — the streets are wide and straight, just like Cleveland. And they were all covered with a mixture of sand, slush, brown snow, black snow and white snow, just like Cleveland.

And the cars and taxis were dirty, just like Cleveland. And they were mostly Toyotas and Datsuns, just like Cleveland. They were, of course, driving on the wrong side of the street. But, that too can happen in Cleveland over a long holiday weekend.

Part of each day it snowed, and part of it was cloudy — again, just like Cleveland.

Most of the houses even have space around them and *no* walls. I can't tell you how nostalgic the whole trip was. I really expected to see the home office pop up every time we turned a corner.

Of course, there were differences.

In Cleveland, there are nowhere near as many Japanese noodle shops as there are in Sapporo. And Hokkaido people don't talk with what anyone would take for a midwestern twang. And the newspaper they shoved under our hotel room door every morning wasn't the Cleveland Plain Dealer.

But, still — with all that — the resemblance is remarkable. On the couple of side trips we took out of Sapporo by train, we were victims of the latest railroad workers' slowdown. Here again, though, when trains were running at all in Ohio, they moved at about the same speed.

Why, even the Kentucky Fried Chicken places were out in little buildings of their own with candy-striped roofs the way they ought to be and not tucked in some depart's B-1 floor the way they are in Tokyo.

One of those Colonel Sander's places in Sapporo had a sign on the side, in English with lettters about a foot tall reading ''Remember Hokkaido and Japan — Chicken ¥ 150 Each Piece''.

Even if they gave away the chicken for nothing, I'm *sure* I'll never forget Japan.

## SOME SECOND THOUGHTS

You can say what you want — you know *I* often do — about Japan's garbage, its pollution, and the impossible prices in Tokyo.

But, for each and every unkind thought I've ever hatched about this country's garbage, pollution and prices, I've had fifty or more *kind* thoughts about the Japanese people themselves.

Actually, the people of Japan are so courteous and helpful to us Gaijins — foreigners, if you're one of those sensitive ones — that they all too often give me a more than sukoshi guilty conscience.

Every single time a Japanese goes out of his way to lead me by the hand to where I want to go, I can't help but think what sort a reception this same Japanese would get back in Cleveland if the situations were reversed.

Let me use just the incidents of a recent few days to illustrate my point.

As I've mentioned before, the international schools in Tokyo don't let the kids off on the same Japanese holidays as I'm off from work.

So, I have all too precious little off-duty time together with our children. A couple of weeks ago, I temporarily rectified this by taking a couple of days' vacation while the kids were on their Easter holidays.

Because the whole family has more than somewhat of an interest in Japanese folk crafts, we planned a trip to Tajimi (near Nagoya) where we heard there were some great porcelain home-factories; to Takayama because we read that Takayama is the home of the great lacquer ware craftsmen; and on to Kanazawa (on the Japan Sea) where the Kutani pottery comes from.

Wife Sarah casually mentioned these plans to a Kamikitazawa neighbor a few days before we left.

The next day, the neighbor came over with a list of places that were "musts" to see in those three cities. She even included names and telephone numbers of friends of hers in Tajimi and Kanazawa and told us they would be more than happy to show us around.

She knew they would, she added, because she had called them the night before about our upcoming visit.

I smiled, thanked her profusely, and jammed the list in my pocket. I had no intention of calling anybody anywhere. I'd be too embarrassed.

When we all arrived at our first stop in Tajimi, I abruptly changed my mind. Before the train pulled out of the station, we were lost. I took out the list and had Daughter Barbara call our neighbor's friend.

In five minutes, she was at the station to pick us up. She drove us all around Tajimi and stopped in family pottery kilns (I think that's what you call them) operated by her friends. We got the red carpet treatment everywhere.

They showed us how the clay (?) was mixed, demonstrated the pottery wheels on which the pieces are formed, let us see the huge kilns where the pottery is baked. They cheerfully answered our questions — through Daughter Barbara.

The owner even let each of us decorate our own cups which he will glaze, finish and mail to us — all at his expense.

Our neighbor-introduced guide even took us to dinner at her husband's restaurant.

At Kanazawa the story was practically the same. We had been told that the hotel was right at the station. We arrived after dark and couldn't see it. When we asked a kimono-clad lady where it was, she told us to follow her.

She turned in the opposite direction from which she was heading when we stopped her, led us up and down the usual assortment of Japanese railway station stairs, through a tunnel and up another four-score-and seven steps to the hotel door. She bowed and disappeared.

Once in the hotel, another friend of our neighbor took over. She treated us to dinner and the next day furnished a guide and private-car transportation to be certain we saw Kanazawa.

In Takayama, there was no neighbor friend, but the treatment was repeated. This time by a girl in an information booth at the station who arranged for us to visit all Takayama had to offer.

The nicer everybody was, the guiltier my conscience became. Except for the sightseeing taxi we hired ourselves in Takayama, no one would take any money. No matter how we insisted.

We couldn't begin to imagine how we could possibly thank our neighbor for making the trip so great. And Wife Sarah told her that when we returned to Kamikitazawa.

Her reply made me feel like a million 360-yen dollars. And, if you're an American, it should warm your heart, too.

"Please don't think about thanking me," she said. "During the month my husband and I spent in America while his job kept him near New York City, the American people could not have been kinder to our totally confused Japanese family. I'm glad to hear that in some small way, I've had a chance to partially pay them back through you. My friends were happy to help."

So — for this weekend, anyway — no complaints about the plight of the Gaijin in Japan. Only much appreciation and affection for a very kind people.

58

And that goes for all Japanese I associate with daily — with only one possible exception: Tokyo Taxi Drivers.

# III.  HOME LIFE

Exactly where the frustrations begin for the foreigner in Japan, I'm not really sure. Sometimes I think it's the collections of all those little frustrations that really get me; other times I think it's only the big ones.

One of those "biggies" is looking for a house, one of the first things almost *every* expatriate businessman has to do when he gets to Japan. Many times, a new arrival comes here to fill the wash-and-wear kimono of some departing member of his company's overseas adventurers.

And, in some of those cases, he inherits the house and all the furniture his predecessor leaves behind. I feel sorry for those guys. They miss one of the more interesting aspects of moving to Japan. That's the "looking for a house" frustration.

In Tokyo, there are dozens — or, for all I know, hundreds — of companies who devote all of their corporate efforts to finding a place to live for the "Gaijin."

I'll digress here for just a moment. "Gaijin" is a word you hear very soon after you get here — and forever after.

It's a sort of contraction of the word "gaikokujin" which means "outside person." I produce only indignant looks when I suggest to my Japanese friends that the contraction was hatched along the same lines as our "Jap" for "Japanese." They don't say it *isn't*, they just look indignant.

You'll hear it most often from native kids who shout it while they're pointing a finger right at your nose. It really upsets some of my fellow foreigners. They think it's a nasty, nasty word.

One thing certain — whether they call you "Gaijin" or "Gaikokujin" — you're *not* one of the locals. You might don a beret in Paris and pass for a Frenchman for awhile. With the help of a derby and cane in London, you might even be mistaken for an Englishman.

But, kimono, wooden clogs, samurai sword and all, you'll *never* sneak by here as a Japanese. As one friend put it: "We Gaijins can attend all the meetings, but we'll never be members." And, in a country that only recently really welcomed outsiders, a foreigner is still much of an oddity.

I used to mind only the stares, not so much the finger pointing and the "Gaijin" calling. But, then, I remembered back to Cleveland when everybody just ignored me. I like "Gaijin," pointing and staring better.

But, back to house hunting. It sounds like it ought to be a simple chore, right? After all, the company has told you how much you can spend. You know how many bedrooms you need. And, hopefully, you know where the office is and where the schools are. You also know the kind of neighborhood you're used to. So, you pick up the morning paper, circle some of the promising ads and you call the Gaijin house specialist.

Your first "only in Japan" experience is then about to begin.

# THEY SPELL IT ALL OUT — OR DO THEY?

Some years back, when I was living in New York, I used to get a big kick out of reading the classified ads in the New York Times.

Not the "Help Wanted" columns, but the ones that offered houses and apartments for rent. Because almost every word was abbreviated — the headings themselves, for instance, read "Apts, Furn-Unfurn" — reading the ads offered quite a challenge.

Only former OSS or CIA agents could really be counted on to decipher the code used in those columns. Either that, or you have to be a regular apartment-changer. Or just an ad-reader like I was.

A typical ad, for example, would read: "Apt, furn, Lge Brnstn, 2 Blk Wk Sub. BMT-IRT. Mbl Fpl. Kit. Bthrm. Shr. 2 BR. Liv-Din Comb. Tel 210-0111 aft 5 Sun onl."

Any ad-reading New Yorker worth his salt knew immediately that this described a furnished apartment in a large brown-stone building that was only a two-block walk from the subway. Either the BMT (Brooklyn-Manhattan Transit) or the IRT (Interborough Rapid Transit) line.

And, the apartment had a marble fireplace, a kitchen, bathroom with shower, two bedrooms and a combination living-dining room. And, you could only call about it after five o'clock on Sundays.

Even though I never really looked for an apartment in New York, I used to telephone sometimes just to be certain I understood the abbreviations. I must confess that "Mbl Fpl" threw me the first time I saw it.

Anyway, what I'm getting at is that they don't abbreviate like that in Tokyo's classified ad columns for houses and apartments. They spell out every word.

But, don't be misled. I've found out the hard way that it's a lot tougher to decipher the real meaning of a Tokyo spelled out classified than it ever was to unscramble a New York abbreviation.

I discovered this when I first looked for a place to live in Tokyo three years ago. I rediscovered it again last week accompanying a new Gaijin about to set up house-keeping here.

After much wasted time and motion. I decided to come up with a Tokyo house ad de-coder for the benefit of other newcomers.

Here's how it goes:

First off, watch the way they describe locations. If the ad says "convenient to St. Mary's and Seisen International schools," it *really* means that you'll be one hell of a long way from the office.

And, if it says "a six-minute walk to the station," it could mean the

62

*police* station. The subway or train station might be an hour by taxi.

If the ad says "near ASIJ bus stop," that could be anywhere. All Tokyo international schools, seems to me, have more bus drivers than teachers. I've always thought, for example, that it would probably be more effective and cheaper to park the busses in Roppongi and have the classes right there on the busses.

Sometimes, the ads say "Close to Aoyama supermarkets, only ¥150,000 a month." Don't be confused. ¥150,000 is *not* the monthly house rent, it's what it costs each time you shop in those supermarkets.

Another thing you have to watch is the garden descriptions. If the ad says the house has "a beautiful large lawn-garden," they mean there is actually enough space between the house and the wall around it for you to walk through.

If, on the other hand, it says "nice small garden," then only the pre-school kids in the family will fit between the house and the wall around it.

When the ad describes a place as a "combination Japanese Western-style house," you'll find it probably means that there is no heating, plumbing or appliances (that, in the ads, makes it "Japanese") but that the price is still ¥ 500,000 a month (like Westerners pay).

There are some other house terms worth learning. Like "cozy house." That means you'd *better* get cozy, 'cause there's no heat and there's only one room. "Studio apartment" is another way of saying there's only one room.

The words "modern bathroom" usually mean that you can flush it. Maybe it doesn't *go* anywhere, but you *can* flush it.

If it says the house has a "good commanding view," it either means a taxi knocked down the concrete wall in front of the house or that they won't start building the 26-story fish cannery across the street until next summer.

A "mansion" in Tokyo, you should know, is a lot like an apartment. The "mansion" rent, however, is twice as much.

Sometimes, the ads close with "¥450,000 monthly, negotiable." Now "negotiable" only means that they will discuss whether you pay one year or two years in advance or whether you pay on the first or the 15th of the month. Whatever, you'll pay the ¥450,000. *That's* not the negotiable part.

As soon as the complete decoder is ready, I'll let you know. In the meantime, clip this out for the next time you or your associates are house-hunting in Tokyo.

And, for when that time comes, I have an old New York wish for you: Gd Lk.

# OPEN HOUSE

Whether or not I can tell you this story in print remains to be seen. Even when I'm face to face with listeners and drawing sketches along with the story, it's difficult. Mainly because the whole thing is so preposterous — and so thoroughly Japanese.

But, it's too good to pass up, so I'll give it a try.

First, you'll have to picture the front of our Kamikitazawa house. The only entrance is via a cement walk about 10 feet wide that doubles — or triples — as a driveway and carport. This concrete strip from the street to our front steps — is exactly the length of two cars.

Because we're in Japan, of course, the house is completely surrounded by a stone wall. An iron gate that swings in is at the entrance. Now mark ''that swings in'' very carefully. That's really the whole story.

You see, when we had only one car, that gate — 10 feet wide — offered no problems swinging in. I just backed my car way back toward the house and there was plenty of room to swing the gate open and closed with the car in the driveway.

Then, a year ago September, I bought a second car — a Toyota Publica — for Wife Sarah. Now, with two cars in the exactly two-car driveway, the gate couldn't swing in.

No serious problem, I thought. I'd simply call the landlord, explain the situation, and have the gate changed so it would swing out.

From this little seed has grown one of our more intersting Oriental frustrations. First of all, the gate man came and explained that Tokyo fire laws would not put up with a gate that swing out into the street. After all, the 10-foot arc it would make would completely block our street when it was opened.

I bought that, and advised him to, dozo, fix it anyway he'd like. Just fix it. He said he'd come up with something and then disappeared.

Well, there's no sense in trying to explain *all* that followed. Briefly, it went like this:   Men came and measured — and measured and measured. Nothing.

Then more measuring. And more nothing. I called the landlord weekly for a progress report. Oh, there were plenty of reports, but no progress. Fall turned into winter;   winter into spring;   and spring into this past summer. All this time, the gate remained open — swung in against the wall so the cars could be parked in the driveway.

Finally, in the beginning of June, I ran completely out of what Japanese patience had rubbed off on me. I delivered an ultimatum to the landlord:   Fix this damn gate so that we can open and close it while the two cars are in the driveway or else. And fix it while we're on home leave in the United States. I really couldn't come up with a good "or else," but I was firm.

Well, we returned to Kamikitazawa in early August. The two cars were in the driveway. And, for the first time in 11 months, the gate was closed. I remarked to Wife Sarah that it was too good to be true.

It was.

Oh, the gate was closed all right. They had taken it down, cut it in half, hinged it in the middle. Now the arc when opening it — after you folded it in half at the hinge — was only five feet. But, it still swung in. And, with two cars in the driveway, you couldn't swing in a gate that needed only a *one* foot arc. Both cars, it appeared, were trapped in the driveway forever.

I told the landlord what I thought of this marvel of Japanese engineering. He assured me that he would have the gate man return and explain how it's done. He did come the next day. And, because my battery went dead since the car was idle for 10 weeks during our home leave, so did the man from the gas station with his portable battery charger.

They both tried to open the gate. No luck. I was losing my Irish temper and the gate man was losing his face. The gas station man didn't know what the hell was going on. "How did you get the cars in there," he wanted to know.

Me, too, I told him. And, more important at the moment, how the hell were we going to get them out?

With his face completely gone, the gate man explained that they had re-hung the gate, after hinging it, with the cars still in the driveway. He asked me to back Sarah's car up. It had to go right over some lovely bushes and up to the front steps of the house. Using a jack provided by the gas station, they jacked up my car and turned it sideways in the driveway as much as they could.

All this allowed just enough room for the folded-in-half gate to swing in and release the cars. The gate man, head bowed to his knees, apologized himself to death. He said that they would come up with a new solution right away. In the meantime, he advised, the gate would have to remain open. He drove off.

That was four months ago. It isn't that they haven't done anything about it since then. There have been at least six measuring trips — but no solution.

If all this isn't clear, please come out to our house and take a look for yourself. And, while you're there, drop in and say hello.

Our gate is always open.

# EVERYBODY, IT TURNS OUT, HAS A GATE

In the previous article, I told you the story of the gate out at our Kamikitazawa house. I outlined in detail my futile fight to simply get the gate altered so we could open and close it when the two cars were in the driveway.

Very clearly, I remember the day that battle started — it was September 18, 1971 when Wife Sarah's little Toyota Publica was delivered.

Well, another date is now forever fixed in my mind. That's January 28, 1973. It was a gorgeous Sunday, you may recall. The sun was bright; the air was clear. You could even see the outline of Mt. Fuji from Tokyo. Not the actual Mt. Fuji, but an outline at least.

It was the day the cease-fire in Vietnam was effected. It was the day when four of our Japanese friends were over for a pleasant dinner party. It was a day that our fireplace worked without smoking up the whole house.

Yes, all of that — and one more: It was the day they fixed the gate! Two men arrived at our house at about 11:30 while we were at church. They cut, welded, bolted, chipped, hammered. And, at precisely 5:08 p.m., they rang the bell and announced that "The gate is now OK."

I rushed out front. Wife Sarah, the kids, the maid, our guests — even the dog — rushed out right with me. We took turns opening and closing it, *with* the both cars in the driveway.

It worked like a real gate.

Of course, there are a few details that still have to be ironed out. Like, for instance, the men only brought enough paint to cover the areas of the gate that they cut, welded, bolted, chipped and hammered. This paint doesn't match the color of the old paint and our working gate is two distinctly different browns.

And, after I open it and get in the car to drive out, the gate slowly swings closed by itself and so has to be propped open with a large brick.

But, after all, I didn't *say* I wanted it all one color or that I wanted it to stay open long enough for me to drive out. I merely said I wanted it to open and close and it does both — quite well, indeed.

What amazed me about the whole gate story was the knowing sympathy I received from so many foreign friends in Tokyo. It seems everybody has similar problems of their own.

There is, for instance, a friend in Meguro who decided he wanted to pay for his morning paper delivery annually because he's not always home when the newspaper boy comes to the door with his monthly bill.

He called the paper, told them his problem and explained he wanted to send them a check for an annual payment in advance. They told him the amount and he sent the check. Starting a few days later, *two* copies of the newspaper now arrive every morning. And the newspaper boy *still* comes for his monthly pay for one of them.

At last report, my friend hasn't been able to shut off either copy.

Or, there was the friend in Harajuku who complained when he found out that his telephone was on a party line and that calls to his phone or to the other party's phone rang in both places. He told the phone company that he couldn't stand this and that he wanted to be the *only* party on his telephone.

The phone company's solution? Simple. They moved the other phone on his party line into his apartment, too. At last report — both are still there. And they're billing him for both.

Or how about the friend in Shibuya who always received calls for whomever had the phone before he moved in? These calls usually came in the middle of the night, too. When he complained, the phone company suggested that he get an unlisted number. Then only people who knew the number could call him. He agreed.

They came one day while he was out. They changed the phone. The new one had no number in that space in the middle of the dial. So, the next day he called the phone company, thanked them for making the change and asked for his new number.

No soap. The phone company does *not* give out unlisted numbers to anybody. At last report, his phone *never* rings.

And on and on go the stories. One thing sure, they helped me get my own problems with my gate into proper perspective. It all boils down to the one common bond shared by we foreigners who live in Tokyo.

It's simply this:   Everybody has a gate.


## THE DAY THE TOILET PAPER RAN OUT

When the United States announced some time back that they would cut off — or cut down, I forget which — shipments of soy beans to Japan, I was a monument to utter calm.

What the hell, I reasoned, I got along on as little tofu — the bean curd food made from soy beans — as possible up to then and I was certain there would be no future difficulty whatsoever for me in a no-bean-curd menu.

And, when I heard that gasoline might be hard to get, I was not really *that* upset. Quite the contrary, I was filled with some feeling of joy over the prospect of even *one* less Tokyo kamikaze taxi on the road.

The news that ¥1 and ¥5 coins may have disappeared forever because of short supply never ruffled me either. Especially since I don't recall anyone ever offering *anything* to me in Tokyo for ¥ 1 or ¥ 5.

I wasn't even *that* shook up over my discovery soon after our arrival in Japan that liverwurst sandwiches would be no more. Or that autumn Saturday and Sundays would have to be spent some other way than marathon football-game-watching on TV.

I weathered all these assorted crises with a minimum of cool-blowing. But, that all changed last week.

That's because, last week, we ran out of toilet paper.

I was going to say that this toilet paper thing hit me without warning. But that wouldn't really be true. Actually, there were definite signs of impending disaster in our house, but I ignored the danger signals.

For one thing, I can look back to last Tuesday when I noticed that the roll in our bathroom was *pastel green.* Now pastel green toilet paper is no big calamity, I know. But we have a pink bathroom that looks just like the outside of Tokyo's Akasaka Tokyu Hotel and — under normal circumstances — Wife Sarah would rather die than hang a pastel green roll in there.

Usually, of course, it was a matching pastel pink. On isolated occasions, I remember an old-fashioned white roll hung there.

But pastel *green? Never.*

It was there, however, and I just ignored it, preoccupied as I was at the time with the business at hand.

Then came Wednesday. And on Wednesday there was no pastel green paper. No pastel pink, either. Or white. *Nothing.* Well, nothing but the empty cardboard toilet paper roll tube that used to serve as such a great prop for a million make-believe games I played as a kid back in Teaneck, New Jersey.

"Where, oh where," I yelled out to Wife Sarah, "is the toilet paper?"

Talk about keeping cool, Wife Sarah casually answered, "There isn't any."

"What the hell do you mean, 'There *isn't* any'," I bellowed. "There *has* to be toilet paper. Even if it's pastel green."

"Well, there isn't any now. And, there might not be any tomorrow either," she warned.

"Send one of the kids to the store *now,*" I insisted. "I can't just sit here until tomorrow or the next day."

"You don't understand," came the voice thru the door, "the store doesn't have any either. There's *no* toilet paper in Tokyo."

"How about the people next door?" I asked. "See if you can borrow a roll from them."

"That's where I got that horrible pastel green roll the other day. And I know they don't have any more, anyway. They all just left a little while ago to use the john down at the Hilton Hotel."

68

"How about the guy on the truck with the loudspeaker? Doesn't he give out toilet paper in exchange for old newspapers?" I wondered. "He used to," Wife Sarah acknowledged, "but this week he's giving money. I'm sorry I didn't keep the newspapers."

"What about Kleenex," I pleaded. "Is there any of *that* around this house?"

"No luck," sighed Wife Sarah. "Kleenex must be out, too. I even noticed two hired cars on Meguro Dori this morning without a box of it in their back windows."

My God, I thought, this *is* serious. Then I got a bright idea. "Please, Sarah, see if there's any air mail writing paper down in my desk."

"I know there isn't," apologized Wife Sarah. "I just wrote a letter to my mother this morning on the last sheet. I told her to send us a couple of rolls of toilet paper for Christmas instead of the pudding cake mixes the boys had asked for and the Gaijin-sized bras the girls wanted. There's another ray of hope, too. I just read that the Japanese have bought millions of rolls of toilet paper from the People's Republic of China. I hope some of it is pink."

"Good Lord, Sarah, how can you be so calm? This is a very serious matter. I mean it's not like being out of soy beans or mercury-less tuna fish. This toilet paper thing strikes at the very seat of American family life. *Do* something."

"Well," she volunteered, "the new liberated Sears Roebuck catalog came this morning. Let me see if we can order toilet paper by mail. I never tried it before, but I imagine that's the way some farmers in the United States have to get toilet paper."

With that, a very bright light dawned. "Never mind, Sarah," I said, "I *know* what the farmers in the United States do. Just bring me the Sears catalog."

## YOU MAY HAVE ALREADY WON — OR LOST

I never thought the day would come, but one of the things I'm really beginning to miss in Japan is that daily healthy pile of so-called "junk mail." I mean it's been so long since anybody sent me the wonderful news that I "may already have won $25,000 a week" for the rest of my life.

If you remember the kind of mail I'm talking about, you'll also remember that, while you may already have won that $25,000 pension plan, they're not going to tell you "yes" or "no" for sure until you subscribe to the magazine and send in your check and your list of computer-selected special numbers.

Since you know what I'm doing for a living these days, you've probably guessed that while I "may already have won" on all too numerous occasions, I never actually did. I probably spent $25,000 for magazine subscriptions to find out, but the answer was always negative.

Of course, we do get a fair share of junk mail in Tokyo, but since I can't read a word — or I should say, a kanji — of most of it, I'll never really know how close I came to may already having won anything here.

Not all of the junk mail here is in Japanese — we do get an English one now and then. Usually, it's from one of the posh department stores announcing a once-in-a-lifetime sale on gold ingots or rough-cut diamonds or something like that. And, it promises, if Wife Sarah will go look at the gold ingots or rough-cut diamonds in the flesh — *and,* bring along the envelope the annoucement was mailed in — they have a very special gift for her to take home.

That very special gift, needless to say, *never* even vaguely resembles the ingots or the diamonds, but they do give it to Wife Sarah if she shows up. No maybes about it. And, as far as I can determine, she *always* shows up.

Back in Cleveland, I could tell just by the envelope that the mail was junk. Like if it was a brown wrapping paper, unsealed, rubber stamped "YOUR LAST CHANCE", and addressed to "Occupant", I had a pretty good feeling that it wasn't from a lawyer telling me that a rich uncle had died and left me a small fortune.

Unless it was a real slow mail day, I never even opened those kind.

On the other hand, if the Cleveland mail came in a white sealed envelope with a cellophane window and my name and address was spelled out in computerese with a long number after my name, I knew it was trouble. I knew that inside would be listed what I owed from last month and what the finance charge on that amounted to, what we charged this month, and how much minimum payment they expected in the next 48 hours or something like that.

Anyway, I *had* to open those window kind.

Every once in a while, the junk mailers would fool you by using your real name and sticking their thing into a white sealed envelope with a window, but that first "you may already have won" sentence blew the whole thing.

What I'm trying to get at is that junk mail is a different thing here in Japan. When you can't read anything in it, you're *never* really sure which is junk and which is for real.

For instance, my tax bills come in a brown wrapping paper envelope. The phone bill comes on a post card. So does my gasoline bill. The other day, an ad for a special sale on kimonos came in a window envelope.

Now, when you can't read a word, how the hell do you know which to pay, which to throw away? We've tried a couple of solutions.

In the beginning, I used to bring all of yesterday's mail to the office and have my secretary read it to me.

You know: She'd tell me this one's the electric bill, pay it; this one says the price is going up at the neighborhood public bath; this one wants to sell you the top ten Japanese records every month; this one wants you to buy a directory listing all the blowfish restaurants in town that have a legitimate license — and so on and so on.

That system didn't work. It was noon everyday before we got yesterday's home mail out of the way. Then, we had to start on today's office mail the same way. That shot the afternoon, because the only mail that came to the office in English was either from the home office or the Hong Kong tailor who was going to be at the Hilton Hotel all next week. Anyway, that left no time for business in the office.

Now, I've settled on a new system. If the inside of the letter is all printed, I throw it away.

If *most* of it is printed, but there are some blank spaces that have been filled in with numbers by hand or computer, Wife Sarah takes it down to the bank or post office to pay it. But that's only if the filled-in numbers have five digits or less. If it's more than five, I still check it out with the secretary-next-morning system.

This system isn't fool-proof, of course. Sometimes, Wife Sarah goes down to the bank only to find out that she's trying to pay a receipt. And once we paid a neighbor's phone bill that got dropped in our mail box by mistake. Plus I've found out at times that I've thrown away invitations to gala grand openings of one kind or another and missed freebies.

And maybe I'll never ever know that I "may already have won ¥ 25,000,000 a year for life."

But there is one big plus in all of this: We've never subscribed to a single Japanese magazine. Nor do we belong to any Asian "Samurai Sword of the Month Club."

Maybe, at last, I *really* have won.


## SAYONARA, KAMIKITAZAWA

Mark down today's date. For today, like Okinawa and Iwo Jima before it, Kamikitazawa reverts to the Japanese. The Maloneys have moved into Tokyo.

It wasn't easy to do. We'd been in Kamikitazawa for all of the first three years we've lived in Japan. And, because of Kamikitazawa, we were *really* close to the Japanese people. Especially on the train and the subway back and forth to town. *Very* close.

Despite all of the trials and tribulations spawned in Kamikitazawa, I

71

really hate to leave the place.

Especially, I guess, I hate to leave the local shopkeepers there whose infinite Japanese patience got us through those first few months alive. During those beginning days when we didn't know "ichi" from "ni" or "san", they never lost their cool.

Like I remember the day Wife Sarah sent me up for five kilos of rice. Now I had no idea how to say "five kilos" in Nihongo, so I just held up five fingers on one hand and pointed to the rice with the other. Before I got back home, the rice man had delivered five *bags* of rice, five kilos each.

And the time I wanted some of those "Spring Rolls" at the local Chinese restaurant. The phrase book said they were *"harumaki."* But when I ordered eight of them, it came out *"haramaki"* which is that knitted wool belly-band Japanese laborers wear.

The confusion resulting from that one was unbelievable.

Once I spent an hour in the meat market trying to simply get a piece of fat to grease the sukiyaki pan with. There *is* no sign language for a piece of fat.

We wound up trying a lot of Japanese food for the first time because of similar sign language difficulties. After all, when they wrapped up something I *didn't* ask for — or didn't *think* I asked for — what could I do but accept it?

In the beginning, our maid in Kamikitazawa came only three days a week. Nobody ever came to our door on those days; they always came when she wasn't around.

My solution to the language problems that resulted from these doorway confrontations was to say "Hai" to everything. Actually, that's not too good a system. Once, I damn near bought some property in Hakone by agreeing with somebody.

We got to know the mailman well, too. *Everything* sent to *anybody* in Kamikitazawa addressed in Roman letters was stuffed in our mail box.

I've told you in detail before about our problems with the front gate and about our impossible confrontations with the gas station up the corner. I won't repeat all that.

I never did get to learn the Japanese language, but all of the locals in Kamikitazawa eventually learned my sign language. It finally got down to where I could get only one five kilo bag of rice at a time, the sort of Sushi I wanted, and the very fruit I pointed to. I could even get a piece of fat for our Sukiyaki. And we were able to close our gate with the cars in the driveway.

But we still couldn't quite negotiate that train trip to Shinjuku, the change there, and the subway ride into town.

The only alternative to all that was to drive down the Koshukaido Highway which, unfortunately, has been under repair since 1943 and won't be completed — apparently — in this generation.

So, however sadly, we're giving back Kamikitazawa. As sad as we feel, however, the local Japanese residents must be happy. I can only imagine how they had that "there goes the neighborhood" feeling the first day our troop of Gaijins came down the street.

However, we never saw one "Yankee, Go Home" sign in town. Maybe they *were* there, and we just couldn't read the Japanese Kanji.

In any event, we're off to our new in-town Tokyo neighborhood. I'm in stark terror at the thought that the first thing Wife Sarah will send me to the store for is a five kilo bag of rice.

I hope the new rice man learned his Japanese from the same book I did. Or, at least, understands Cleveland sign language.

# I HOPE NOTHING HAPPENED TO YAMAMOTO SAN

I've given it a fair amount of thought lately, and I've finally come to the conclusion that one of the most troublesome things I brought to Japan with me is my name. I'm sure the same is true for any other foreign businessman.

I wasn't off the plane for five minutes at Tokyo's Haneda Airport when I realized that — for the length of my stay in Japan, anyway — I would no longer be "Maloney," but "Maroney." That's what the immigration man called me; the customs man pronounced it the same way. The Japanese businessman who met us welcomed me as "Maroney San," and that's the way we were checked in at the hotel.

Once I got used to the sound of it, I kind of liked it. And, anyway, it's not the first time that name gave me trouble. When I was a little boy, the other kids used to love to call me "Baloney" or "Macaroni" or some other such name in an effort to get my Irish up. I never disappointed them.

But the real name problems began after we moved in our house out in the Tokyo suburb of Kamikitazawa. In the first place, one of the people from our Japanese partner's company gave us a brass plate with our name on it in Kanji. They are the complicated characters based on the Chinese, not the more simple "Katakana" alphabet characters usually used by the Japanese for foreign names.

I was very proud of that nameplate and immediately hung it on the front gate. A few days later, I met one of our sort-of-English-speaking neighbors. The conversation went like this:

"Are you Maroney San?"

I admitted it.

"Do you live there?" he asked, pointing to our house.

I admitted that, too.

73

"Are you Chinese?"

"Heavens, no," I assured him. "I'm from Cleveland, Ohio — in the United States."

"Ah so," he smiled, "Creverand."

"Why are you so surprised?" I had to know.

"Well," he explained, "a group of us were talking the other night. We looked at your Kanji nameplate and knew 'Maroney' was not a Japanese name. And, since it was written in those old Chinese characters, we decided you must be Chinese."

I finally convinced him we were Americans. At least I convinced him *I* was. But — what with her black hair, brown eyes and five-foot-two frame — I think they still have their doubts about the origin of Wife Sarah.

On the day of our arrival in Kamikitazawa, I was warned by the real estate man that I'd better appear at the local post office, show them what my name looked like, and get some assurance that they understood which house was mine. If I didn't, he predicted, I'd never get my mail.

So, with his bilingual help, we did just that.

A few days later, the first letter appeared in our mailbox. It was addressed to "Shigeo Yamamoto," or some obviously Japanese name like that. I brought it back to the post office. This time I was on my own, and — although he gave me plenty of "Hai, hai's" — I knew he didn't understand.

Next day, I got two letters. One was really for me; the other was the same Yamamoto one I'd brought back the day before. Since Yamamoto San's house number was also on the letter, I simply had Son Donald go over there on his bike and drop it in Yamamoto's mail box.

The day after that, Time magazine came — four of them — all addressed in English. One was mine and the rest were addressed to Japanese neighbors. Included, of course, was one for our friend Yamamoto.

I had Son Donald deliver the magazines where they belonged on his bicycle.

Day after day, the strange mail kept coming. And, day after day, Son Donald did his delivery thing.

Finally, I mentioned the situation to the sort-of-English-speaking neighbor. Now, having — as a result of birth — a much deeper insight into Japanese logic than you or I will *ever* have, he figured it all out in ten seconds.

"You see, Maroney San," he explained, "if *you* can read the names and addresses on those misdelivered letters and magazines, they are obviously written in Roman letters from your alphabet. Since, written like that, the mailman probably can't tell 'Maroney' from 'Yamamoto', he plays it safe and delivers anything addressed in English to you."

I guess my friend was right, 'cause it went on like that for the three years we lived out there.

When we moved into downtown Tokyo, a whole new chapter was written. Of course, I went to the Kamikitazawa post office and told them of our move. And, I gave them the new address and asked them to forward our mail. They agreed.

Better than before, they also understood me — *almost* completely. Problem is, that while they are forwarding all *my* mail, they are also forwarding to me the mail that is addressed to the poor Gaijin who moved into the Kamikitazawa house after we left — even though his name is nothing like "Maroney".

The first time it happened, I gave it back to our new mailman and told him to send it back to Kamikitazawa.

No use; it comes back to me again in three days.

Certainly, I'm not going to send Son Donald out there on his bike. But, we did find a man in our new neighborhood who works in the same foreign company as that new Gaijin who lives in our old house. He's been good enough to hand deliver the mail.

The only thing that worries me now is that they are not forwarding Yamamoto San's English-addressed mail to me.

I hope he's all right.


## ALL GAIJINS HAVE FUNNY NAMES

In the previous article I was telling you some stories that illustrate the kind of problems you can have in Japan because you have such an obviously foreign name.

Well, since then, I've heard a foreign-name story to end all foreign-name stories. And, since it involves a situation that could easily happen to you, I decided I'd better tell you about it.

It goes like this:

One of our foreign friends has a wife who teaches English on the side (nothing new so far, right?). And, on her way home from "work" the other day, she stopped in a Roppongi coffee shop.

Please excuse the fact that I don't have all the finer details like the name of the coffee shop, whether she just had coffee or whether she went all the way and ordered a cucumber sandwich, too. I don't even know if she looked thru one of those thick "X"-rated comic books all coffee shops supply.

But, I do know the one fact that is most important to this story: When she left for home, she forgot her purse. And, it wasn't until she got home that she realized it.

75

Because she didn't want to walk all the way back to Roppongi for it, she telephoned the coffee shop. (Sorry, but I didn't ask her how she got the number.)

They said yes, they found the purse. She said good, hold it for me. They said nonsense, we'll send it over to your house. She said never mind. They insisted.

OK, she said, and told them her Alien Registration — the little booklet all us resident foreigners must carry always — was inside the purse and that they would find her name and address right in there. Now it was their turn to say OK, and they did.

I should digress long enough here to assure you that she had no trouble with all this conversation. Any poor soul who wants to survive with a coffee shop in Roppongi needs *somebody* around who can speak English, and it was that particular coffee shop's "somebody" that she was talking to on the phone.

Anyway, a little while later there was a knock on her door.

Now, if you are going to follow this story properly from here on, it would be better if you had one of these Alien Registrations to refer to. OK? Because, on page 4, you'd see in that heading on the first box on the top of the page that there is some Japanese writing printed and next to that, in English, the translation, "Name in full."

Well, in almost every Alien Registration book I've see in Japan, there is rubber-stamped in that "name in full" box, some more Japanese writing and some English that says "SAME AS AT PAGE 1."

Anyway, try to understand what it looks like. Now, back to the knock at the door.

She answered, and there stood a little man with a big brown envelope that contained her left-behind purse. He handed it to her, bowed low, and disappeared during her thank you.

Before she opened it up, she read the address scrawled on the outside. The numbers were right;   the apartment was right;   even the block was correct. But her name? You guessed it by now, I hope.

It was marked "To:   SAME AS AT PAGE 1 *SAN.*" They *really* believed that was her name!

Now I know you think I'm pulling your Occidental leg. Honest to God, I'm not. And, as further evidence of how something like this happens, listen to this one:

Last fall, I ordered some custom-made suits from a Yokohama tailor. You know, made-to-measure and they even embroider your own name inside.

Well, I picked out the materials and had my first fitting in the office. For some reason I can't recall right now, however, I asked the Japanese tailor to deliver the finished suits out to my Kamikitazawa house rather than to the office.

Because he was convinced he would get lost, he didn't like that idea at all. Finally, I found one of the little cards I had printed for Wife Sarah. It's one of those cards with her name on the front and a map of how to get to our Kamikitazawa house on the back.

"Just follow this map," I assured him, "and you'll find us."

He agreed. And, sure enough, he found the house. He brought the two finished suits and insisted I try them on. As I was putting in my right arm, I saw it over the inside pocket — in gold thread, yet: "Made especially for Sarah Maloney."

"Why, oh why?" I asked him. "That's my *wife's* name."

"I thought it was strange" he said, "but it was printed on that card you gave me." My wife sews in the names and I warned her that 'Sarah Maloney' was a funny name for a man.

"But," he went on, "my wife said she was going to put it in anyway. Because, as she explained, *all* Gaijins have funny names."


## TO SLURP OR NOT TO SLURP?

Lately I've been reading a lot in the newspapers and hearing a lot from Japanese business associates about a rising tide of pressure being exerted on traveling locals to improve their overseas behavior and so help erase the "Ugly Japanese" image that some think is projected abroad.

There's a flood, I'm told, of pamphlets and booklets around advising Japanese not to act like Japanese when they take to the foreign road.

They're warned, for instance, not to slurp their soup, not to pick their teeth at the dinner table, and, the men especially, not to consider telephone poles as outdoor sanitary facilities. The more I hear and read about all of this, the more I'm confused and the less I'm certain about how to counsel Son Donald on the way he should conduct himself manner-wise in private or public while we're living in Japan.

I mean I've been bringing up Son Donald according to the same rules that my mother insisted I follow under threat of severe bodily harm. And, as consistently practical under the circumstances, we've carried all those same rules to Japan.

But, now, I'm wondering if we are doing the right thing.

After all, what all those books and pamphlets are telling the Japanese is to follow the old rule about "When in Rome, do as the Romans do." Come to think of it, that's what many Gaijins around here have been telling me to do.

You know what I mean — I've been advised to quit complaining about the price of melons, steak and Old Grandad and settle down with local substitutes such as mikans, soba, and Suntory Red. You are, they remind me sternly, in Japan and should be willing to adapt rather than constantly trying to transplant your little corner of Cleveland's East Side to Tokyo.

Now what bothers me is how to work all this out.

Let's say I switch from steak to that soba noodle soup. Can I slurp my soba the way the locals do? And, if any of that stuff usually floating on top of the soba sticks between my teeth, can I pick it out right there at the table? Isn't that what the Japanese do?

Heavens, no, say my confused advisors.

"We are civilized and civilized people don't slurp soup and pick teeth at tables", they say. "Have you ever seen — or heard — anybody in Cleveland slurp soup?" they ask.

If I ignore some temporary lapses in my own children's table manners, I have to answer "No, I haven't."

But, I also have to add the often ignored fact that I've never seen *anybody* in Cleveland eating soba at all, slurp or non-slurp.

That "civilized" argument doesn't move me, either. Contrary to what some superior-feeling Occidentals might care to admit, the Japanese *do* have a civilization. And it dates back far further than most of ours.

The point I'm trying to get at is this: If the Japanese who visit the west must conform with our ways and *not* slurp their Campbell's Vegetable Soup over there, then — while we're here — shouldn't *we* conform to Japanese ways and slurp our soba? Doesn't that make sense to you?

I mean it seems to me we have to take a stand on this sort of thing right here and now. We have to get off our position of double standards. Like I notice many Gaijins get a kick out of bowing when they meet people here instead of shaking hands. (I even pulled that a couple of times by mistake back in Cleveland during our last Home Leave.)

There's also a group of get-with-it Gaijins who end almost every English language sentence with a "desho" on the end and who say "Ah so desu ka" a lot.

Generally, these are the same people who have kicked Winstons for Hi-Lites, collect woodblock prints, say they like sushi, and can pronounce all the names of Sumo wrestlers.

But these same people frown on the idea of soup-slurping and teeth-picking and telephone-poleing.

So where do we draw the line?

Do we say, "When in Tokyo, do as the Japanese do — but only sometimes. Other times do as the Romans (or the Clevelanders) do?"

I'm afraid that's not going to work. It's too complicated, and Son Donald will never understand rules like that.

Certainly you have some ideas on the subject. How about dropping me a line with your version of whether or not it's OK for Gaijins to slurp?

78

But, please hurry. Son Donald is dying for another bowl of soba and I've been steering him away from such gastronomic cultural exchanges until I got all this settled in my mind.


# COOL IT, YOU "IRATE FOREIGNERS"

Boy, I'm telling you, that was really something the way all those "Irate Foreigners" jumped all over poor Japan Air Lines.

Surely you remember the story: JAL decided to pay something like ¥500,000 to each of the Japanese passengers who went thru that four-day-long hijacking ordeal on a JAL jet in the Mediterranean — but *only* to the Japanese passengers.

This sort of "Mimaikin" payment, JAL reasoned, is strictly a Japanese traditional expression of concern and those foreigners who were hijacked along with the natives would never understand it.

Well, the "Irate Foreigners" took pen in hand and raised Occidental hell with JAL through the letters-to-the-editor columns of the Japan Times. Foreigner — the "Irates" wrote — do, indeed, understand getting ¥500,000 payments from anyone, anyplace, anytime.

And, apparently as a result of those letters, JAL changed its mind and paid off — or said they would pay off — the five foreigners on the ill-fated flight as well as the Japanese.

I, for one — maybe the *only* one — am very, very sorry to hear about JAL's reversal. I hope all you "Irates" are satisfied now. And, I hope you remember — when the Japanese around here start treating all us Gaijins just like they treat all the other Japanese — that *you're* the ones who started it with your letters. I know *I* won't forget what you've done.

Let me explain: The *last* thing I want in this country is equality, and *that's* what you're writing those irate letters in behalf of. You want us to be treated like everybody else instead of the minority we are.

Why if you have your irate ways, the Japan Times will probably be printed only in Japanese — not English. Why not? Why should you have a special newspaper? Is there a Japanese language edition of the New York Times?

And remember the next time you go to the police box with a parking ticket and the cop *doesn't* tear it up just because you're a foreigner. Wait till he runs you through the Japanese justice mill like everyone else and tells you to shove your badly-pronounced "gomennasai" apology up your glove compartment.

Because of you, they might even run McDonald's and Shakey's Pizza Parlor right out of town. They'll probably replace them with more raw fish counters and curry rice stands.

JAL itself might go all the way and stop answering their information phones in English. Then, you'll never know what time that home office visitor's plane is coming in. And you know what will happen if you're not at the airport to meet him.

What are you going to do if JAL decides to get even by pushing the Japan Travel Bureau into cancelling all their English-language tours and make you follow the same Nihongo flag as everyone else? How will you ever find your way to Nikko or Kyoto or Mt. Fuji again?

I can't wait until you ask some Japanese man where the nearest men's room is and he directs you to the same telephone pole he uses.

If you have your way, we'll all be working Saturdays and be limited to one-and-a-half day vacations that can only be taken in Golden Week, New Years, or August 15.

Supposing you never have to go down and register as an alien again and lose that day off you take to do it everytime you come back from a trip?

If you think I'm getting carried away without just reason about all of this, think of how terrible it can be here when you *are* treated equally. Everytime you are, you know, it borders on tragedy.

Like how about at the check-out counter at your favorite supermarket where you pay the same $15 for your mini roast beef as they charge the Japanese? If you really want to be of service to your fellow foreigner, get irate about *that*. Write a letter and say you don't understand $15 for beef ' cause you never paid that much back home.

And, when your Japanese income tax becomes due, stamp your irate feet and tell them you want to pay the same taxes you paid back in wherever you were in your non-irate days.

Same goes for your Johnnie Walker Black. Don't pay more than you paid in Scotland.

Don't you feel even a little irate when you're pushed on and off the train like everybody else? Shouldn't there be special cars or the subways for foreigners who aren't used to pushing?

By God, *those* are the things you ought to be writing irate letters about. You ought to be demanding *more* discrimination, *more* bias and *un*equality — not campaigning to be treated like everybody here treats the Japanese.

I hope for your sake — and for mine — that JAL hasn't mailed those ¥500,000 checks to those foreigners yet. In case they haven't, get going and write some more letters-to-the-editor. Tell him you thought it over and decided that JAL is an OK airline, but only if they *don't* pay off the foreigners.

If you don't take it back they might wind up treating all of us foreigners around here exactly the way the Japanese are treated back in Cleveland. Or, worse than that, the way people who are *born* in Cleveland are treated in

Cleveland. Then what?

Of course, JAL — even after you all write cancelling your previous irate-ness — might decide they *still* want to do something for those hijacked foreign passengers. Why not, instead of the ¥500,000 cash, give them each something of equal value?

Like a night out in Tokyo.


## LOVE IT OR LEAVE IT

This may come as a shock to many of you, but I enjoy living in Japan. In fact, I'm having the time of my life.

I guess this is because, back in Cleveland, I had some 40 years' experience living in the U.S. more I spoke the language rather fluently; less I never got lost on the train; and I seldom rode in a taxi. All that, *plus* I knew instantly exactly what those people at my Cleveland door wanted.

My point is, it was pretty much a routine existence back there. Even at the office, there were no "We's" and "they's", only "us". And, I learned to become quite comfortable in that routine. I *liked* Cleveland.

Then came Tokyo.

Here, I can't speak the language fluently. Hell, I can only ask questions — simple questions, at that — in this language and I understand only about five per cent of the answers. I get lost on almost every train trip I take. I try to ride in a taxi, but only score occasionally, and I *never* know what the little people at the door want.

As a result, I might describe my life in Japan with a whole lot of adjectives, but one of them certainly would *not* be "routine." In the office here, I'm the only "we" — *everybody* else is "they." But for my money — even at ¥265 to a dollar — the collection of all that non-routine is what makes everything in life here worthwhile.

Now for many foreigners (I'm sure you know at least *one*), it's the little things that cause them to join the ranks of the "Japan Haters" that I've talked about before and set them off impatiently counting the days until they can re-join the routine life back in Cleveland or wherever. My conversations with some of them lead me to believe it's because they are convinced that the long list of Tokyo-spawned frustrations are directed personally against them.

It's probably too late to convince those already into their countdown that it's not that way at all, so I'm directing what I have to say today to the more recent crop of newcomers. I want to get at them before they join up with either the "Haters" or the "Lovers" — while they're still active members in the "Just Confused."

First off, I want this fresh crop to know that nobody else can open a Japanese milk bottle, either. Don't laugh. I know many who started their countdowns the moment they first tried to get the cap off the bottle.

Back in Cleveland, I just used to get my index fingernail under that little tab on the cap and pull it off and pour the milk. By now, you must know that there is *no* such half-round tab in the middle of a Japanese milk bottle cap.

So, I tried to get my nails around the edge. No go. A Japanese milk cap is a marvel of precision Oriental engineering and there's no room for finger nails around the edge. Then, I pushed down, ever so easy, on the cap. It resists, but finally lets go and goes down into the neck of the bottle. And the milk that was in the neck of the bottle comes out — in surprisingly vast quantities and with amazing coverage of both your clothes and the kitchen floor and cabinets.

What's worse, the cap lodges firmly in the neck of the bottle and prevents you from pouring out what little milk remains inside.

Later, I got on to the little thing that looks like a miniature ice pick which the milk companies provide for such emergencies. The idea is that you pierce the cap with the pick and impale it. Then, when you lift the pick at an angle, the cap comes with it — *most* of the time.

Son Donald Jr., of course, has found any number of his own applications for that pick, like stabbing caterpillars out in the garden and busting other people's balloons. So, even after I finally found this pick thing as the answer, I can almost never find the damn pick.

And don't think you're going to end all this by switching to milk in cardboard containers. You'll see containers in the store, all right. And, they look just like the containers back in Cleveland. You simply pull apart one side at the top and it forms a spout, right?

*Wrong.*

The same Japanese dairy engineering specialists who came up with the bottle cap minus the tab have invented a milk carton glue that will never, *never* let go. You'll eventually tear the carton OK, but you'll pour milk from an unpredictable ragged edge, not from a friendly spout.

Now, really, does *any* milk bottle or carton in Cleveland start you with this kind of challenge and excitement? Never. And the milk company back there doesn't furnish a caterpillar-killer either.

If the milk thing doesn't get you, the little red public phones will. It's easy enough to place a call on those little red phones. It's *ending* the call where the fun comes in. Just like in Cleveland, you put your money in and wait for the dial tone. Then you dial and your number — or *some* number, anyway — answers. And you talk — for *exactly* three minutes.

Then, with no "your three minutes are up; signal when through" or any other conversation or warning of any kind, the phone goes dead. *That's* how you know your three minutes are up in Japan. And, since the callee has no idea what red phone number you're calling from, he can't call you back; you have to do it all again.

Aggravating?

Hell, no. Quite useful.

Let me give you an example: Some months back, the home office told me that a very important U.S. customer of ours, with his wife, would be coming to Tokyo for the first time on a pleasure trip. They said they gave him my office number, that he would be calling me, and that I should, with Wife Sarah, take them out to dinner.

Well, the warning was weeks in advance and I forgot all about it. Then one day, he called me — from a little red phone. He was just talking about the weather and the plane ride across the Pacific and shrines and things, waiting for me to spring the offer for dinner he'd obviously been promised by the home office. Because I forgot to ask Wife Sarah which day would be OK, I stalled and talked with him about weather, planes, shrines and things, too — until the three minutes were up and he disappeared in the middle of a sentence about some temple he'd seen.

Now, knowing it would be awhile before he would figure out what the hell happened, I immediately called Wife Sarah on another line, established that dinner the next night was OK (we always leap at any chance to charge off roast beef at the Hilton's Keyaki Grill to the company) and waited for his call back.

It came, and I apologized (believably) for not warning him about the rather abrupt finish on the red phones before inviting him to dinner the next night. He acted surprised (also believably) and accepted immediately.

How can you get mad at such a helpful little red phone?

And, sure as hell, you'll forget where you put that damn ticket you have to turn in at the end of your subway or train ride. And, you'll change trains at the wrong station or forget to change at all. And, the empty taxi will pass you by in the pouring rain. And, your Japanese collapsible umbrella won't collapse when you want it to and *will* when you *don't* want it to. And, on and on.

But, I guarantee you one thing: In Tokyo, you'll *know* your alive.

In Cleveland, sometimes, you can forget.

You'll notice that this is the smallest section of this book. That's because the social whirl — or, more accurately, the social ripple — doesn't really take up much of your time in Tokyo.

It has it's moments, of course. Seems like every month one foreign bank or the other opens a Japanese Branch and has a big cocktail party to mark the event. And, you can't ignore the Wednesday night movies at the American Club or the Press Club (if they didn't both show movies on the same night, the social life would double).

It isn't that there isn't plenty to do in Tokyo. It's a jumping town — until about ten o'clock each night.

But, the cost is high, and only native Japanese expense-account-type businessmen seem to be able to afford it. Of course, when Home Office visitors are in town, it's the custom to take them out. That ritual serves two purposes: First, it gives you an opportunity to show them that what you've been telling them about Tokyo prices is really true. Second, whether the Home Office visitor picks up the check or you do, the company pays for the cost of the demonstration and you and the wife get a night on the town.

Mostly, though, social life in Tokyo is what you contrive to make it. And — as you'll soon read — contrive we do.

# NOTHING TO DO

If you've been in Japan any length of time at all — like more than two hours — you're probably not neutral about this country. At least, I've never met a neutral foreigner. Foreigners either love Japan — make that LOVE, all capitals — or they HATE it. That's all capitals, too.

Probably because my mind is just sick enough, I enjoy antagonizing both the Japan Lovers and the Japan Haters. When I'm in the midst of Lovers, I recite all the terrible things about Japan's that the Haters have taught me. And, when surrounded by Haters, I speak of nothing but the Oriental paradise that is Japan — according to the Lovers, anyway. In a mixed group, I talk only about the prices of American cake mix in Japanese supermarkets. *Everybody* agrees about that.

Anyway, last Saturday night, I found myself with nothing but Haters. There we were, in one of those million-yen-a-month apartments, sipping the best of duty-free booze, munching on the finest hors d'oeuvres, all served by a bartender and two "hors d'oeuvre tenders" (I think that's what you call them).

After everybody first established which company everybody else was with (that seems to be extremely vital information in Tokyo), the subject for the evening's discussion settled on "Resolved: There's Nothing to Do in Tokyo."

For over an hour, I listened to evidence piling up supporting the fact that the world's largest city was a cultural and social Asian Sahara. All the participants were speaking for the resolution. All agreed that "Nothing to Do" was the foreigner's number one problem.

Now, you know how dull an evening can be if everybody is going to agree on everything. So, I decided to strike a blow for the Lovers. "I'm sorry," I interrupted. (I really wasn't sorry, but I don't want to come off a complete troublemaker. So, whether I'm acting as a Lover or a Hater at one of these things, I always start with "I'm sorry.") "I find quite the opposite is true. There's just too much to do in Tokyo".

"Like what?" challenged the Haters' leader who started the whole thing earlier.

"Well, let's take just one day—this coming November 23rd. It's a Thursday."

"What's to do on a Thursday?" Hater scoffed.

"Everything. That's my problem. From morning until night, there will be so much to do on November 23rd that I don't know what to plan. I never had problems like that back home."

"For instance?" Hater wanted to know.

"Well, for one thing, it's Thanksgiving. Do we go to the American

Club for the buffet? Or do we go to one of the Hotels for their dinner? Or do we stay home? And, even if I settled that question, there's still a problem.''

''Do tell us about it.''

''There's a big Agricultural Festival that day at Meiji Shrine. Farmers from all over Japan will be there with farm products from every district. They'll pray for a better crop next year, then throw all the fruits and vegetables into a parade of cars and go from Meiji to Shimbashi to Ginza and wind up at Isetan in Shinjuku.''

''Big deal. What's the conflict?''

''On the same day, at the same time, there's an Issa Festival at Entenji Temple in Adachi-Ku. There'll be another big parade there, featuring a person representing Issa, one of the most famous masters of the 'Haiku', the Japanese poems of exactly seventeen syllables.''

''You really *have* a problem,'' the Haters agreed.

''Especially since it's a Thursday,'' I added, ''and I'll be already worn out from trying to make a decision Wednesday night about whether to go to the Press Club movie or the American Club movie.''

The Haters were really steaming up now. Finally one of them exploded:  ''Why don't you just get lost?''

''Now,'' I smiled, ''You're arguing on my side.''

''What the hell are you talking about?''

''You can get lost in Tokyo any time or any day. That's something else to worry about for Thursday.''


## THE PLEASURE OF YOUR COMPANY


You can't help but notice that just about every Gaijin-type organization and English-language newspaper in town goes out of its way to tell the innocent newcomers everything we Old Japan Hands think we already know about Oriental survival.

Like the American Chamber of Commerce publishes ''Living in Japan,'' a hard cover book that gives advice and facts about coping with almost everything. The American Club has all kinds of classes, it seems, on Asian pursuits from rice cooking to kite making. The Press Club is even sponsoring language lessons.

Depending on their individual specialities, columnists about town are always telling the new arrivals things like where to get their luggage repaired for less money than the airlines paid them in damages, how to cook octopus so it tastes like filet mignon, and on ways to live without grapes, melons, and Johnnie Walker Black — if they really try.

But, it occurs to me, nowhere can you newcomers get the straight dope on how to behave under certain circumstances you're bound to find yourselves mixed up in while you're here. So, I've decided to take it upon myself to clue you in on some of these subjects that others find taboo.

The first situation I want to handle — and the most potentially dangerous one — is the cocktail party. Because, sooner or later, somebody is going to invite you to one while you're here, and — believe me — they are not like cocktail parties back in Cleveland.

Don't for a minute consider throwing one of your own until you attend one given' by somebody else. There are too many rules to learn any other way than by personal experience.

Probably your first invite will come from somebody your wife has met at Judo lessons somewhere. Or, from somebody one or the other of you talked to at a PTA meeting or sat with at a luncheon sponsored by the Chamber of Commerce.

First impressions made at these affairs can be vital to repeat invitations from others you'll meet at the party. For instance, if you have a driver, then — of course — be driven right to the door. If you *don't* have a driver, don't ever admit it. Have the taxi let you off a block away. If anybody sees you walking that last block, tell them that you were afraid your big car wouldn't fit in the narrow street.

Don't ever come by subway, because you might meet somebody else on that subway who is going to the some party and spoil both your Japanese futures.

After the party, unfortunately, some one will find out there's no driver waiting out front for you. Tell them his wife or kids were ill and you thought it a crime to keep him hanging around.

When you get inside, surely you and your wife will be separated. Therefore, always thoroughly rehearse with her answers to questions you're likely to be asked so that your answers agree. That's pretty easy to arrange because the questions are always the same.

First, of course, will be your name. That should offer no problem although some may ask you to spell it. That's because they plan to look you up in one of the club directories they have at home to see, A., If you belong, and B., If all the other answers you gave check with the directory info.

Then comes, ''What company are you (or your husband) with?'' That's crucial, so you'd better answer right or you could be at your last Asian cocktail party. It's a toughie, because, while that company of yours might control the whole economy of Kokomo, Indiana, it doesn't mean a thing to the New Yorker you're talking to.

Don't lie about it, of course, or make up a name. But, think of other ways you might field the questions. Try, ''Well, he came over here on the advice of IBM because they told him there might be a good market here for our interfacing software." Or, "His company is involved somehow with Mitsubishi." (That works even if you just fill your tank at a Mitsubishi gas station.) Of course, if you're really with IBM or Mitsubishi or General Motors or some big outfit like that, spit it out without explanation.

Next question is usually divided into two parts. Part One: "How long have you been in Japan?" Part Two: "How much longer will you stay in Japan?"

Watch part one, because if you say a long time and they've never seen you at a cocktail party before, that raises a red flag. Part two is trouble, too. If you say a short time, then they won't think there's any sense in talking further with you and they'll move on to the next person. If you say a long time, then they might get the idea that you can't hack it with the company back home. Be careful.

Your answers to "Where are you from?" and "Where are you living now?" are optional. Seldom a problem there. Same with "What school are your children attending?" Truth is always OK there, too.

Best watch, "Who's sitting with the kids tonight?" Unless it's their daughter, answer, "One of the maids."

Best stratagem of all, probably, is for you to come on strong and early *asking* the questions. That way, you can collect all the answers and later — when *they* start asking *you* — you'll know the flavor of the group and can give your replies accordingly.

One question you must *never* ask the host is, "Is the company paying for this party?"

The company seldom knows, so there's no reason why you should.


## OH, HOW THE TOKYO SOCIAL WHIRL GOES ON!


Recently, the Japanese Prime Minister's Office published the results of a world-wide survey they sponsored which was designed to measure what they called the "consciousness of youths of the world."

The survey people asked a lot of questions of a lot of youths between the ages of 18 and 24 and covered 11 countries.

Results of the survey, I'm told, caused quite a ruckus in older Japan circles because Japanese young people, when compared to their counterparts in foreign countries, showed a rather high degree of frustration with life in general, particularly with the Japanese society and the Japanese state.

The kids' views of life in general, I agree, didn't look too good. For example, 30.6 per cent of Japanese youth is dissatisfied with family life, 42.5 per cent with school life, 40.0 per cent with their place of work and 73.5 per cent thought their social life in Japan left something to be desired.

Now I don't want to stick my Gaijin nose in the affairs of the native youngsters around here. And since I live in a bamboo house, I don't want to throw stones.

What I mean by that is there are certainly times when at least 30.6 per cent of my own kids are dissatisfied with our family for one reason or another. And I can vouch for the fact that occasionally at least 42.5 per cent of them are fed up with school. I myself, occasionally, would join with the 40.0 per cent who would have things sukoshi different at work.

But, I do feel well qualified to give some advice to that 73.5 per cent who are unhappy with their social life in Japan. Gee whiz, what could they want that you can't do — socially — in Japan?

I mentioned this to Wife Sarah the other day — who coincidentally was just warning me that we'd better cut down on our entertainment because we're getting over-socialized. Why don't you, she asked me, tell the Japanese youths about how *we* spend our social hours during a typical week in Tokyo. Maybe they'll try the same things and get to be as socially satisfied as we are. Then, too, Wife Sarah went on, maybe they'll even be as happy about their Japanese social life as the American kids are about theirs (only 35.7 per cent of *them* were unhappy socially).

Map out last week for them, she ordered, and show them how it's done. So, that's the theme of today's column. It's addressed to those unhappy 73.5 per cent.

First off, kids, loosen up with the neighbors. It's easy in Japan. We talk to our Japanese neighbors every day — and always a different conversation. That happens when we meet them on the street. Sometimes we say, "Konichiwa" (Good Afternoon). Sometimes, "Ohayo Gozaimas" (Good Morning). Sometimes, even, "Konbanwa" (Good Evening). *Always* a different conversation.

And, sometimes, the Japanese even answer back as they go by. Is that social life or isn't it?

We even had two of our Japanese neighbors call at our home last week, in person. True, one only wanted us to make our dog stop barking. And the other one was collecting for community chest or something. We'll never know. But that's not important. The neighbors *did* call on us. *That* counts as social life.

Actually, now that I try to get it all down on paper, last week *was* rather slow for us socially. There wasn't, for instance, a single foreign bank opening or the social hour at one of the hotels that goes with it.

I can't deny, however, that we *did* socialize up at Yasukuni Shrine Monday night. There was a big festival up there. We got to see all the ladies dancing around some statue. Why, they even had canvas covered stands selling all kinds of things.

We had some barbecued squid, ate corn-on-the-cob drenched in soy sauce, and bought the kids cotton candy made out of *real* cotton.

Now, if you Japanese kids would have joined in all this, your replies to the survey might have been different.

What the hell, American kids *never* get a chance to see people in kimonos dancing around a statue in 95° heat. And, they probably *never* ate barbecued squid *or* soy-sauce-covered corn. Even their cotton candy is just candy.

Still, only 35.7 per cent of them are complaining. Think about it.

Don't feel bad if you missed the festival at Yasukuni. There'll be another one next week, and the week after that, and the week after that, and... Just don't feel bad.

Another thing, we did that very big Tokyo social thing last Saturday — we went to the Tsukiji Fish Market at five in the morning to watch them sell the fish. Of course you're complaining about no social life; I didn't see *one* of you 18 to 24 year olds there.

There's one more reason why I don't understand your dissatisfaction. Sunday afternoon I took my kids up in Tokyo Tower. It was a great day. We could see all the way to Roppongi — about three blocks away. I know you kids were there. About two million of you, in fact. How come you didn't find that experience acceptable socially?

And don't you know how to spend a social evening at home around the TV like we do? We watch the baseball games. Of course, we never know how they end because they're cut off at 9:25, but what we see is fun.

Oh, there are so many other social highlights of last week I want to tell you about. About walking down Ginza when they close off the street. About a visit to the Oriental Bazaar or Kiddy Land stores.

And how about going to chat with one of the Hong Kong tailors who has set up shop in the Hilton? Don't you get a personal letter of invitation like we do? I bet you didn't even go over to Kasumigaseki and watch the farmers demonstrate against the government.

Or, if it's *real* excitement you want, how about a taxi ride?

Good Lord, there's a whole giant social world right around you here if you'll only get with it. Really, I can think of only *one* legitimate reason that you 73.5 per cent are not tickled-to-death socially.

And that could be because, since you were born here and are now between the ages of 18 and 24, you've just been in Japan too long.


## VISITING FIREMEN

If you had some home-office people over during mid-August, I hope you realize that your fringe benefit progress has been set back 20 years. I did

91

have visiting fireman, and my personal set-back may be more like 30 years.

First of all, you know that the one thing that annoys most of us about living and working in Japan is money. We all thought that "overseas bonus" or "expatriate allowance" — or whatever each company calls it — was going to let us, at last, salt away a few bucks for the first time in our lives. That was while we were back in Cleveland or New Paltz or wherever.

Then, we came to Japan. And came the realization that everything here costs so damn much that we really had to *spend* that overseas allowance. Then, each in his own way, we opened our campaign to get the home office to increase that allowance. We bitch regularly. We clip articles out of the paper about pollution and Xerox 50 copies so that everyone back there reads about our sacrifices. We send surveys from the American Chamber of Commerce that shows how generous those *other* companies are. We send the latest Japanese government statistics on cost-of-living. We cry about the yen revaluation. When they send somebody over here, we plot their social tour to demonstrate all these hazards to life and pocketbook.

Well, in mid-August, they came.

I decided that I'd bring them right to the house for dinner. And not by car (I'm doing *my* part to fight pollution in Tokyo), but by Monorail, then Yamanote commuter line to Shinjuku and the Keio Railroad Line to Kamikitazawa. Their plane landed at 5:00p.m. Perfect time for the transit crush.

There *was* no crush. You probably read about it. For the first time in Japanese history, almost 70% of the workers took a real vacation in August. Because it was "Bon Festival" time, they all took it *that week*. The trains were damn near empty. *We all got a seat*. Much nicer than Cleveland trains, the firemen said.

When we got to the house, the gardener was just leaving. One of those guys who usually charges so much for nothing. He announced, in perfect English that I didn't even know he knew, that there would be no charge for the bushes he put in today. "Service," he said. "How generous," the firemen said.

My wife served roast beef for dinner. Great, I thought. What an opening to remind them about beef prices in Japan and that the little roast beef they were eating was about 12 bucks worth. Before I saw the opening, however, Wife Sarah livens up the conversation by announcing "I hope the roast isn't too tough. It's been in the freezer for awhile. The kids just don't care for beef anymore. They like Japanese Soba and Katsudon and Yakitori. Thank god. Japanese food is cheap."

During dinner, the doorbell rang. The maid announced that it was the man delivering my new tape deck and did I have ¥90,000 for him. The fireman observed that that "was half the U.S. price for such a tape deck. How lucky to be stationed in Japan!"

After dinner, I decided to attack. To walk them up to the shopping street and point out Melon for $8.00 each and Papaya for $5.00 each.

Would you believe there was *no* Papaya and that the Melons were on sale for $1.00? Still not cheap, but only one-eighth of the $8.00 I'd been complaining about. The other fruits? "Much cheaper and better looking than the ones back at the A&P", was one fireman's reaction.

For the next two days, there was not one serious traffic jam in Tokyo. And our Japanese partners picked up every lunch and dinner check. We never even saw a menu or the prices on them. I thought of explaining that they only do this when firemen were in town, but I decided it wouldn't ring true.

And, of course, you know the "we have to work every Saturday in Tokyo" bit. Not *one* Japanese partner was working that Saturday. We had no appointments.

In pure desperation, I planned Sunday dinner at that restaurant on top of the New Otani that goes round and round. Two birds there, I thought: High prices and an excellent view of the surrounding pollution. Well, the Otani had a special buffet-only deal of all-you-can-eat for half their usual prices. Three straight days of high winds had Tokyo air so clear that you could see Hawaii.

The parting shot came at the airport the next afternoon as the firemen headed home. They picked up a copy of the Japan Times with a headline that said "Japan to Import Two Billion Dollars of U.S. Goods to Balance Trade."

"Just get half of that for us," The firemen said, and headed east from this Oriental Paradise — on the last plane out before the worst smog we had in two months.


## ALL THAT FOR ¥100

The other day, while catching up on all the local Tokyo news I'd missed while we were on home leave in the United States, I came across an editorial in a June copy of the Japan Times newspaper about leisure.

It seems that the Japanese Government's Ministry of Trade and Industry — we all know and love it as "MITI" — did a survey designed to find out what the Japanese do with their leisure time. And, the editorial writer was slightly put out because the survey ignored Pachinko, the pin-ball-parlor pastime so popular in Japan.

I was surprised, however, to read on in that editorial that the writer thought Pachinko "may be less respectable in some eyes." Surprised, because for a long time after we first arrived here in Japan, Pachinko was the big social event for some members of the Maloney family. Son Sean, anyway.

First hint we ever got that the game existed was out in suburban Kamikitazawa one night when he asked for ¥100 after dinner. In those days, ¥100 was only about 27 cents, but I still decided to find out what he intended to do with it before we coughed it up.

"I'm going to play Pachinko," he said.

"What is Pachinko," I asked.

"It's a game. For ¥100, you get a plastic box full of little steel balls. You dump these in a tray on one of the Pachinko machines and you flip the lever with your thumb." To Sean, it all seemed perfectly logical.

"And what do the little steel balls do?" Wife Sarah wanted to know.

"They go flying up a little loop, spout out into an area of the machine filled with hundreds of little nails, bounce off the nails, and — if you're lucky — fall into one of the little holes just big enough for the ball."

"I don't understand," I said — and I *didn't*. "Why are you *lucky* if the ball goes in the hole?"

"Because," Sean sighed, "when a ball goes into one of the little holes, lights light, bells ring, and in another tray on the machines, you automatically get about another dozen balls — *free!*"

"*That* makes you lucky?"

"Sure, it makes you lucky. Because, if you put a ball into one of those little holes — besides winning a new supply of free balls — the little hole opens wider and, next time, it's easier to get a ball in there."

"So," I assumed, "the next time you get a ball in the wider hole, it gets even wider."

"Oh, Dad," Sean exasperated, "of course not. When you get a ball in one of the holes a previous ball made wider, the hole closes up to be smaller again."

"Now what is the sense to that?" I asked.

"Because, if it stayed wide or got even wider, you'd get too many free extra balls and win too many prizes."

I had to find out, "What prizes?"

"Well," Sean listed, "You can turn in all your little steel balls at the end of the game, and — depending on how many you have — you get a chocolate bar, a pack of Hi-Lite cigarettes or a can of abalone or something."

"But, Sean," I observed, "you said you don't *like* Japanese chocolate; Hi-Lites only cost ¥80 — ¥20 cheaper than the original supply of balls — and nobody really eats canned abalone, do they?"

"No, of course not. They sell these prizes to a guy around the corner."

"And then what?"

"And they take the money back to the Pachinko parlor and buy some more balls."

Then, I wondered out loud what they do if they lose their original supply of balls before any of them go into those little small or temporarily wider holes. "Then," Son Sean announced, "they need another ¥100 like I do now."

I could see Wife Sarah was about to veto the whole ¥100 idea. "Do you mean," she turned to Sean and asked, "that you intend to sit around a Pachinko Parlor all night?"

"No, Mom," he assured her. "You *stand* in a Pachinko Parlor."

"Stand?"

"Yes, it's a stand-up game."

"Like pool!" Wife Sarah decided.

. "No, no," Sean was insulted. "A pool table is flat; a Pachinko machine is vertical."

I decided I'd better step back in and settle all this. "Tell me again, Sean. You want ¥100 to go up to a Pachinko Parlor where you buy a bunch of little steel balls, pour them into a machine, hit a little lever, hope the balls bounce off nails and go into holes so you'll get more little steel balls, bigger holes to aim at, free Hi-Lites, chocolate and canned abalone that you can sell to somebody to get more money to buy more little balls and start all over again. Is that right?"

Sean insisted that it was.

"Give him the ¥100," Sarah gave in.

"Are you sure?" I asked.

"Certainly, I'm sure," she confirmed. "Now that I hear all this summed up that way, I have to admit that I didn't think you could make that much happen in Tokyo for $100, much less ¥100."


## IT'S ALL THERE IN BLACK AND WHITE


It always amuses me to hear about things that make Gaijins mad. The other day, at a small social get-together down at the American Club Stag Bar, the gripes were really pouring out.

"Did you know that they stopped playing the chimes on those little red public phones?" asked one annoyed gentleman.

"What the hell are you talking about?" asked another. "What chimes?"

"Don't you know that those little red phones used to play chimes — bong, bong, bong — about 30 seconds before your three minutes were up to warn you that you'd soon be disconnected? Then, at exactly three minutes, the chimes would sound again and you'd be cut off?"

"Oh, yeah," came the answer, "now I know what you mean. That's a great idea.''

''That *was* a great idea,'' said the griper. ''Now, no more chimes.''

''But I read that now you can extend calls from little red phones over three minutes just by putting in ten more yen.''

''You can. But, no more warning chimes. At the end of three minutes they cut you off without a bong — unless you remember to put in the extra money. No chimes. No 'Your three minutes are up; signal when through'. No nothing. Just cut you off.''

''Who cares about the bong-bong -bong on the telephones?'' snapped one of the older men. ''You guys better start worrying about the *big* picture. That's what's going to finish us off over here.''

''What *big* picture?'' was the unanimous question.

''What those 'Japan experts' back home are printing about doing business here. Have you read any of it lately?''

''Like what?'' everybody wanted to know.

''Like, listen to this,'' he ordered as he pulled a copy of one of those subscription newsletters out of his pocket. ''It says that the Japanese businessmen are so successful because they make instant decisions, because they're flexible, and because they're creative and imaginative.''

Everybody's lower lip dropped at once as they lunged for the newsletter. ''My God,'' confirmed the first to grab it, ''that's exactly what it says.''

All agreed that a report like that certainly was at odds with the information and excuses they have been sending back to the home office.

''That's all I need is for the guys back in Chicago to read some drivel like that. As it is, they're driving me crazy because no foreign businessman in Tokyo has been kidnapped yet and held for a half-a-million-dollar ransom.''

''Why the hell does *that* bother them?''

''They figure that if we're all as good as the American Chamber of Commerce in Japan says we are, why doesn't somebody get kidnapped? Why do they only kidnap guys in South America? Are they *that* much better than those of us in Tokyo?''

That started everyone wondering just how much their respective companies *would* pay in ransom.

An old Japan Hand shut that thinking off with, ''Hell, it costs them a half-a-million a year to keep me here, if I listen to their story. So, why wouldn't they pay that much to ransom me and send me home.''

''Maybe they'll send you to South America.''

The only guy in the place who was quiet up to then completely changed the subject with ''Never mind kidnapping and start worrying about the Pandas.''

''The *Pandas*?'' screamed the kidnapping worrier. ''Now what's with the Pandas?''

"Good Lord, don't you *know* about the Pandas?"

"Know what?"

"About their new house."

"Yeah, I read they are about to move into a new home out in Ueno Zoo. So what could that possibly have to do with us?"

"Do you know how much it cost?"

"I remember something about 40 million yen. I repeat, so what?"

"It was *exactly* 40 million yen, and *that's* what."

"What's what?"

"For 40 million yen, the Japanese built them a new house with a pool, with bullet proof glass, a medical treatment room, a bedroom and an outdoor playground."

"So?"

"Forty million yen bought all that plus air conditioning. And that's about $155,000 at today's exchange rates."

"C'mon," everybody insisted, "get to the point."

"That *is* the point. The United States also just finished a house for their Pandas in the Washington Zoo and it cost over $400,000 for what sounds like the same thing."

"But. . ."

"But *nothing* . That's not all. The Pandas' upkeep in the Washington Zoo is costing $550,000 a year. The Japanese say they only spend about ¥ 3000 a day — or $12 — to feed theirs. Even if you add the cost of keepers, Tokyo's cost doesn't come anywhere near that of Washington."

"We miss the point," everyone agreed.

"The point is just this: The Pandas are foreigners, Gaijins. They live for a hell of a lot cheaper in Tokyo — about a third as much — as it costs the other two Pandas who live in Washington. That makes the Japanese government's recent cost of living figures sound right. Don't you see what that will mean when our home offices put all those Panda figures together for themselves?"

I'm afraid I couldn't stay interested in where the discussion went from there. I was too busy wondering:

How much ransom *would* Harris Corporation pay for me?


## IT REALLY *WAS* A BASEBALL GAME!

I've tried — Oh, believe me, I've tried — to get into Japanese sports to beef up our social life.

After watching two or three Japanese Sumo wrestling tournaments on television, I even decided to go see one in the flesh. And that's not just an expression; Sumo matches, you know, are done in as much flesh as you'll ever see in a sporting match anywhere, anytime.

After I got into the Sumo stadium in what appears to be uptown Tokyo, I got my first shock: We were to sit on the floor in our "box".

Now we took a whole "box" because my Japanese friends told me a box holds four people. Well, it *does* hold four people, but it's very necessary that these four people be four *Japanese* people — not oversized Gaijins like me.

Fortunately, I took Wife Sarah and two of our kids. By Western standards, they are all of normal size. By Sumo box standards, we had a hell of a problem squeezing in. Finally, after contortions I didn't even know I could perform, we made it.

As soon as we were settled, they brought shopping bags of obento box lunches, fruit, beer and soda — all arranged by our Japanese friends who arranged the box. Then came the inevitable pot of green tea and cups to match.

Since there was absolutely no space for all of this, we piled it on our laps. That was OK for awhile. But then we decided to start eating and drinking to clear our laps, and that was a tragedy. We all just got bigger and the box got tighter.

Well, for more than four hours, the Sumo wrestlers paraded around in the nearly altogether. They squatted down, bowed, threw tons of salt around, drank water from bamboo cups, stamped their feet and clapped their hands.

For a brief — very brief — few seconds now and then, they even wrestled.

My legs and back ached so bad that I felt I'd actually been involved in every match.

All I could think of as I was dying of muscle spasms was that I must be missing something that other Gaijins see.

After all, all my friends collect Sumo woodblock prints at great expense. They read the English-language Sumo magazines. They've bought wrestler Takamiyama's new book about what it's like to be a Gaijin Sumo wrestler (he's from Hawaii). They also leave work early on tournament days to go home and watch the matches on television.

And then it hit me — *they watch it on television.* They sit in an upholstered chair, drink cold beer and eat Ritz crackers and Velveeta cheese. Of course.

They are *not* sitting on understuffed pillows balancing a hot cup of green tea on their lap with their neighbor's knees in their back, drinking room-temperature Pepsi and trying to swallow dried squid without tasting it.

Next time I go to see these matches live, I'll sit upstairs in the cheap seats that I hear are *really* seats — with backs, arms, everything.

As it was, I'm afraid that I couldn't really enjoy Sumo. Funny part of it is, neither did most of the Japanese in the stadium. They were too busy enjoying the spectacle we created trying to adjust to our environment.

Now baseball is something else again.

Actually, I got into Japanese baseball via television, too. Even with the sound off, a Gaijin can understand the game. In fact, *only* with the sound off.

For months, of course, I thought all games ended at 9:20 or 9:25 every night when they are cut off television — even if it's the bottom of the ninth with the score tied, bases loaded, and Nagashima (the Japanese Babe Ruth) at bat with a 3-2 count and two outs.

Then I went to the real thing at Korakuen Stadium in Tokyo.

First off, it doesn't end at 9:20. They play to the end. It looks just like an American baseball field — a pitcher's mound, three bases, nine guys on a team, dugouts, the works.

The umpires even call "strike," "ball" "foul," etc. Of course, all these words have "u's" on the end — but you *can* understand them.

Each side gets three outs to an inning, too. And if the ball is hit over the fence, it's a "Homu Run."

As you might expect, though, it's not *exactly* the same in all respects.

For instance, the boy running around the stadium with a big box hung in front of him is yelling "Hot Dogs." And what he's selling *looks* like Hot Dogs. That's why I tried one.

I won't plague you with the details. Just accept that they are definitely *not* Hot Dogs. But they *are* definite clues to what the Japanese do with whale meat.

Another thing you'll never see in Yankee Stadium is the obento boy selling those marvelous Japanese box lunches. It's kind of difficult to root for the home team while eating barbecued eel and rice with chopsticks, true.

But, it's easier than rooting while eating one of those Hot Dogs.

And one more thing: Do you believe that when a "foulu" or "homu run" ball is hit into the seats that the Japanese give the ball *back?*

Well they *do.* Without a fight.

And, nobody argues with the umpires. But they don't bow to them either.

One thing appears to be the same. The Pepsi-Cola is *really* Pepsi-Cola. And the people cheer the good guys, like Nagashima, and boo the bad guys.

Going to a Japanese ball game is, indeed, very much like watching the Cleveland Indians. I had a great time.

For one thing, you don't have to sit on the floor.

# FIRST DOWN, 10,000 MILES TO GO

After the initial thrill — and shock — of living in Tokyo has been ground off, it's perfectly natural, I guess, to begin making mental lists of some of those things back home that you *really* miss.

I remember, quite vividly my own personal initial list of those things I thought I could never do without. In no special order, that list included things like television, liverwurst sandwiches, pizza, steak, street signs I could understand, cooked fish, hamburgers with only meat in them, all those guys back in the home office, people with blue eyes, American flags, taxi drivers that talk to you and football games.

Well, as each week of the two and a half years we've been in Tokyo slipped by, things were dropped from the "can't do without" list rather rapidly and regularly.

For example, I ran right out and bought a color TV. I even bought one of those magic boxes that would change the Japanese audio into English. And I watched it every night. Only "Marcus Welby, M.D." came out English from the magic box. Back in Cleveland, I never watched "Marcus Welby, M.D." when he came out English *without* the magic box. Pretty soon, I realized why.

So, I switched to things that didn't need a magic box. Fabulous shows like kick boxing and baseball and sumo wrestling. I don't know which one of those shows deserves the credit — maybe it's a combination of all three — but I don't watch TV any more. And I don't miss it. And I pledge that if the good Lord returns me safely to Cleveland, I won't watch it again.

Just a few days of absolute withdrawal broke the liverwurst sandwich habit. I'm glad. There was too much cholesterol in one, anyway.

Soon, Japanese pizza tasted like real pizza. When we were on home leave this summer, I couldn't take American pizza.

As for the steak, ¥2,000 a pound eventually began looking like an A & P price and we eat it often enough now.

I also found out that Japanese drivers who *can* read the street signs don't read them anyway, so I no longer feel bad about that. Just scared stiff.

And McDonald's finally came with meat-only hamburgers.

Raw fish suddenly seemed quite normal. And quite tasty. And a hell of a lot cheaper than rare steak.

The guys back in the home office? They make sure I don't get a chance to miss them anymore.

Now, if I want to see blue eyes and American flags, I drive out to the military bases at Yokota or Tachikawa and watch the people go in and out of the bases. If I don't feel like a drive, I can see the blue eyes at Roppongi where all the foreigners live and the American flags at the department store fairs.

100

Now that I *can* talk to the taxi drivers, I'm sorry. My Japanese is pretty good, but — unfortunately — not many taxi drivers in Tokyo studied at my language school so we each have no idea what the hell the other one is talking about.

Anyway, on January 15, the social "miss list" was down to football games. And on that very day, the University of Hawaii team was in Tokyo to play the All-Japanese All Stars.

We bought our tickets and Wife Sarah and I went out to National Stadium with some friends.

It looked just like the Cleveland Browns stadium back on Lake Erie. It was cold. It was sometimes snowing, sometimes raining. Always cold.

Some friends brought a thermos of hot-buttered rum and a jug of Scotch. Others brought some beer. We brought some hot soup.

A gang of G.I.'s from Camp Zama were in front of us with jugs, bottles and thermoses of practically everything.

Across the field the band was playing. The scoreboard was spelling out the lineups. The coin was tossed.

For all the world, it looked exactly like a football game. This will do it, I thought. Off the "want list" goes football, at last.

But then came the kick-off. What you call what went on after that, I'm not sure. But a bunch of 6-foot, 250-pound guys mauled some 4½-foot, 100-pound guys for three hours. The little guys' biggest ground-gainer was the official who caught the big guys off-sides about 51 times. That held the big guys down to a merciful 43-0 win.

When it was all over, I had my fill of hot rum, luke-warm soup and cold beer.

But, believe me, I still miss football.


## PARLOR GAME, AZABU STYLE

The other night, at a cocktail party in a friend's apartment over in Azabu, I joined a group over in one corner just in time to hear one man dismiss another's statement with: "The trouble with you is that you've been in Tokyo too long."

I never *did* find out exactly what brought on that remark, but the conversation from there on was most fascinating.

"How," I asked, "does one discover that he's been in Tokyo too long?"

"For one thing", snapped the apparently oldest man in the group, "you've been here too long when you know what initials like MITI, JCP, and LDP stand for."

"Another danger signal," volunteered by the first man I heard speak, "is when you find that you *didn't* already see any of the movies at the Press Club and the American Club before you came here."

That tickled some funny bones and everybody had a chuckle. I could see a "You've been here too long" game beginning.

"How about," asked the man on my right, "when you don't know which teams played in the last World Series?"

"How about," asked the man opposite him, "when you don't *give* a damn who played in the World Series?"

More laughter.

Another player said he thought the too-long turning point was when the Japanese yen bills and coins started looking like *real* money. "The second stage of that," he added, "is when the dollar bills begin looking like Monopoly money."

Still more laughter. Enough to bring two more players in from across the room. As soon as the game was explained to them, one said, "I think you've been here too long when it seems perfectly normal to be driving on the left side of the road."

Everybody laughed except the transplanted Londoner in the group. But he quickly countered with, "I actually had a Gaijin explain to me recently why Tokyo taxi drivers were justified in passing up foreigners. You *know* he's been here too long."

As the laughter died down, he brought it back with, "Me, too. I *agreed* with him."

One of the women who were now part of the group observed that, "My husband has been here too long. He never calls my attention any more to taxi drivers who jump out of their cabs and do you-know-what over at the side of the road."

An up-to-now non-player joined in with, "I'm worried about myself. Last month, when the gas company raised their rates about 40%, I didn't ever curse Japan once."

"That's nothing," chimed in one of the original players, "I don't even cut out those price raise or cost-of-living rise notices from the newspapers anymore and send them back to the home office in Chicago."

One man, quiet up to now, said we'd better count him in as a too-longer. "Now, it seems perfectly logical to me to have to go and get a new alien registration every time I leave Japan, even if only for a day in Seoul."

By now, the laughter after each contribution was coming in torrents.

One of the ladies again: "I didn't even notice the last two Tokyo earthquakes. First I knew was when I read about them in the papers."

The group's youngest member — who had been waiting for some time to get a word in — admitted that he didn't even realize the last railroad slowdown was over until he read the other day that a new one was beginning.

"That's nothing," assured a New Yorker. "When I was talking to the home office the other day trying to explain a position taken by our Japanese joint venture company, I started by saying 'Now *we* think . . .' "

Suddenly, the group noticed that I was *not* laughing and just staring out the window at the lit-up Tokyo Tower.

"What's the matter with you, Maloney?" they wanted to know.

"To tell you the truth," I answered, "I just don't think all this is anywhere near as funny as you all do."

"You know why?" the game's inventor asked. "You've been in Tokyo too long."

People used to say: "Those Japanese copy everything from the West." I'm not going to get into a long discussion on that subject right now, but I bring it up only for the opportunity to mention that I know one thing that the Japanese definitely invented all by themselves: *Inflation*.

Before there *was* such a thing as the "oil crisis," we were paying more for our gasoline than Americans are paying now. I was always certain that there were places in this world where you could buy a farm for less than we were paying for a box of grapes here in Japan.

But, with a thing called "overseas allowance" (or a name something like that), we foreign businessmen learn to cope. How the Japanese do it, I'll never know.

Anyway, if you think that prices wherever you are can't get any higher, reading through the next few stories should give you no hope at all. Believe me, they can.

And, in Japan, they will.

# CALL ME A TAXI

Just a week or so after the United Nations irresponsibly listed Tokyo as the most expensive city in the world, the Japanese Ministry of International Trade and Industry decided it was time to finally turn loose a survey completed a year or more earlier.

And so, last Saturday morning, they released the facts that showed — without a doubt — that Tokyo was one of the cheapest places on earth to call home. In fact, MITI says, Tokyo — costwise — places a mere 21 on a world-wide list of 34 cities.

If you want to get off cheaper than you do here, you have to head for places like Nairobi or New Delhi or Istanbul.

You can thank your lucky Tokyo supermarkets, says the survey, that you're not trapped in cities like New York (1.7 times more expensive than Tokyo), or Stockholm (1.6 times as expensive) or Chicago (more than 1.5 times dearer).

In cities like that, the report goes on, you'd pay a lot more for cameras or TV sets (probably imported from Japan, although the survey didn't mention that).

Even moving around those other expensive cities costs a fortune compared to Tokyo. A five kilometer taxi ride, for instance, that costs only ¥380 in Tokyo would set you back ¥924 in New York and ¥768 in Stockholm.

All in all, the prices of a list of 101 items were checked around the world in the survey. And, with a long list like that, you can't expect MITI to lengthen it by including such frivolous things like perishable foods and land prices or eating out and things like that, so they weren't considered.

Besides, comparisons of the prices of things like that only makes such a survey more difficult to reconcile, they said.

Prices in Tokyo only *seem* high to me, I guess, because I concentrate on things like my weekly food bill instead of keeping track of my ridiculously low weekly camera and TV bill.

Probably I have everything out of focus simply because I paid more for my last roast beef than I have ever paid for a camera.

And costs are probably distorted in my mind because each month's rent totals more than the cost of three color TV sets. That's three *console* models; it's more like six or seven portables.

Even if I took one of those Tokyo taxi rides over to the supermarket, bought a melon and a bottle of Scotch and took another taxi ride back home, the total cost of that trip — taxi, melon and Scotch — would be one hell of a lot more than it would be in that nasty city where the taxi alone costs ¥924 each way. (If I decided to buy an Eye Round at the supermarket, I'd have to forget about the melon, the Scotch, *and* the taxi.)

106

Of course, we shouldn't be too harsh on MITI about all this. After all, they only reported the figures last Saturday. After all, the survey was actually taken last year by the overseas offices of the Japan External Trade Organization.

Maybe, just maybe, JETRO's employes overseas purposely left out things like food prices so they could agitate for a higher cost-of-living allowance from their home office back here in Tokyo. Or maybe they just wanted to show cameras and TV sets were cheaper in Tokyo to stave off any dumping charges that may be brewing in Europe or America.

Whatever it's all really about, the report only confirms a notion I had the last time I read the results of one of these MITI-is-quicker-than-the-eye cost-of-living surveys. And that's this:  I'm going to move my family out of our house and into a taxi. We would live half Western style, half Japanese style with Wife Sarah and I on the seats and the kids on the floor. We could, at Tokyo's bargain prices, maybe afford a Summer taxi in the resort areas of Shimoda or Karuizawa.

What the hell, at ¥380 for five kilometers, we can ride more than 5,000 kilometers for the cost of one month's rent.

And, the way traffic is in Tokyo these days, we probably wouldn't be able to cover more than 3,000 kilometers in a month's time so we'd have enough left over each month to buy a new camera or TV set.

Some months we could skip the camera and TV and buy a melon for the kids or a bottle of Scotch for Wife Sarah and I.

So, we're definitely moving this time into a taxi. Maybe this month, maybe next.

It depends on how soon we can get one to stop and pick us up.


# A PERFECT DAY, MITI STYLE

If you read the previous article, you already know that the Japanese Government's MITI (Ministry of International Trade and Industry) recently released a survey that showed Tokyo to be one of the least expensive cities of the world in which to live.

And, you know that I had a feeling that the report was just slightly misleading.

Well, a Japanese friend of mine suggested that I was perhaps too harsh in my judgement. I should, he said, get hold of a copy of MITI's complete report. In that way I could discover, he was certain, how to live cheap in Tokyo.

After all, he pointed out, MITI listed 101 everyday items in the survey, covered the whole world, and Tokyo wound up number 21 in cost of living on the list of 34 cities.

He's right, I decided. I got the list and, last Saturday, Wife Sarah and I spent a perfect day in Tokyo — MITI style. We stayed away from those bad expensive things and took advantage of all the wonderfully cheap things in town.

First off, we left the car home (gasoline costs twice as much here as in the most expensive American cities) and took the train to town (less than one-third the cost of a train ride in London). It's only fair to add, I think, for London's sake, that their trains only have one-third as many people in them.

We didn't eat lunch in a restaurant (sorry, MITI says, that's a Tokyo no-no). Instead, we bought a tomato (only ¥31 here compared to ¥40 in New York) and a ¥130 loaf of bread (that would set you back ¥205 in Bangkok).

Sarah wanted an egg (eggs are more expensive almost everywhere) but I talked her into a cabbage (only one-fourth the cost of a Paris cabbage).

After we made our sandwiches, we found we had to drink beer with them (¥150 here; ¥266 in London). Milk (more expensive only in Accra in Africa) and coffee (half again more costly than in Paris) were out of the question.

While Sarah got herself a permanent (a MITI permanent is only ¥1,810 here compared to ¥3,410 in London), I bought a suit (no big deal, but no more expensive than New York). I even bought a new shirt (¥1,840 here vs. ¥3,234 in New York).

Then, we went on a consumer durable goods shopping spree. We bought some fluorescent lights (lowest cost in the world) and a refrigerator (cheaper here than in Africa).

Sarah found it hard to pass up a piano (less expensive than in the West). We already have a color TV, but at ¥153,000 here against ¥223,718 in Bangkok, who could do without another one?

I had to stop in the department store's men's room. That reminded me that toilet paper is cheaper only in San Paulo, Brazil. And that *nobody* in New York will give you a fresh roll of it for your old National Geographics the way the old paper man here does.

We stopped into a real estate office in the afternoon to ask him to show us one of the "high rise three room plus kitchen" apartments that the survey said was available in Tokyo for ¥78,000 per month (that's a lot less than the ¥91,630 for three rooms in New York).

The only three room apartment he had at ¥78,000 was under the railroad tracks near Shimbashi station. Sarah didn't like it just because we would have to share it with another family.

He did show us an apartment for ¥519,000. But, be fair, it had *four* rooms. *You* pay the utilities.

Actually, the only real hole on MITI's list was the utilities. They say utilities in America are up to three times as expensive as they are in Tokyo.

108

I checked back to my Cleveland bills. If that's true, then in Cleveland the exchange rate must be ¥965 to the dollar.

But, to get back to our day, Sarah suggested that this running around saving money all day had really caused her to work up an appetite.

Without thinking, we turned into one of those Akasaka Steak Houses and ordered the works. When it was all over, we got the bill. It read ¥11,260 for food, ¥1,126 for service and ¥1,126 for tax.

At today's rates, Sarah pointed out, that's almost $50 for dinner. What, she wondered, are the people in New York doing tonight (where MITI's cost of living index is 175 compared to Tokyo at 100).

"They're doing the same thing," I guessed. "For about half the price."

With that, I could see I was getting bitter again and that we had better head for home in one of those cheap Tokyo taxis (a ¥380 ride here costs ¥924 in New York).

Only one thing went wrong. We had to pay ¥2,000 extra to get a taxi driver to let us in.

The end of a perfect day. MITI style.

## THE BIG BARGAIN SALE

It was one of the most depressing Saturday mornings I remember in my two-plus years in Japan. The weather was cold and damp. The man who roams our street with his loudspeaker offering a roll of toilet paper for our old newspapers and magazines was earlier than ever and had his loudspeaker turned higher than ever.

Because our company was involved in a trade show out at Harumi convention center, I'd have to work both Saturday and Sunday. *That* didn't help the mood I was in.

There were three home office visitors in town. (No comment.)

I reached for the morning Japan Times in hopes of finding some cheery news.

None.

The foreign exchange bank, the Times said, was still closed — for the twenty-something straight day. The closest place my dollars were welcome was Guam. And, I didn't have enough yen to buy a one-way ticket there, anyway.

A page two story really further upset me. It reported that the latest issue of the United Nations' Monthly Statistics Bulletin showed Tokyo to again be the city with the highest cost of living in the world.

With New York at 100 on the UN index, Tokyo is 117. Even Paris could only score 103 and Bonn 99.

Oh I wondered as I read down the list, what do foreigners in London (85 on the index), Pnompenh (61) Santiago (61), Ankara (79) and Sydney (85) do with all their money?

To hell with it, I thought. I'll have a Bloody Mary to cheer me up. Well, the thought only made matters worse. I like my Bloody Mary's made with V-8 juice and the maid explained that the Japanese Government had determined V-8 was bad for some reason and she couldn't buy it anymore. "You mean the cans are blowing up ?'' I asked.

No, she assured me, that was the American soft drinks. This was another problem. The cans were OK but the juice was supposedly hazardous to your health.

Well, I certainly haven't been here long enough to go anything heavier than a Bloody Mary in the morning, so I went back to the newspaper.

There was an ad for one of those supermarkets we all love so well. The headline on their ad *really* sent me into a frenzy. It read:    ''While the Yen floats and the dollar dips, our prices hold firm.''

Now, damn it, that's not the idea. At least, I don't think it is. As I understand it, when the yen floats and the dollar dips, prices of imported things, anyway, in Japan are supposed to be *lower,* not ''hold firm.''

I decided to go down there and tell them right to their shopping carts what I thought about all this.

Unfortunately, however, I never got to *that* supermarket. Because, as I was driving up Aoyama Dori (I *had* to drive;   the railroad was on strike again — but that's still another story), I saw this big banner on the front of another supermarket that said, ''With New Uniform and New Mood — A Fiscal Year End Big Bargain Sale.'' In English. Just like that.

I turned into their parking lot. I was dying to see what a ''Big Bargain Sale'' was like in a Tokyo Supermarket. I must share the experience with you (at ¥ 260 to $1).

There certainly were bargains. Those Hershey Bars that are 40 cents back in the U.S. were not being sold at the usual Tokyo $1.73. They were slashed to only 98 cents. Mayonnaise was only $1.28 a jar.

Melons were as low as $9 and $10 each and Avocados were a steal at $2.75 each. Some melons were as high as $18, of course, but they were offset by the $2.50 each Papayas.

Johnny Walker Black Label was practically a giveaway at $21 a bottle. (It wasn't all great news at the booze counter, though. Jack Daniels Black Label has creeped up to $38.46 a copy, on sale.)

Best news was at the meat counter. The ''Big Bargain Sale'' caused meat prices to really tumble. Eye Round, for instance, was only $7.10 a pound — a good alternative to Tenderloin which had only skidded to $15.30 a pound.

As I said, I had to get to work out at Harumi so I didn't have a chance to buy much. I just picked up a Sara Lee Cheesecake ($2.89) and a half-pound jar of nuts ($3.84) and a box of brownie mix ($1.65).

So much for the ''Big Bargains'' promised by the sign out front. The ''new uniforms'' mentioned were true. Every employe had a new outfit.

The ''new mood'' I missed. Certainly the local women in the store still pushed their shopping carts like kamikaze pilots of old.

And nothing I saw in that store changed *my* mood.

## EAT 'EM AND BEAT 'EM

Let's face it: It's not possible for the average foreign businessman to make his Occidental-style ends meet on how much ever the company is giving him for an ''overseas allowance'', ''cost of living adjustment'' or whatever it is that your corporate procedures manual calls the ''little extra'' you're getting for being in Japan.

At least that's what you always tell them back at the home office, right? (And that's why you're going to Xerox this article and send it back to Cleveland or wherever, right?)

I'm on your side because I know it's true. In many Tokyo-based foreign families I know, the high cost of living here has *everybody* poor these days. The husband's poor, the wife's poor, the kids are poor, the driver's poor, the maid's poor — even, in some cases, the gardener's poor.

The obvious way to remedy all this, of course, is to get the home office to increase that allowance. Obvious, maybe. But possible? Unlikely. With just the housing allowance they're paying, the guys in the accounting department back home are certain you're living inside the moat in Hirohito's old house.

You *could* fire the maid and the driver. But, that would upset the whole Japanese system of ''lifetime employment'' and you certainly don't want to go down in history as the Gaijin clod who did something like that. Besides, with no maid and no driver, it would make this place entirely *too* much like home.

So, *how* to beat them?

By eating out, *that's* how.

Now I know that sounds stupid. And I know that — back home — eating out is a sometimes luxury you pull off when there's some extra money in the till. But, hear me out for a couple minutes and I'll explain how you can eat yourself to riches in Japan.

First off, I'll give you a perfect example: Let's say you plan to serve your family of four a roast beef tonight. And, to do this — and have enough left over to fix the kids a snack to eat on the school bus tomorrow — you buy a four-pounder.

At ¥ 400 a hundred grams — FOB delivered you-know-where — this brings a pound to something like ¥ 2,000 and four pounds to ¥ 8,000 or about $30. I won't even suggest that you and your wife have a couple of Scotches before dinner. Or, that you all have a piece of melon for dessert. That could only triple the cost. Nor, will we assume you eat anything else at all — just the roast beef.

Now, if instead, you take the family of four out to a Japanese noodle Soba shop, you could *all* eat for a total of about ¥800 or only $3. That even assumes that the kids each have a Pepsi to wash down the onions they're going to sprinkle all over the Soba.

I didn't allow for beer for Mom and Dad, because I don't know if you can handle a Soba shop beer or not. While they always seem to have that little size can of Pepsi they always have the super Bowery size bottle of beer.

As a matter of fact, it wasn't until I tried myself to down a whole Soba shop bottle of beer that I realized exactly why Japanese men can't make it home and have to stop by the side of the road.

Anyway, there are some other things I have to tell you about a Soba shop before you try it on your own.

For one thing, people who work in Soba shops understand *no* English — except "Beeru" and "Pepusee" — and they don't understand the brand of Japanese you've been learning, either.

So, until you become an "Old Soba Hand", stick to the shops with the bowls of plastic soba in the window out front. Understand, please, that there are as many varieties of soba as there are people standing on the 8:21 Yamanote commuter train out of Shinjuku each morning, so the window only shows a fraction of the different kinds available.

But, don't get fancy. Stick with the ones in the window.

Also, don't expect the real one to have anywhere near as much chicken floating on top as the plastic one did out in the window. You can't expect *that* anymore than you can expect the "spacious Japanese garden" in the real estate ads to have room to plant a rose bush.

When you've made your choice, go inside and grab the first waitress you see, by the sleeve and drag her outside. She'll probably be sukoshi reluctant, but you be firm.

I'll digress for just a minute here to tell you that the most reluctant one I've found *really* didn't want to come. It wasn't till I finally got her through the door that I found out why:   She was a customer on her way back from the wash room to her seat. They *do* all look alike, you know.

In any event, when you get her out there, point to the one you want and hold up a finger for each bowl you're ordering. It'll be much easier if you can get the whole family to agree on a single variety.

Then, go in and sit down. And, watch out. A special feature of *all* tables in *all* Soba shops is that they have little shelves or, at the very least, tie rods of some kind *under* the table. And, they are *all* Gaijin-knee-high. So, as you pull in your chair, your knee cap will meet this shelf or tie rod with extremely painful results.

When that happens — and it will happen because you'll forget about this warning — go ahead and yell out your most appropriate word for such circumstances. Unlike at Howard Johnson's in Hackensack, the people in the Soba shop won't understand those words, either.

Soba shop chopsticks deserve a mention, too. Because they are made from old railroad ties, they tend to splinter a trifle. Remove these splinters from your lips and tongue as quickly as possible or the creosote from the ties may cause infection.

While you're eating the Soba, slurp all you want — even *more* than you want. You look strange enough to the Japanese just sitting there without sitting there silently. This slurping will cause the loose ends of the Soba to whip around and spray Soba juice on your clothes — and on your wife's, if she's sitting across from you — but you can prevent that.

In fact, all Soba shops have a complete collection of comic books which you'll notice that all Japanese men read while they're eating. They are all in Japanese, of course, but it's no matter. You don't really *read* them, you hold them in front of you to catch that slurp spray I'm talking about.

After it's all over and you face an assault suit for grabbing the waitress, contract tetanus from the chopstick splinters, suffer water on the knee from hitting the table, have a knot on your head from hitting the top of the doorway on the way in (I forgot to tell you about that), stop in the department store to buy everyone new clothes to replace the Soba-spotted ones, and are still hungry anyway — after all this, you'll probably ask yourself if it was all worth it.

Why not? After all, you *did* beat the company out of 27 bucks.


## SOUR GRAPES

There's no doubt about it — Autumn *has* arrived in Tokyo. The unmistakeable signs of the season are everywhere.

St. Mary's School has already had the first parent-teachers' meeting;   the railroad is doing one of its quarterly slow downs;   the home-office visitors are arriving in droves at Haneda;   the college kids are raising hell;   the foreigners — *not* the natives — are restless;   and you can buy those big green grapes that cost about as much apiece as we used to pay for unliberated grapefruit.

In case you missed the meeting, you'll be glad to hear that everything is all right at St. Mary's. We were assured that the tuition won't go any higher this year than last and that the boys' hair won't be allowed to come down any lower. (Thank God — and the good Brothers at St. Mary's — for both.) And, some kids have already been thrown off the school bus for the semester.

I never could understand why people would pay five bucks a bunch for those big green grapes. I tried to count the grapes in each of some of those five dollar boxes over at the supermarket the other day. You may be interested to know that it seemed to me that there was an average of 20.3 grapes in each box which, if true, brings the per-grape going price to just under 25 cents. In any event, one box was ¥1,300, and that wasn't the most expensive one.

Now I could never understand why anybody — especially the Japanese — would pay 25 cents for a grape. I say "especially the Japanese," because we New Yorkers and Clevelanders eat almost the whole grape. I say "almost" because as kids, we were warned that if we ate the seeds, an entire grape arbor would sprout in our stomachs and we would be vined to death in a matter of days.

But Japanese mothers have obviously told their kids not to eat either the skin *or* the seeds. So you watch one of them eat a 25 cents grape and you'll see him spit out 18 1/2 cents worth.

Anyway, this is the fourth fall season in a row for me in Japan and, so, the fourth time I've seen the five buck boxes of grapes appear. I was anxious to try them every time — just to get some idea of why they could cost so much — especially back when they were only two 360-yen dollars a box.

But, I always managed to put down the desire. As I stood there with a five dollar box in my hand the other day, I decided I really should take the plunge now. After all, the way things have been going in Japan, it might cost seven or eight bucks a box next year.

And, there will probably be only 17.4 grapes in each box.

Finally, I decided, what the hell — buy it and try it and get it over with.

I selected the one box with the most grapes over the 20.3 average and carefully placed it in that little upper basket section the supermarket thoughtfully supplies in their shopping carts especially for valuables.

Instantly, I could tell that Wife Sarah didn't approve. "What in the world are you buying *those* things for?" (That's not *exactly* what she said, but that's what she meant.) "Don't you realize that ¥1,300 comes to about five dollars — just for a bunch of grapes."

I told her that I *knew* that, and that I'd been quietly counting and dividing, and that I just *had* to taste them.

"But, think," she suggested, "what we could do with that five bucks you're about to waste on grapes."

Well, I had to admit that she had a point. And, I began to think of what we really *could* do with the five bucks.

"You're right, Sarah," I told her straight out. "Let's see."

First, I suggested that we could buy a half of one of those big green melons instead of the box of little green grapes.

114

No go.

Or, I pointed out, we could buy almost three quarters of a pound of beef. If she'd prefer to go first class with Kobe's finest, we could even get a little less than a half-pound of steak.

Why, hell, we could buy *two* packages — well, a little over a package and a half, maybe — of ice cream.

We might put the ¥1,300 as a down payment on a bottle of Scotch and lay it away. After we passed up the grapes five or six times more, we would have saved enough to pay off the Scotch and take it home.

Then I noticed that it would also be possible to spend the money on some Italian cheese. It *was* a much better buy. There was enough cheese in that package to make a sandwich for Son Donald for each of the next *two* days' lunches. He'd eat the grapes on the bus the first morning.

On an even more practical side, I noticed that we could pick up a can of deodorant spray and have enough left over for one of those baby-food-size cans of mushrooms.

Wife Sarah was not impressed with any of these ideas and it showed.

"OK," I backed down, "we don't have to spend it here at all. We can go over to Roppongi and get a small pizza. Or, one of us can go to the American Club for brunch next Sunday."

No reply. No audible reply, anyway.

"I get the distinct feeling, Sarah," I observed, "that you're getting mad at me." I always, as a matter of policy, face these situations head-on.

"Believe me," I went on, "I'm *not* trying to make you mad. It's just that I wanted to try those grapes. *You* are the one who told *me* to think of what else we could do with the five bucks, and that's *exactly* what I've been doing. You're not being fair getting mad at me."

"I'm *not* getting mad at you," she said. "It's just that I, too, have been thinking about what we could do with the ¥1,300. *That's* why I'm mad."

Now I don't want to see Wife Sarah mad about anything. That's why I said, "Please, relax. Just tell me what I can do to make you happy again. I'll do *anything.*"

"Are you serious?" she checked.

"I'm serious," I assured here. "Just name it."

"OK," she smiled. *"Buy* the grapes."


## NOT EVEN HONORABLE MENTION

I followed with a great deal of interest the recipe contest that ran in the Japan Times recently. Since the contest was sponsored by some dairy group up on the northern island of Hokkaido, the idea was to submit recipes that called for milk.

Not only did I enter the contest, but I was sure I'd won it hands down. The recipe I submitted was for a breakfast dish. And it uses loads of milk.

First, you have two bowls of Kellogg's Corn Flakes with one cup of milk on each. You follow this with three or four milk punches, each of which comprises a cup of milk, mixed with one and a half ounces of Old Granddad Bourbon and a pinch of nutmeg.

Such a breakfast can use up six cups of milk. And the early Old Granddad helps smooth the edges of another day in Tokyo.

Anyway, as you probably know now, a recipe that called for only a half cup of milk — and no bourbon — took first prize. I didn't even get honorable mention.

Actually, I'm not all that hurt, My best Tokyo recipes use no milk and that's why I didn't enter them. For nothing, I'll give them to you now. But, before I do you have to understand the philosophy behind them:

First off, the way I look at it, there's no sense cooking *great* meals at home in Tokyo. They take too damn long to prepare and the wife is too pooped-out to sit down and really enjoy them with you. Or, if the maid cooks in your house, you've got to be nuts to give her a ¥15,000 roast beef to cook when she's spent most of her life eating things raw. I say get out to the Keyaki Grill in the Hilton, or some place like that, for those ichiban meals.

You pay just about as much for eating the Kobe beef out as you do buying it raw at my favorite supermarket, anyway. So why worry about doing the dishes or take the chance of spilling some of the au jus on the dining room rug?

Besides, I can charge the Keyaki meal on my American Express Card and get the bill two months later, buried in with the rest at, maybe, a better exchange rate. Good old supermarket wants my cash — *all* of it — right on the barrelhead.

And, besides the ichibans, there's no sense cooking the cheapie meals at home, either. I mean not when you can have Soba and that sort of thing delivered right to your door, already cooked.

All you have to do is telephone the corner Soba-ya San and he zips up to the house with all of it hanging from all those springs on the back of his motorcycle. Or maybe he delivers twelve orders of Soba on four tiers of trays balanced in one hand while pedalling his bike. Anyway, I'm certain they deliver it.

So, *no* ichibans and *no* cheapies cooked at home.

Well, then, what's left? The mediocres, that's what, the meals that can be put together by any expatriated gourmets.

Try this one, for instance. I call it:

*Gaijin Atsui Inu*

Go to the corner store and buy:

1 Head Chinese Cabbage
2 Lotus Roots, medium size
5 Bamboo Shoots
1 Bag Moyashi (Bean Sprouts)

Then, go to the supermarket and buy:

1 Can Sauerkraut
1 Package U.S. Imported Hot Dogs
1 Package Hot Dog Rolls
1 Jar Mustard (Again, U.S.-Made. Be careful not to get that "Chinese Dristan" variety, unless your sinuses are really blocked.)

As soon as you get home, give the maid the Cabbage, the Lotus Roots, Bamboo Shoots and Moyashi and tell her to get rid of it. The whole idea of buying it up at the corner was to impress your Japanese neighbors and the storekeeper with the idea that you're an OK Gaijin who's really getting with it.

(You may think it's an awful waste of money to throw that stuff away — but only *until* you see how much if costs to *keep* the Sauerkraut, Hot Dogs and Mustard.)

Now, boil the Hot Dogs in the Sauerkraut until they look as bad as the ones they sell at the baseball games back in Cleveland. Put them in the rolls with the Sauerkraut and top with Mustard. Eat them.

If you cook them right, one package of Hot Dogs will serve two Gaijins. If you cook them wrong, one package will serve twelve Gaijins *and* all the neighborhood dogs.

I call this "Atsui Inu" because my Naganuma dictionary says that means "Hot Dog" in Japanese.

Now, here's another one I call:

### The ¥2,095 Lunch

For this, probably you have to go back to the Gaijin supermarket because you need:

1 Can Campbell's Soup (any flavor, *don't* pay more than ¥95.)
1 Piece Kobe Beef (¥2,000 worth)

If you picked a can of the Soup with the label in English, you won't have any trouble cooking it the way the label tells you. Broil the Kobe Beef to your taste. Serve together, but on separate plates. The can of soup serves four; you're lucky if only ¥2,000 worth of Kobe Beef serves anybody. (If you forget the Kobe Beef, and you probably should, call this "The ¥95 Lunch".)

Now, one last one. It's the:

### Roppongi Gourmet

This one requires:

1  Bucket Kentucky Fried Chicken and/or
1  Bag McDonald's Cheese Burgers, and
1  Big Bag McDonald's French Fries

You have to go down and pick these up yourself because both the Colonel and Big Mac are foreigners and don't know about the motorcycles with the hanging springs on the back. Nor, could they balance one hamburger on top of *one* bucket and pedal their bikes at the same time. If you're out in the "Real Japan" country, you probably have to order stuff like this by mail. Anyway, get it over to your house and eat it. Serves as many as you bought for.

And one more thing:  Since I didn't win the contest, I owe nothing to the Hokkaido milk people. I tell you this because you should know that if you don't have any milk for that breakfast recipe I gave you in the beginning, it's OK. Just pour the bourbon, in that case, directly on the corn flakes.


## ALL THIS, PLUS: IT'S OK TO DRINK THE WATER

The other day, I read in one of the papers that Japan Air Lines — along with some other outfits that depend on the tourist trade for a measure of their livelihoods — were in the midst of planning some sort of promotional campaign in the U.S. designed to attract more Americans to visit Japan.

According to this article I read, these people really know what they're up against, because they've already decided that the number one problem is to convince these would be visitors that Japan is not so expensive for vacationers — despite what they might have heard.

Now, if people back in the United States are walking around with the idea that Japan is an expensive place, it occurs to me that it's probably as much the fault of foreign businessmen here — like you and me — as it is anybody else's.

After all, *we 're* the ones who are always complaining to the home office about how much everything costs here and *we 're* the ones who say we can't make our Oriental ends meet with our Occidental allowances.

And, apparently, these home office people must be talking to the non-expense-account travelers and repeating our tales of Asian financial woe. Obviously, frightened off by this sort of hearsay, Americans are heading someplace else.

If that's the case, I think we ought to accept some of this responsibility and do what we can to correct any erroneous impressions about what it's really like here. As I examine my own conscience, for instance, I see that I have complained about many things that temporarily went awry in the past.

118

But, I never once wrote again when wrongs were righted to report the good news.

For instance, when we couldn't get any toilet paper here, I included that bit of information somewhere in every letter that headed back to the USA. Now that I can sometimes get a four-roll pack — even if it's almost never in Wife Sarah's favorite color — I haven't yet told anybody the toilet paper shock has apparently been wiped out.

I'm going to spend this entire Sunday afternoon doing just that. And you should do the same. I don't see any reason why you have to do anything but report the fact of toilet paper availability, either. I mean, don't get involved with details like now-available toilet paper costs twice as much per pack as it did before the shortage. That has nothing to do with it.

Another thing I think back to are the stories I used to write home about how unliberated grapefruit used to cost $2.00 or more for each one. I *never* once reported the liberation of grapefruit, however. And I most certainly will as soon as I can. Of course, you can still buy even liberated grapefruit for $2.00 or more, but now the label says it's flown here by Pan Am and it used to come by some unnamed boat.

And how about all the times we complained in the past about how much it costs to eat out at night in Tokyo? I always used to write and tell everybody how the simplest of meals could run as high as $7.00 per head without any problem.

But I'm the first to admit now that this $7.00 doesn't have to be the case anymore. I know it to be true because I took the whole family out for Pizza the other night in Tokyo and it only came to about $6.50 per head.

I always griped in the past about those big grapes that used to cost the equivalent of about $6.00 for a small box. And now that the change in the value of the yen has cut that cost to the equivalent of only a little more than $5.00 per box of grapes, I never reported it.

To be perfectly honest, however, I don't think I'll report the grape thing. If, indeed, the home office people talked to the potential travelers about Japan, then it's safe to suppose that the potential travelers I write to will talk to some home office people, too. If that happens, and they specifically mention about the grapes and the value of the yen vs. the dollar now, it could start another hassle over my overseas allowance that I'd rather not get involved in right now.

And, since we obviously know much more about what it's *really* like to be a tourist here than anybody at Japan Air Lines does, we should be willing to freely offer as many suggestions for cutting visiting costs here as possible.

For instance, we could probably get all the banks who may be scheduling grand opening parties this year to have them all during the height of the tourist season. Then, they could invite the tourists to partake in the free eating and drinking that goes on during these parties. The banks shouldn't mind, since they probably stand as much chance in getting some business out of these tourists as they do from getting any business from most of the local freebie lovers who attend these things.

And, why don't we buy ads in American newspapers offering to exchange use of our houses or apartments here for the use of theirs over there while we're on Home Leave? Granted, with the rent we pay here it's not exactly an even swap, but we could ask for the difference in cash. Or, just have them bring toilet paper.

We could offer them the use of our cars, too. Driving around here for a couple of days would make some so intent on mere survival that they would forget all about the high prices here. Until, that is, when they have to stop for gas.

Japan, after all, has a lot going for it. Tourists should know that you *can* drink the water. And, in most hotels and restaurants here, it's still free.

But the way things are going lately, the tourists better hurry.


## *THAT'S* WHAT I'VE BEEN TRYING TO TELL THEM

I know that it's not polite to read other people's mail, but last week I did peek at a letter that a fellow — or girl — named "Poor but Rich" wrote to the Editor of the Japan Times.

"Poor but Rich's" letter was taking exception to my discussions about Tokyo prices.

Some of the figures he mentioned in his letter were slightly in error, I know for certain, and I want to correct them. Others confuse me and I'd like to have some further explanation.

So, if the rest of you will excuse me, I'd like to devote the remainder of this piece to "Poor but Rich." Since he didn't sign his real name, or at least "Poor but Rich" isn't listed in the Japan Times Directory, I know of no other way.

Besides, if we can confirm some of the things he wrote, we'll all benefit considerably. So here goes:

First off, "Poor but Rich", I'm extremely flattered that you're convinced that my income is ten times more than Japanese earn. Even more flattered that you've decided I earn more than four times the ¥300,000 that you spend every month.

But, alas, I'm afraid it's not true. After all, for you to have more than ¥300,000 left over to spend every month after taxes, you would have to earn about ¥10,000,000 — or $40,000 annually — according to my Japanese tax table, anyway.

I'm afraid I'm still waiting patiently for my first $160, 000 year (even

120

with your "all that included")

And I'm sorry that you're not a regular reader. If you were, you'd know that I don't live in what you think is the "concrete jungle" down in Roppongi.

My home is out in Kamikitazawa, much more than 30 minutes from the Ginza. In fact, on some days, Kamikitazawa is 30 minutes from downtown Tokyo by telephone.

But these are minor points. Let's get to the heart of what I want to know. First is about this restaurant where you get the one-pound steak "with all the goodies" for ¥1,500.

Since I often pay the supermarket more than ¥1,500 for a pound of raw steak with none of the goodies, I'm interested. Is this *beef* steak? I mean, is it from a cow or some other animal?

If it's beef, would you please ask them if they'd sell it to me raw with none of the goodies, or table service, or dirty dishes or anything for, say, ¥1,200?

And about your house. You described it in your letter as "completely Western-style" with a living room that measures 20 mats or 360 cubic feet.

Now, if that living room has a Western-style eight-foot high ceiling, then it can only measure about nine feet by five feet in length and width (8ft×9ft×5ft = 360 cubic feet, no?)

After you get the 20 Japanese tatami straw mats in that small room, where do you and the wife and kids sit? In the stainless steel kitchen? Or are they place mats, not tatami mats?

I was really interested in your idea of growing tomatoes out in your 1,080 sq. ft. "Japanese standard" garden. Ours is nowhere near that size but I see no reason why we couldn't grow something, too.

However, I think we'll skip the tomatoes. They're not too expensive. Instead, I'm going to plant some melons. And, I see no reason why we can't have some chickens, too. That would help both our egg *and* meat budget. I give you that suggestion for nothing.

I appreciate your list of the weekly menu you follow in your house. That's a help, too.

I'm not too sure I'd like lamb every Monday night, however, and I know the kids would hit the ceiling if we had liver every Tuesday.

And, chances are that we'll probably move the hamburger from Wednesday to Thursday. Otherwise, we'll certainly give your diet a try.

Just clear up one thing there for me. You said "All this is spliced with desserts such as Jello, pudding, ice cream, etc."

With a ¥300, 000 monthly budget, I assume that you only served *one* of those desserts with each meal and not all with every meal. Is that correct?

And why — or how — do you "splice" desserts?

As you may have discovered by now, "Poor but Rich," my feelings are hurt. I really like it here and I'm sad that you don't include me in the same class with those Gaijin friends of yours who "reallly know their way around here."

I'm also sukoshi put out that just because I like Hershey chocolate bars and New York steak that you call me "stupid."

Although, I'm probably not near as upset with you as the Keyaki Grill Wine Waiter with the key around his neck that you call "gay." I've been there, and he never impressed me that way.

But, anyhow, no hard feelings — from me, anyway. The waiter will contact you separately, I'm sure.

I even sent your letter, as you suggested, back to my home office in Cleveland. I want them to see that a guy who spends ¥300,000 a month (or $1,200 at today's exchange rates) has to grow his own tomatoes, eat tuna fish and baloney sandwiches for lunch, dine out at McDonald's when he's on the road, and live in a 9×5 living room full of mats.

Good Lord, *that's* what I've been trying to tell them all along.


## THE HIGH COST OF LEAVING

That's not a typographical error above. I'm talking not about the often-discussed high cost of *living* in Japan, but about the never-discussed high cost of *leaving* Japan after the foreign assignment is over.

Just to find out exactly what is involved in cushioning the reverse cultural shock of returning to the homeland, while on Home Leave this summer I interviewed an ex-expatriate couple I knew in Tokyo at their new home outside of Cleveland, Ohio.

To protect almost everybody involved, I won't use real names — we'll just call them John and Mary.

"Gee, John," was my opener as we sat on his spacious patio and sipped Martini's, "what a beautiful lawn. You don't see anything like that in Tokyo."

"No you don't," he agreed. "In our six years in Tokyo, I never saw a lawn like that. And I never had to mow one, either. You know a guy wants twenty bucks just to run the lawn mower here? Thirty bucks if he trims the edges. In Tokyo, the guy used to take care of our six-foot square garden for ¥2,000 a shot. And, when he collected the money he used to give Mary a plant worth ¥2,500 as a present."

I decided to change the subject. "Well at least, John, you don't have to pay those outrageous Tokyo prices for your booze."

"That's another thing," he fumed. "I never did pay Tokyo prices for booze. Either my Japanese friends bought it for me at the PX or the overseas visitors brought it to me from duty-free shops. And, that reminds me," he continued, "You know those home-office visitors that used to come over and bug me every six months? Well, they're on my back every day now."

Again I switched, "You have a gorgeous home, John."

"You're right there. It's terrific. And the monthly payments are only one-fifth of the rent of my Tokyo house. I hate the place."

"You *hate* it? At one-fifth the price?"

"Of course. After all, in Tokyo the company paid the rent. Here I pay it."

I decided to attack. "Now come on, John, you make good money."

"That was in Tokyo. Mary had that great thing going with the English teaching on the side. Do you know that it's impossible for her to get an English teaching job in Cleveland, Ohio?"

"Why, then," I suggested, "doesn't she teach Japanese cooking here to make some extra money?"

"What the hell does Mary know about Japanese cooking. We only ate at the American Club or at one of the big hotels."

"Surely you went down to Ginza for dinner once in awhile during your Japan stay."

"Sure we did," John admitted, "to McDonald's or Kentucky Fried Chicken or Dunkin' Donuts or maybe some Pizza Parlor."

"You can't just think of money, John. Isn't there anything better about being back home? Certainly the subways, for instance, aren't as crowded here as they are in Tokyo."

"Cleveland has only one municipal rapid transit line and, I agree, it's not crowded. But, it's so damn expensive that we can't afford to ride it. We have three cars."

Looking for some silver lining, I asked, "How about the kids?"

"They see no difference," John admitted. "Just like in Tokyo, they spend half their life on a school bus."

John looked up at the cloudless Cleveland sky. "I miss everything about Tokyo. Even the pollution. Even the Japanese people."

That did it. I knew John too well to let *that* go by unchallenged. *"You,* John, miss the Japanese people?"

"Well," he said, "I miss two of them, anyway."

*"Two* of them?"

"Yeh, the maid and the driver."


## BACK TO THE $5,000 ELECTRIC FRYING PAN

One more of those unmistakable signs that you are becoming an "Old Japan Hand" shows up when you notice that you are being invited to more and more "Sayonara Parties" thrown for Gaijins going back home after their Japanese assignments are over.

When you first get to Japan — like moving to any other new neighborhood — it takes a while for you to get to say hello to people for the first time, never mind to join in saying goodbye to them.

I remember in the beginning reading in the local social columns about Sayonara Parties. The pictures accompanying the Sayonara stories always showed a group of smiling, happy people. It *must,* indeed, be a joyous occasion, I thought, to finally say goodbye to all this and to return to the normal, familiar mother country's womb.

Anyway, that's what I used to think.

Now, I've been to a few Sayonara Parties and I know better. Those smiling faces in the party pictures don't belong to the people who are going back. They belong to the people who are staying behind in Japan.

"Sayonara" when a Japanese says it — means "goodbye." But, when it's used as a name for a Party thrown by Gaijins who intend to remain in Japan for a while for Gaijins who are leaving, "Sayonara" means "Better you than me."

You never see that second translation in any language book, so let me tell you about it.

We went to a Sayonara the other night for a couple who — by Tokyo social column standards, anyway — were our "intimate friends."

Excuse the digression, but "intimate friends" is another term, like "Sayonara", that must have two meanings. I say this because I've read of parties thrown in Tokyo for as many as *fifty* "*most* intimate friends."

If I understand the old Stateside definitions of "intimate" and "friends," it's highly unlikely that anyone would have enough time to devote to fifty different people on a regular basis to keep them intimate *or* friendly.

So, in Tokyo, "intimate friends" are those people who are willing to show up for a shindig at your house and, in turn, to someday invite you to theirs.

These reciprocal parties come even more often if your "intimate friends" can work out some way to charge the whole thing off to their company account. Deals like welcoming a visiting fireman, a new foreigner in the office, or — like we started out to talk about in the first place — to say Sayonara to somebody.

Anyway, at the other night's Sayonara, a group of us settled over in one corner to hear the parting remarks of our departing intimate friend.

Because he looked sukoshi sad, I decided to cheer him up with a "Well, John, must be good to think about getting back to the midwest, huh?"

"Getting back to what?," he asked. "To the rotary lawn mower and the snow blower?"

"But, John," another intimate reminded "You never really *liked* Tokyo, did you?"

"Of course not," John snapped. "I hated this place. But I loved living here."

"But, John," I joined in, "You *never* said you liked living here before."

"How could I have said anything like that before. Nobody would ever have invited me to another party. You know you have to be careful about saying good things about Japan to other Gaijins. They'll put you down as some sort of a kook and you'll have to go it alone."

"But, John, what about the train strikes, the garbage, the pushing on the subways, the $40 bottles of Scotch and all that you used to bitch about?"

"Of course I bitch about those things. But, let's face it. I've never taken anything but the first class green car on the Bullet Train. The maid takes out the garbage — I never see it — and I don't even know *how* to get on the subway. As for the Scotch, I buy it — or it's bought for me by incoming intimate friends — at the duty-free shop."

I wanted to know, "Are you trying to tell us, John, that you're sad about leaving Tokyo?"

"You'd better believe I'll miss it. I can speak freely now. Look, for instance, at the social life of Tokyo. And, at just *one* aspect of that social life — bank openings.

"Do you realize that my wife and I have helped open about two dozen banks — maybe more — during our years in Tokyo. We went to their opening parties at the hotels, drank their booze, ate their buffets, took home their presents — all for free."

There was a tear in John's eye. "And do you realize that they will probably *never* open another bank after we get back to Cleveland? And, worse than that, even if they do, their "party" will be right at the bank — no booze, no buffet. And if they *do* have a gift, it will probably be an electric frying pan and I'll have to deposit $5,000 and leave it there for two years just to get and keep the damn frying pan?"

Now, John was actually crying. It was all too depressing for words. I could see my other intimate friends felt the same way at that point.

We decided we'd better go and let John and Mary get on with the job of packing up their Sumo woodblock prints and Mashiko pottery and all the last minute Japanese things they bought at the Oriental Bazaar.

John shook my hand and gave me a choked "Sayonara."

I patted him on the back, gave Mary a hug and said my own, "Sayonara, John and Mary."

Better him than me.

125

# VI.  ECOLOGY

The Japanese appear to me to be more concerned about Ecology than any people on earth. They seem to be doing more to preserve their environment then any people, anywhere. And, it's no wonder, because they have so little environment left worth saving.

In Tokyo alone — if I read the statistics correctly — they put out tons more garbage each day than the city can possibly dispose of. A lot of Japan's Ecology problems are exaggerated in the foreign press, however. For instance, I've read in the U.S. that Tokyo streets have little coin-operated devices where you can buy a whiff of oxygen every few blocks. That's not true. Not that they couldn't *use* such devices, but you probably wouldn't be able to find them in the smog.

And besides man-made Ecology problems like garbage and smog, the Japanese have to learn to live with some other ecological features like earthquakes and typhoons. And, of course, if you are going to live here with them, *you* have to learn, too.

As you can read in what follows, we're still trying.

# GINZA GOMI

There was a story in the paper recently about the "Garbage Display" in Ginza (the Oriental Times Square). I saw that story and was certain that something was lost in the translation. The Governor of Tokyo could not possibly have been dedicating a display of garbage.

Well, I went down to Ginza the next day to see for myself. "Where," I asked the policeman, "can I see the garbage?"

"Anywhere in Tokyo" he assured me.

"No," I said, "I want to see Governor Minobe's garbage."

He suggested that I go to the Governor's house in that case. He was certain that the Governor wouldn't bring his garbage all the way down to Ginza. "Besides," he added, "we have enough Ginza garbage in Ginza and we export only, not import."

"Maybe," I suggested, "that the pile of garbage over there in front of the Sony Building is the one I'm looking for."

He doubted it. If it was variety or quantity I was looking for in garbage, he suggested I look under the railroad tracks near Yurakucho Station. The best selection there, he said, can be viewed before noon. After that, the quantity goes up but the variety tapers off.

It couldn't be Yurakucho, I told him, because I've seen the Yurakucho garbage many times and it didn't look like the picture I saw in the paper with the Governor speaking while wearing his "Stop Gomi" ("Gomi" is "garbage" in Japanese) lettered Happy Coat. I held out for the pile in front of the Sony Building.

"It can't be that one," the officer insisted. "That garbage has been there since I was transferred here in 1968."

I thanked him for his help and went over to Sony anyway. There it was, just like the picture. All kinds of garbage. Real garbage and sculptured garbage. Pictures of garbage and paintings of garbage. All under the sponsorship of the "Stop Gomi Committee."

"Gee," I told a Committee spokesman, "I want to bring my children down to see this garbage. It's much better garbage than we have out near my house."

He wasn't surprised to hear that. "After all," he observed, "your garbage is probably just home-made, ordinary garbage. Our garbage has been produced by some 70 celebrated artists — photographers, potters, designers and sculptors. And, the Governor himself saw that our garbage exhibition received ¥1,500,000 assistance from the metropolitan government."

He had me there, and I had to admit that our neighborhood garbage was produced by ordinary housewives and businessmen who work at other

128

jobs for a livelihood and produce garbage only in their free time.

"If you're bringing the kids, " he warned, "do it soon. We're moving the exhibit to Osaka in November and then we're exporting it to New York and London."

I warned him that he was really leaving the Japanese wide-open for American and English complaints of "dumping" if he exported the Gomi. He pointed out that the recent agreements between Nixon and Tanaka in Hawaii mentioned nothing about garbage.

"Don't feel bad," he added, "if the kids don't get to see this garbage. Next month we're piping in some polluted air from around the factories down in Kawasaki. They'll probably enjoy that more, anyway."


## THE GROSSEST NATIONAL PRODUCT

In the previous story, I made rather light of the garbage situation in Tokyo. I thought it was a laughing matter. I've changed my mind.

That's because I've just read the Japanese Government's White Paper on the Environment. We're not only already up to here in garbage, but — if everything goes the way the planners predict for the Japanese economy — continued prosperity for Japan will lead to refuse reserves that will make the current dollar reserves look like a Sunday collection basket in a mission church.

Here, says the "White Paper on Garbage" (that's not the contradiction it appears to be) is where we stand: In 1960, there were 10 million people in Tokyo and the average income was pretty low. During 1960, the average Tokyoite tossed out about 1/3 of a kilo of garbage per day.

Now, each Tokyo resident is throwing away 1.1 kilos — three and half times as much — of garbage every single day. Why, the White Paper asks? Because the population has increased three and a half times? No, population is only up 18.9%. Garbage is up, the White Paper says, because income is up. People are making more than three times as much money — and so, garbage — as they did in 1960.

The amount of garbage, the White Paper states clearly, is directly proportional to prosperity. Tokyo people alone now create five million truckloads (that's the White Paper's number) of garbage every year. If the White Paper's diagnosis is right, and if the unions win another average 14% raise for Japanese workers next spring, where does that leave us? It leaves us buried under 5,700,000 truckloads of garbage, that's where.

Well, I decided to check this whole theory out — right at the grass roots on our street in Kamikitazawa.

"Do you have the same number of people in your house now as in 1960?" I asked the woman across the street.

"Yes," she said. "My daughter got married but my husband's mother moved in."

"Is your husband making more money now than he was in 1960?"

"Certainly", she proudly announced, "more than three times as much."

Everything checked out that far, so I let go with the five-million-truckload question: "How about your garbage? How does that compare with 1960?"

"Well. . ." She thought for a minute. And then, "My 1960 garbage couldn't have been anything special. At least, there's no vivid recollection in my mind. It was just garbage."

It's not the quality I was worried about, I assured her, but the quantity.

"Well, there's certainly more of it, that's for sure. And it's *your* fault, *not* my husband's, just because he makes more money."

"My fault?" I gasped.

"Not yours personally. It's all foreigners in general." She led me out front to where the Friday pile of garbage was still waiting for one of those five million trucks. "Look," she directed, "at the variety of our Kamikitazawa garbage. It's all Western style. See all those old shopping bags? We used to carry cloth furoshikis, and when we got home, we'd empty the furoshiki, fold it up, and use it again tomorrow. *You* introduced paper shopping bags. If they survive one subway change at Akasaka Mitsuke station, you're lucky."

I started to back away.

"And look here at these cans, bottles and Kentucky Fried Chicken paper barrels. We used to order Soba from the corner. The boy would deliver those noodles on his bike in real dishes. Next morning, he'd come back on his bike and pick up the empty real dishes to use again and again. That system was, if you'll pardon the pun, honest-to-God recycling. All we threw away in 1960 was the chopsticks. Now, look."

In a desperate effort to get the foreigners off the hook, I admitted, "Sure, some of that is Western-inspired garbage, but isn't the *real* cause of all this garbage increase the fact that you're so prosperous now as compared to 1960?"

"Look," she insisted, "my husband might make three and half times as much money as he did in 1960, but that doesn't mean prosperity."

"Why not?"

"Because, our taxes have gone up, more than three times since 1960."

"Oh? Westerner's fault?"

"You better believe it. For one thing, the city has to buy five million

130

garbage trucks.''

I decided to give up the neighborhood survey. I went home ordered a bowl of Soba from the corner shop (as penance, I guess) and settled down to read the Japan Times. I was resigned — for whatever the cause — to our eventual burial in the grossest of gross national products.


# RANCID TRANSIT

Some time back a Japan Times reader wrote a letter to the Editor suggesting a final solution to Tokyo's garbage problem. For those of you who missed it, the gist of his suggestion was to have people bring their garbage to their local subway station rather than just leave it out in front of their homes or places of business.

This way, our corresponding sanitation engineer thinks, the garbage could be moved more efficiently by subway train than it is now in those five million little blue and white garbage trucks.

Now I have my own reactions to such an idea, but — since I'm only a victim of Tokyo's garbage problem and not an expert — I decided to find out what the involved metropolitan officials thought about his garbage-by-subway method.

First thing I discovered in my search for Tokyo's #1 garbage man is that, Japanese style, there is no *single* man responsible for disposing of the city's leftovers. These sort of things are handled by groups.

Finally, I located the nerve center of the garbage department in a slick new building overlooking Tokyo Bay. The center's office has an excellent view of one of those man-made islands being built out of garbage.

I passed up their offer of a cup of green tea and got right down to the business of my interview. Surprisingly enough, I found they had not only read the suggestion in the Times, but had pretty much decided to establish the underground garbage system.

''We have even decided'', the youngest member of the group beamed, ''on a name. We called in an American advertising man and he came up with the idea that we re-name the subway the 'Rancid Transit System.' We like it.''

Aghast, I asked, ''After less than *two* weeks, you actually made a decision?''

''Absolutely,'' they chimed together. ''At least, we'll test market the plan. The first load of subway garbage will be put on the Marunouchi Line at Kasumigaseki Station by the Governor after appropriate ceremonies.''

''To where?'' I wanted to know.

''Well, that's one of the problems we're thinking out now,'' they answered. "Obviously, the garbage — like everybody else — will have to change trains at Akasaka Mitsuke."

"Change? To what?" I asked.

"To the Ginza Line, of course."

"But won't the Ginza Line already have its own garbage?"

"We thought about that," they assured me, "but, we'll solve the problem by keeping the pushers overtime. They'll see that each subway car will hold four times as much garbage as it was designed to hold."

I couldn't believe they were serious.

"Won't this cost the city a lot of money?" I wondered.

"On the other hand," they proudly stated, "that's what we like *most* about the whole thing. The city will actually make money. Each person using the service will have to buy a regular subway ticket for his garbage. If you send garbage by subway everyday, we'll offer you a garbage commutation ticket. In other words, garbage will have all the advantages currently offered to people. It's only fair."

"But what about people like me who don't live near a subway station?" I asked. "Out in Kamikitazawa, I have to ride fifteen minutes on the Keio Railroad to Shinjuku before I get to a subway station."

They were ready for my question. "That's one of the definite benefits of the Rancid Transit. You're probably turning out garbage at a record clip now since you just dump it in front of your house. But, if you have to lug it down to Shinjuku you'll think twice before you throw something away."

"But what about the present subway riders?" I questioned. "Do you really think they'll continue to ride to work in subways that have been carting garbage all night?"

"Of course they won't," the group snapped. "But, we've already thought of that, too. We're converting those five million little blue and white garbage trucks to mini busses. They'll pick up the people in the morning where they used to pick up the garbage."

I stared in disbelief. "When," I asked, "does all this go into effect?"

They sat up proudly in their chairs. "We started today on a test basis."

Just then, the telephone rang, interrupting our discussion. The youngest group member picked it up. With each "Ah so desu ka" he turned a little paler. Then, the receiver slipped from his hand as he rushed to the window.

"What's the matter?" I gasped.

"Disaster," he said. "The governor, because he's always had a car and driver, couldn't find the subway station. Instead, he put the garbage in the first class green car on the Bullet Train."

"Oh, no."

"That's not all," he muttered. "Nobody explained the system to the drivers of the garbage-trucks-turned-mini-busses and they have been

132

dumping all of their passengers on the island out there,'' he said, pointing to the Bay.

"What about the garbage on the subways?"

"That's the worst of it," he sighed. "All the tickets for the garbage got mixed up with the garbage itself when it changed at Akasaka Mitsuke. None of the station men will let the garbage out of the subway without a ticket."

"Well don't just stand there looking out the window," I suggested. "Do something."

For the first time during our talk, the oldest member of the group stood up in an obvious signal of taking charge. "Gentlemen," he announced, "we'll have to reconsider all of this at another series of meetings next week."

"Next week?" I asked.

"It will take us until then to get those six million people off that island."

## RULES ARE RULES

Because almost every set of printed-in-English rules I've been handed since we arrived in Japan uses the language in a very similar way, I've always been convinced that the same person runs up and down these islands turning Japanese into English. Word for every single word. At least, that's what he thinks.

First set of rules I saw was given me as I entered a little monkey zoo out on top of Mt. Takao, about an hour out from Tokyo. The monkeys run loose there, as so it's deemed necessary by the management that visitors follow what is headed "Rules to keep in this place." Before these rules got down the business, a short paragraph tells why they call this place "Monkey Paladise" — because "there are about more than thirty monkeys are left free."

The rules ordered, among other things, that visitors "Don't close your face to monkeys." If you did close your face, the monkeys, you are warned, think that "Closing face means threat."

Another rule ordered that you "Don't show your fruits." The monkeys, the sheet said, will "steal them from you, thinking that you have brought them food."

One rules sheet I see all the time is generally posted in Japanese hotels. They tell you not "to give annoyance to the others by making a great noise or disgusting behaviors." They also ask you not "to bring visitors into the room and let them use the furnitures and fixtures without a sufficient cause."

But, no matter how quaint the translations, I do try to follow the rules in Japan. I've never — I don't think — closed my face or showed my fruits to monkeys. And I never make disgusting behaviors in hotels or let visitors use my fixtures without what I honestly feel is sufficient cause.

And, I never thought I was breaking any rules the other night at home when I decided my old brown shoes had had it and simply told Son Donald to please throw them in the garbage can.

Wife Sarah, visibly upset at my request, snatched the shoes from Donald's hands and said, "Don't you *dare!*"

"Sarah!" I shouted — shocked at her reaction, "Look at them. The heels are shot; there are holes in both soles; the uppers are covered with scratches. I couldn't wear them again."

"That has nothing to do with it" she pointed out. "Tomorrow's Tuesday."

"So, it's Tuesday. I wouldn't wear them on Wednesday or Thursday, either."

"You can't throw shoes out on Tuesday," she announced, "Or on Thursday or Saturday."

"Why not?" I had to know.

"Because they're leather, and leather — according to the rules — can only be thrown out on Monday." She was reading right from a set of rules posted on the wall near the back door.

Again, I asked, "Why not?"

Wife Sarah explained that, according to the garbage rules, only regular garbage like food leftovers and paper could go out on Tuesday, Thursday, and Saturday.

"Who says I can't throw away my old shoes except on Monday?"

"The Tokyo Metropolitan Government, *that's* who," Wife Sarah answered, "And we're not going to break the rules."

"Now seriously, Sarah," I asked her, "Does it really say I can't throw away old shoes except on Monday?"

"Yes, it does. And it also says" — she was reading it — "you have to wait for Monday to dispose of thing like toothbrushes, chopsticks, buttons, rubber hose, clinical and regular thermometers, batteries and fluorescent lamps. In fact, all plastic, glass, rubber, leather or 'other' products have to wait for Monday."

"But, Sarah, at these prices we don't throw out as much leftover food as we do plastic products, do we? So why do they pick up food three days a week and all that other stuff only once?"

Wife Sarah insisted she didn't know why and that it didn't make any difference. We were going to follow the rules. "You can't put food or paper in plastic bags anymore, either," she volunteered. And she went on to explain that *anything* that won't burn without "noxious gases" — I know

134

she picked *those* two words right off the rules sheet — has to wait for Mondays.

"OK, Donald," I backed off, "please put the shoes in that old bookcase we're getting rid of and remember to put them both out next Monday."

"Oh, no you don't," Wife Sarah stormed. "Bookcases and big things like that are *not* for Mondays."

Son Donald looked as confused as I felt and asked, "Can I put the shoes out on Monday and the bookcase Tuesday?"

"No," Wine Sarah checked the rules, "bookcases and big things can be thrown out by appointment only."

"By *appointment?*" I asked. "With *whom?*"

"With the garbage man's head office. Do you want the number?" Wife Sarah asked.

Showing one of my infrequent signs of being sensible, I decided to change the subject and announced that I hadn't had a chance yet to read the morning paper.

It was just as well. I noticed that Wife Sarah was "closing her face" and, like the monkeys, I took that closing as some kind of threat.


## IT SOUNDS FISHY TO ME


There's this Japanese friend I met some time back right after we first arrived in Tokyo.

He, along with his wife and her parents, used to live out near us in Kamikitazawa.

After they moved in closer to town, we met — on a fairly regular bases — for lunch in a little sushi (raw fish) shop over in Akasaka.

For one reason or another, a couple of months had gone by since our last meeting before he called me the other day. He didn't sound like himself on the telephone. But, yes, he wanted to have lunch. No, not at the sushi shop in Akasaka. Not at any sushi shop anywhere. He asked if we could make it a hotel this time and I agreed.

The first sight of him in the hotel coffee shop confirmed his telephone impression. He *wasn't* himself. For the longest time, he just puffed away on his Hi-Lite cigarettes and nodded agreement — Japanese style — to everything I said.

Then, right in the middle of some profound statement I was offering, he blasted, "Don San, *please* help me."

"What's the problem?"

"You know my mother-in-law never really liked me or approved of my

135

non-arranged marriage to her daughter."

"Look, Shuji," I consoled him, "no mother-in-law *ever* really approves of her daughter's marriage partner — arranged or not arranged."

"I know that, but it's really getting serious in my case." Then, checking around the room, James Bond-style, to see if anyone in the coffee shop was listening, he leaned over and whispered, "I think she's trying to murder me."

Now there was no concealing my shock. My sushi shop conversations with Shuji up to now had centered on the important Japanese versions of English conversation. You know, like "Have you ever seen Mt. Fuji?" and things at that level. Never murder. "Why in the world do you say something like *that?*"

"Because she *is*. I'm certain of it."

"Tell me about it."

"Well, last night, she served Ika for dinner. In English, I think you call it squid or cuttlefish. She even insisted that I have second helpings. It was fried. DELICIOUS."

"So?"

"So? Don't you realize what I'm saying? *Second* helpings of Ika?"

"No, I don't."

"I *thought* you read the papers. Didn't you see the story the other day about how the Japanese Ministry of Health and Welfare warned everybody not to eat too much fish because of mercury poisoning? They even published a list of how much of each fish to eat each week to avoid being poisoned."

"What has *that* got to do with your mother-in-law?" I asked.

"Well, she saw the Health Ministry's permissible weekly list, I know. And on it, it clearly showed that the most number of Ika anyone could eat in any week, and still avoid being poisoned, was 2.3. She *knew* that, but was offering me seconds anyway. She's trying to poison me."

"Oh, c'mon now, Shuji. Even if you ate the seconds, surely you wouldn't have consumed 2.3 Ikas," I pointed out.

"That's true. But, I had already had a Prawn Cocktail for lunch."

"I'm not following," I admitted.

"Of course you're not. That's obvious," he shrugged. "The simple fact is that Prawns were on the Ministry's list, too. And you can only eat 6.6 of them each week and not be poisoned."

"Well," the suspense was killing me, "had you eaten 6.6 Prawns for lunch?"

"Fortunately, no. We went to the American Club for lunch and they only give you 3.0 Prawns in a cocktail so I was all right. But," he added, "What worries me is that the list showed you could eat 6.6 Prawns *or* 2.3 Ikas each week and survive. What it *doesn't* make clear is what happens when you mix and have 3.0 Prawns *and* — my guess, anyway — about 1.75

136

Ikas.''

"Let's get back to your mother-in-law," I suggested. "Did she *know* about the Prawn Cocktail?"

"No, but I mentioned the day before that I'd meet you for lunch this week. She *knows* we always go to the sushi shop."

"I think, Shuji," I charged, "that you've blown this thing all out of proportion. Chances are, your mother-in-law doesn't even *know* about this permissable fish list from the Health Ministry."

"Oh, yah," he jumped, "her own cousin down in Osaka wrote her a note and then tried to commit suicide last week by eating 53 pieces of Maguro — that's Tuna fish sushi — in five days. She knows *all* about it."

"Fifty-three pieces of Maguro?"

"Fifty-three. On the nose. And the Ministry list says that 47 Pieces of Maguro sushi in one week is the limit."

"How about your father-in-law," I wanted to know, "And your wife and herself. Don't they all eat the same thing you do?"

"Look," Shuji reminded me, "this is a Japanese family. My father-in-law *never* comes home for dinner. My wife and mother-in-law, like all good Japanese women, wait until I'm finished eating before they do. And they only eat my leftovers."

"And?"

"*And*, the way she was shoving the Ika at me, there couldn't possibly be 4.6 Ikas left over for them. And that's how much it would take for there to be enough for them to have 2.3 each."

"Well, why don't you switch to beef?" I wondered out loud. "Or vegetables?"

"You know damn well," he steamed, "that the vegetables are covered with poisonous sprays. And, that beef is full of cholesterol. Even if the beef *is* O.K. now in Japan — besides the prices, of course — soon all this poison scare will result in a surplus of fish and they won't know what to do with all the extra fish."

"And, so?"

"And, so, with the increased demand for beef, they'll have to find some way to feed the extra cows and they'll probably feed them the surplus fish — mercury and all."

"Maybe," I suggested, "I'd better come out and have a talk with your mother-in-law. But I think you've got yourself carried away."

"Thanks, Don. I knew you'd help. In fact, I made arrangements for you to come out tonight for dinner. My mother-in-law says she would be glad to have you." Shuji *really* looked relieved.

"What are we having for dinner?" I asked. "I don't want to have the same thing for lunch now."

"Good thought," Shuji agreed. "I'll call home."

He did, and returned to the table with the some look of shock he had on his face when I first arrived at the hotel.

"Well, what did she say? What are we having?"

"Mackerel," he whispered. Then repeated, "Mackerel."

"Good," I said, and picked up the menu.

"Good? *Hardly*. Mackerel is on the list and you can only eat 1.2 Mackerels a week."

"So, only eat 0.8 or 1.0 tonight and relax," I smiled.

"It wouldn't make any difference," Shuji sighed.

"Why?"

"Because, she told me, in honor of your visit, she's going out and buy all the fixings so we can start with a Prawn Cocktail."

## NOW HEAR THIS

Lord knows the Japanese Government has the supporting statistics someplace, but — because I can't find them — you'll just have to take my word for this: Japan has more loudspeakers per capita than any country in the world.

If there is any doubt in your mind about the accuracy of that statement, I offer you last Saturday as evidence. It all began promptly at seven a.m. Outside our Kamikitazawa house, a mini-truck rolled slowly by, all sides plastered with campaign posters picturing one of our local candidates in the upcoming elections.

And on top of the truck was the world's largest — if not the largest, the loudest — loudspeaker. In one of those screeching public-address-type female Japanese voices, somebody was being described as, I'm sure, "the man who," or, maybe "the woman who." You couldn't tell from the posters whether the candidate was a man or a woman because the pictures of the Pandas on the poster were bigger than the candidate's photo.

Anyway, anybody who screeches within my earshot at seven a.m. on a Saturday is damn lucky I can't vote in Japan.

Finally, the truck slipped around the corner and peace once more came to Kamikitazawa. Until 7:35 a.m. That's when another mini-truck — from the opposition candidate, I guessed — went by chanting more campaign promises. The chanting, of course, was also broadcast through a loudspeaker bolted atop the truck.

That did it. I was wide awake and decided to get up and go downtown to do my Saturday shopping tour. I must admit that while I was in the shower, I hardly heard the loudspeaker voice on the eight a.m. pass of the truck offering to recycle our old newspapers instantly by turning them into a roll of toilet paper.

Once in the car, I was caught up in a real jam on the Koshukaido Highway which brought all traffic to a grinding halt with my car at the front gate of Meiji University. It seems the University wants to raise the tuition. Some students are for the raise; most are against. They were hotly debating the issue. With loudspeakers, of course. The police were trying to quiet everybody. With, naturally, more loudspeakers.

At Shinjuku Station plaza, a police car was trying to encourage everybody not to block the intersection. They did this via the loudspeaker that's mounted on the fender of every police car.

Even in the hotel garage — where I decided to abandon the car — loudspeakers are installed every four feet on the ceiling. In the short walk from my car to the elevator, they blared six times telling six different drivers that their bosses were waiting upstairs for their cars.

Once in Shinjuku Station, the real battle of the loudspeakers unfolded. There must be a dozen different railroad lines that come in and out of Shinjuku. The trains on each line are each a different color. The loudspeakers, however, are all the same; continuous.

Even on the train, the beat went on. Not only do the loudspeakers tell you the next stop, but they tell you on which side the exit door will be and repeatedly warn you not to forget anything. It's all in Japanese, of course, so I only understand one thing for sure: They never shut up.

I decided to walk down Sotobori Dori street and so got off at Akasaka Mitsuke station. On the left side. And, I didn't forget anything. Out on the street, it was relatively quiet. Only the din of Tokyo traffic. Until I got to the big intersection where Sotobori Dori goes under the expressway (at that building with the big bulldozer mounted on top). There, big loudspeakers are strapped to poles on each corner to broadcast the shrillest police whistles you ever heard each time the light changes. Further on, as I passed the NCR Building, I could see a group at the gate of the American Embassy. The Ambassador's phone must have been out of order. They were trying to talk to him via loudspeaker.

I headed down toward Shimbashi Station from Toranomon. On every light pole, that same grating voice that started it all at seven a.m. was coming out of a loudspeaker, describing all the once-in-a-lifetime sales in the local stores.

That did it. I ducked into the Dai-Ichi Hotel coffee shop for silent refuge. As I was sipping my iced tea, I imagined the voices I would hear on the department store escalators warning me of instant catastrophe if I didn't hold the hand rail. And I was certain there would be a wood block print show on some floor or other and that the pleading loudspeaker voices on every other floor would be directing me to it. I decided to stay right there.

Over my second iced tea, I glanced through the morning paper. There was a picture of a group of Japanese citizens who went down to the

139

Philippine jungles to plead with Japanese soldiers believed to be hiding there in those jungles since World War II. Naturally — and the picture confirmed it — they were calling to the hiding soldiers over loudspeakers. The soldiers, as you may have read, weren't answering.

Thinking back over that day, and every other day in Tokyo, I decided that the search party was going about this all wrong. I know why those soldiers probably chose 28 years in the Jungle. To avoid the very loudspeakers that were trying to entice them back home.


## IT WAS ONLY AN EARTHQUAKE

Without any trouble, I remember the first taxi ride I ever had in Tokyo. I also remember the first time a taxi wouldn't stop to give me a ride.

Like it was yesterday, I recall the first trip through the aisles of the supermarket and the telephone number prices at the meat department. (You *have* to remember those — no cameras are allowed in the store.)

And who could forget their first morning rush hour ride on the Yamanote Commuter Line? Or how you felt when you first realized that the man facing the telephone pole is *really* doing what he looks like he's doing?

And how about the first time a Japanese actually understood one of your brand new Nihongo phrases?

All of these experiences will remain unforgettable — along with dozens of other Japanese firsts.

But one moment — one absolutely terrifying moment — stands out far and above all the rest. And that's my first Tokyo earthquake.

Now for those of you who have lived on the West Coast of the United States along the San Andreas Fault or in the fault areas of Central and South America and Europe, your first Tokyo tremor was probably a real no-hummer.

But, I'd spent all of my life in and around New York and Cleveland and everyone knows that those cities have absolutely *no* faults.

None that could cause an earthquake, anyway.

And so the first shake here was a real affair to remember.

Wife Sarah and I were over here on our house-hunting trip. We had spent about seven days doing the town with the Gaijin specialists in Tokyo real estate. Finally, we settled on the house in Kamikitazawa, raised the necessary deposit and commission money from our "Friend at Chase Manhattan," and signed on the slanted line.

All that, we decided, called for a celebration of some sort.

So, we went over to a friend's apartment in Mita (not really intimate, just a friend). On the way, we stopped to buy a bottle each of bourbon and

Scotch and the fixings for a we-just-signed-for-a-house party.

To tell you the truth, when I paid that supermarket bill I began to wonder what in the hell we were celebrating about.

But, I digress.

Anyway, we got to the Mita apartment with goodies in hand. Our friends had asked over a couple of *their* friends to join in the goings on. (By the way, since all of them had known each other in Tokyo for more than thirty days, they were truly "intimate" friends.)

Well, we produced our copy of the signed lease, the stamped receipt and the IOU from Chase Manhattan and the party was underway.

Now, I'm normally a one Bourbon-Manhattan-on-the-Rocks man, but this was after all an occasion, and it was during my third such party favor that I was aware of the fact that I was perhaps not in full control of all my faculties.

Oh, how I tried to sit straight in my chair — a rocker, yet. After all, I couldn't embarrass my ordinary friends in front of their intimate friends by going off my rocker.

Just as I felt that I was, indeed, in complete control, it happened. Instead of just going to and fro the way rocking chairs are supposed to, mine started to go from side to side. That probably wouldn't have bothered me, but while it was going from side to side it continued to go to and fro.

I forget who was talking at the time (I know *I* wasn't capable of putting two words back to back), but they shut up tight. Desperately, I tried to hold my Manhattan still, but it started to splash over the sides of the glass and onto my lap and all over my official documents.

Everybody, I was certain, was staring at me. And I was just as certain that my predicament was the same thing I'd seen Ray Milland go through in the "Lost Weekend" movie.

Then, I noticed that I was in such bad shape that everybody else's drink was spilling over, too. The chandelier in the dining room was swinging and the statues of the "Seven Gods" on the bookcase went down like ordinary mortal dominoes.

Any minute now, I was convinced, comes the pink elephants and striped snakes and polkadotted lizards.

Just as I was ready to shout the pledge at the top of my lungs, everything settled down again. The rocker went back to just to and fro. The Manhattan — what was left of it — stayed in my glass. The chandelier just hung there without a swing. The "Old Japan Hands" resumed talking.

I fully expected the "Seven Gods" to return to an upright position. When they didn't, I realized that maybe all this wasn't just me.

Then, as one of our ordinary's intimates was in the middle of telling Wife Sarah to be sure to bring plenty of bras and shoes because neither were available in her obvious size in Tokyo, I interrupted.

"What *was* all that motion?" I had to know. "You all DID feel it, too, didn't you?"

"Oh, sure," assured my friend. "That's an earthquake."

Even though I knew exactly what he said, I repeated aloud "An *earthquake*?" Under my breath, I added a "Thank God!"

"Yeh," he said, "we have quite a few here."

"How many?" I wanted just a few more facts.

"Quite a few. But, they're not half as bad as the typhoons."

"Or," his wife cheerfully added, "as dangerous as the photo-chemical smog."

Well, it was after five o'clock. And it was Friday. No hope, I decided, to try to get my IOU back from Chase. Or to try to break a lease that was only two hours old. And, the home office had already sprung for Wife Sarah's trip over here and we'd been through the American-operated "Sayonara" parties. No, we had to go through with it.

All this deep thought was broken by my host with, "If earthquakes shake you up *that* much, you'd better get off your rocker."

All things considered, I decided that I already was.


# NOBODY WILL BE HERE TOMORROW

I mean like it was one of those once-in-a-lifetime days. I'd met an Ambassador from one of the Arab countries the night before and he smiled at me, 1973 was over and we *didn't* have that big earthquake that was supposed to sink Japan into the Pacific and my friend at Chase Manhattan was getting even friendlier by passing out almost ¥ 300 for a dollar.

And, since I'm not growing any rice or anything out at my house that requires the rain we were not getting for a change, I was tickled to death with another morning of sunshine.

In fact, considering the collective joy of all these omens of good fortune, I was super-tickled.

Then, I picked up the newspaper. As usual, there was nothing on the front page likely to heap any additional joy on the list above. But there was nothing especially dampening, either. Sort of a neutral news day. Like the price of oil was going up, but there *would* be some oil. And like the robbery rate was going up, but robbers were stealing less per robbery. Plus the word that companies who hoard laundry soap and toilet paper in their warehouses were going to get in trouble with the government.

Page two had nothing to erase the smiles either — or to widen them. Except maybe for that round-the-world weather report that showed it was raining in Honolulu. Since I can't afford to go there this winter, I must confess that news of bad weather on Waikiki leaves me with just sukoshi more than normal glow.

Page 3, however, was another matter. There, tucked away under an article about big snows up in Hokkaido and over an ad for some restaurant that was doing its part to fight inflation by holding their price of a steak sandwich under $12, was the story that spoiled my day.

It wasn't a big story. It wasn't, I'm sure, from UPI or AP or Tass or anything like that. It just was a few lines to tell how Japanese housewives have been buying up all sorts of "survival kits" at the local department stores. These things, the article says, come already packed with some cans of Osembe — those little Japanese crackers that have been dipped in shellac — flashlights, extra batteries, plastic raincoats, toothbrushes, and things like that.

Some stores were already sold out on survival kits, it went on, and people were making up their own. For instance, they were buying a lot of canvas knapsacks and transistor radios, canned eels, instant Soba noodles and things like that.

Then the story ended.

Now what the hell kind of yellow journalism is that, I thought. Don't just leave me hanging. Tell me why these women are buying these things. What do *they* know that I don't know? Obviously, they are clued into something I don't know anything about.

Certainly, I remember the story about how Japan was going to sink into the sea on December 1 last year. *That* I did read about. But when December 1 came and had gone, we were still here. I assumed that was that, and we could go back to pushing each other on and off the subway again.

But then came this story.

When I got to the office, I asked my secretary what was new. She told me they were going to cut out the heat in our building at certain hours and that we would have only one elevator running until further notice to save energy.

No, I snapped, I meant what *big* news did she hear.

Well, she said, she noticed the day before that the restaurant across the street began supplying paper napkins at lunch and that they never did anything as Western as *that* before

But that would only effect this neighborhood, I pointed out. I was looking for *big* news that would affect *everybody*.

Oh, she beamed, you mean the taxi rates going up? Or that one of the bullet trains was six minutes late yesterday?

No, no, no, I interrupted while I decided to be more direct. "Has your mother," I asked her, "been buying flashlights, Osembe (those Japanese crackers dipped in shellac), or transistor radios?"

No, she said, she didn't think so. Why did I ask?

No special reason, I said. Just wondering.

Why, she wanted to know, did I ask such a funny question? Her mother, she pointed out, very seldom carried a flashlight anywhere, didn't really like Osembe and never listened to the radio.

Then obviously, I told her, she doesn't know.

Know *what*?

That everybody is buying things like that because Japan is about to earthquake apart at the seams or sink into the ocean or be buried in hot lava or something like that.

She was obviously startled at such news and wanted to know where I heard it.

Right here, I said, and showed her the clipping.

She read it, smiled, and assured me that she hadn't read anything in the Japanese press, heard anything on the Japanese radio, or seen anything on Japanese TV that hinted that any such disaster was just around the corner.

I let her know that I was still unnerved by all this and asked her to call some Japanese friends who might know more about something like this.

When she left my office, I started thinking how stupid I was to get excited. After all, if the earthquake *does* come and it *is* that bad, who could you listen *to* on your transistor radio? And if we sunk into the sea, why would you want to be weighed down by a flashlight and extra batteries? And, Good Lord, can you imagine your last meal ever being shellac-dipped crackers with seaweed wrapped around them? And soggy crackers yet, from being in the ocean?

It was late then and I decided to head for home — considerably relieved that reason had taken over again. As I passed my secretary's desk, she was just hanging up the phone.

"See you tomorrow", I called.

"I won't be here tomorrow", she said solemnly. "Neither will you. Neither will anybody else."

My knees turned to jelly. What, I asked her, had she found out with the telephone calls I suggested.

Oh, that, she said. Nothing. "It's just that tomorrow," she reminded me, "is Sunday."


## YOUR LIFE JACKET IS UNDER YOUR SEAT

There was no doubt about it from the moment he appeared in the doorway, I was going to catch hell about something.

He was a man I'd met a couple of times before at the Press Club bar and the "doorway" was the entrance to that very establishment. I was just sitting there alone, minding everybody else's business, waiting for Wife

144

Sarah to show up so we could get at the biggest decision of the week up to then: Do we eat first and go to the late movie or do we go to the early movie and eat later?

He plowed across the room, slammed himself in the chair I was saving for Sarah, and — without so much as a "Konichiwa" — waded in.

"What the hell is the matter with you? Must you *always* cause trouble?"

I knew it, I thought. He's one of the letter writers who just signs his initials or some cute phrase and has decided to take me on face to face.

"What is it, George?" I asked. "Are you mad at what I wrote about Sumo?"

"Sumo, Shmumo," he snapped, "who cares about naked men?"

"Then it was one of the columns about prices that upset you. Are you *really* 'Poor but Rich,' George?

"You know damn well," he reminded me, "that I work for an American company, and so I'm not here about what you said about Vietnam, either."

"Well, George," I pleaded, "let's have it."

"It's that thing you did about earthquakes a few weeks ago. Good God, is nothing sacred with you?"

"I don't understand, George," I said, and I didn't.

"You could break up any number of already unhappy homes in this town with that scare stuff."

"How?"

"How? *How*, he asks. Look, my wife is about going crazy. It's bad enough she thinks everyone of those snake-dancing gangs with the red armbands, flags and painted helmets are heading right for our house.

"And just the other day, she read about the Japanese who say they saw a 30-foot snake in Tokyo.

"The same day, she read about crows that are supposed to be attacking people right here in downtown.

"On top of that, Senator Muskie came over here to remind everybody again that we're all about to breathe our last breath."

"But, George," I interrupted, "surely you're not going to blame me for the snakes and the crows and Muskie."

"Don't change the subject," he warned, "I'm on you for the earthquakes."

"But, George, *I* don't cause earthquakes. I just simply wrote about my first experience here with one of them. "The whole point of the story was simply that I thought at the time that I had too much to drink and how relieved I was to find out it was an earthquake."

"That's what I'm trying to tell you. Don't you see, for two years I've been telling my wife that there's no such thing as earthquakes. I've been telling her that the Martini she has before supper is what makes her think the ground is shaking. She would have been terrified of earthquakes, but she loves her Martini at night and figures a little shaking now and then is a small price to pay.

"Besides," he added, "they make her forget about the snakes, crows, Muskie and everything else."

"C'mon, George," I laughed, "you're kidding."

"I most certainly am not. Ever since she read that thing of yours, she knows now I've been handing her a line. She wants to go back to New York where she *knows* what Martinis do to you."

I suggested to George that he go right down to Ginza and buy his wife one of those "Earthquake Survival Kits" all the department stores are selling.

"After all, George," I explained, "each kit comes with a flashlight, a transistor radio, a map of Tokyo, raincoat, towels, a toothbrush and some Japanese crackers. Just having all that around in one knapsack that she can grab in case of emergency ought to make her feel better."

"You're absolutely unbelievable", George gasped. "Can you just picture my wife sitting on a pile of post-earthquake rubble in nothing but a raincoat, eating Japanese crackers and brushing her teeth?

"And what would she do with a map of Tokyo? Even if the flashlight worked, it wouldn't translate the Japanese on the map."

"But, George. . ."

"But, nothing. You want her to do all of this while she's listening to her transistor radio?"

"But, George," this time I stopped him, "there's nothing to prevent you from adding a jug of Martinis to her survival kit. That ought to make her feel even better."

I could tell that idea mellowed George a bit. He confirmed the mellowing with: "Maybe you're right. I don't know if the Martinis would make her brush her teeth any better or read the map any easier, but it sure would make the radio sound better."

"See, George. It's not so bad, is it?"

"No, I guess I was a little hard on you," he sort of apologized.

"Besides, George," I threw in, "earthquakes aren't the real problem, anyway."

"Now, what does *that* mean?"

"You'd better read the rest of the papers, too, George. Haven't you heard about the book that's Japan's best seller now called 'Nippon Chinbotsu'?"

"Nippon whattsu?"

"Nippon Chinbotsu. It tells how any day now Japan will just sink into the sea. The title, in English, means 'Submersion of Japan.'"

146

"Good God," wheezed George, "what next?"

"It's not hopeless, George," I advised. "The book also tells how the government will act to protect the people in such a situation."

"What could they do?"

"I can't tell you that, George. I didn't read the book. However, I would guess not much. After all, if Japan sinks, I guess the government would sink with it."

"Well," George sighed, "I'm not going to worry about now. Perhaps tomorrow."

"Why, George?" I wanted to know, "What's tomorrow?"

"If we're lucky, maybe tomorrow there will only be an earthquake!"

# VII.  HOME LEAVE

Depending on what kind of a deal you were able to work out with the Home Office before you left, part of the overseas benefit package includes Home Leave.

This means that every so often, the company picks up the travel tab for you to go back to see what it's really like these days in that little patch of Cleveland or wherever that you've spent all this time and effort — in vain — trying to transport to Japan.

By the time Home Leave comes — usually after you've worked a year or two at trying to adapt to the cultural shock — the reverse cultural shock is usually just as bad.

Oh, the people back home are glad to see you — the ones who have realized you were gone, anyway — and they say clever things like, "Gee, your eyes don't look slanted," or they ask questions that always seem to begin with, "Is it true that in Japan . . . " But, they *don't* want to see your slides and they *don't* believe a word you say about what it's really like living here.

Maybe the following selection of stories will help change all that.

# THE HOMECOMING

This time, it was *my* turn to reverse the normal procedure and *I* visited the home office. In case you haven't done the same lately, I want to advise you of some of the back-to-the-womb cultural shocks you're in for when you do. If, of course, your womb is in the United States.

First of all, I stopped off in San Francisco for 48 hours. This, I've convinced everybody involved, is necessary for me to "adjust to the time change". I get no home office arguments about that layover. That's because it makes them feel better about doing the same thing in Honolulu on *their* way to visit *me*.

The first day there was a tragedy of sorts. For one thing, I invited some of my friends from the company's San Francisco Branch Office to breakfast at the hotel. The check for the four of us — shades of Tokyo — was $15. I grabbed it, of course, since I was the out-of-town man. But, when we walked out, I forgot to leave a tip. I didn't realize that until we were out in the lobby again and one of my breakfast guests pointed it out rather tactfully — tactfully for an American, anyway.

"What the hell is with you?" he asked. "Don't you tip in Tokyo?" I explained how the tip was always included in the check in Tokyo and so it was perfectly natural for me to forget.

"Please go back in there," he pleaded, "and leave 15%. *You* may never come back here again, but *I'm* a regular."

So, I sneaked back to the Coffee Shop. Fortunately, our waitress — I hadn't even noticed during breakfast — was a transplanted Japanese, Hatsu San, and she understood, bowed profusely, and grabbed the $2.25 like a life-long American.

Back in the lobby again, I invited the boys up to my room so I could give them something from my shopping bags full of souvenirs. In the elevator with us was an Oriental man with a newspaper tucked under his arm, printed all in Kanji characters.

Immediately, I decided to show the boys how well I was doing with my Japanese lessons. Leaning over toward the man, I gave him — in near-perfect Book II Japanese — a "Good morning, how are you?" and a "How do you like San Francisco?"

Realizing I was speaking to him, he turned and asked in Oxford English, "Isn't that Japanese you were just speaking?"

"Yes," I beamed, "Japanese."

"I thought so," he smiled, "but, since I'm Chinese, I didn't understand a word of it."

Fortunately, just then the elevator stopped at his floor and he got out.

"I could have told you he wasn't Japanese," one of my San Francisco allies said, "and I spent only two weeks in Japan once."

"How," I demanded of the 14-day wonder, "were *you* so sure?"

"Because," he pointed out, "when that guy got in the elevator downstairs, he *didn't* push the 'Door Close' button."

And that wasn't the worst thing that happened to me on my first day back. I rented a car to drive out to see my sister. And I insisted on a big, new one that I could sit up straight in like the old days.

Well, I got a new one. With only 4/10's of a mile on the odometer. It still smelled like new cars used to smell. And as a further indication I was back home, there was no plastic covering on the doors or the seats or the sun visors.

But, thanks to Ralph Nader, you have to be a graduate electrical engineer to operate a new car in the U.S. these days. If you don't shut the door, fasten your seat belt and turn the ignition key in a certain sequence, lights blink and buzzers buzz and the car won't start.

The seat belt in the front was broken, so the only way I could close the circuit was to pull up one of the belts from the back seat and hook it to the front seat clasp.

Still no start. Just lights and buzzers. I realized that my suitcase, on the seat next to me, tripped off another circuit so I had to put a seat belt on the suitcase.

When I finally got going, the radio didn't work — it just buzzed like a Nader device. Before I got off the Bay Bridge, my left front tire was almost flat. Three gas stations told me that they don't change tires any more. Finally, a building guard — I had stopped to ask him for directions — changed it. For only four bucks.

My sister, that night at dinner, apologized for having only an eye round roast beef to serve. Too late notice, she said, to cook anything better. I'd forgotten that there *was* anything better.

Next day, things began looking up. I had real sausages for breakfast, not little whale-meat hot dogs. I bought a copy of Playboy with no black ink painted over anything. I even watched an honest-to-God football game on TV.

The kids in the street, I noticed, all had braces on their teeth the way kids are supposed to. And I had a liverwurst sandwich and a piece of pumpkin pie for lunch.

Later, back in my hotel room, I decided that — despite the sad incidents of the day before — I *was* home. And I *could* cope. To celebrate, I ordered a Bourbon Manhattan delivered to my room. With another liverwurst sandwich.

It wasn't until the room service waiter slammed the door as he left — hard enough to register 6.3 on the Richter Scale — that I realized the mini-celebration was sukoshi premature.

I'd forgotten to tip him.

# IT'S STILL PARADISE

HONOLULU — If you have been to Hawaii lately, you are probably already aware of the things I'm going to talk about today. It you haven't stayed here recently, I've got some advice for you: Don't believe everything you hear — maybe even what I'm going to tell you.

I give that advice because I almost skipped Waikiki this time on my way back to a home office visit in Cleveland. Almost, because of some bad advice I got back in Tokyo .

At a recent Roppongi get-together, the fresh-back-from-Christmas-in-Hawaii crowd was bemoaning the fact that "Everybody in Hawaii is Japanese. No change from Tokyo at all."

Or they said, "Waikiki is too commercial. It's like Coney Island. Not like it used to be. You have to get away from Honolulu to find the real Hawaii."

And another warning: "Hawaii is too expensive now. It's a go-for-broke vaction spot — *flat broke.*"

They went on and on, painting more and more dark clouds over Diamond Head. Like I said, I almost passed it up this time. Then I took another look at the prospect of a non-stop flight over the Pacific and decided, what the hell — I'll take a chance on Waikiki one more time.

Thank God I did.

In the first place, anyone who thinks Hawaii is over-run with Japanese has never tried the platforms at Shinjuku Station in the morning rush hour during one of those monthly railroad slowdowns.

Certainly there are *some* Japanese here. Or maybe they're Chinese or Koreans, for all I know. But there are just enough to make Waikiki more interesting than ever.

For instance, on two occasions yesterday, I ran into Japanese couples and had a chance to pay off some Tokyo debts. The first two were in a restaurant near my hotel. From what I heard from my table next to them, they were trying to figure out what "Eggs Benedict" and "Breakfast Sausage" were.

In my best Naganuma Japanese (Book One), I managed to explain both to them. They tried both. They loved both. They "Arrigato Gozaimas-ed" (thank you) and I "Do itashimashite-ed" (don't mention it).

Last night, in front of a Waikiki theater, another Japanese couple (from Kobe) was trying, without luck, to find out from the ticket seller if the Burt

Reynolds movie had Japanese subtitles. It didn't, and I told them so in Naga-numa. They went in anyway.

What a great feeling — expecially when I remember the countless times some English-speaking Japanese have bailed me out in Tokyo. I'm certainly not even, but I caught up a little.

Another dividend from the Japanese tourists in Waikiki is that Honolulu's TV Channel 9 shows Samurai movies — with, get this, *English subtitles.* It was fabulous. For the first time since I saw my first Far Eastern-Western two years ago, I knew what it was all about. I wonder if they'd lend Japanese stations the subtitles.

Now about Waikiki being commercial. I realized one hour after I got there that that's exactly why I love the place. Movies — all kinds of movies. Scores of restaurants — all "Western Style". Even the Japanese steak house has Kansas City beef. Hot dogs — *honest-to-God* hot dogs. Not on a stick dipped in Oriental corn bread, but on a bun with mustard, relish and sauerkraut. Liverwurst sandwiches, *everything.*

And, of course, nightclubs. Topless, bottomless, hostessless. Why, Waikiki even has a Woolworth's and a Sears and a J.C. Penney.

Everywhere you go, you get to decide for yourself how much tip you should leave. I loved every commercial minute of it.

As for the "real" Hawaii away from Waikiki, I checked it out. I rented a car one day and drove up to the northern end of the island. The advisers were right; there was no commercialism.

In fact, all that's there are acres and acres of sugar cane and pineapple fields. No Japanese. No commercialism. *Nothing.* You can get the same feeling — for a lot less — by standing in the middle of a rice paddy out in Chiba. I drove right back to crowded, gaudy, wonderful Waikiki and laid on the commercial beach.

One thing they were right about: Hawaii *is* expensive. It's damned near as expensive as Tokyo. But, when you're as fresh from the Aoyama supermarkets and Akasaka restaurants in Tokyo as I was, Hawaii looks like a gigantic open-air discount house.

So, the only thing that kept Hawaii from being its usual Paradise this time was that it was a "business trip" and Wife Sarah had to stay behind in Kamikitazawa.

Now, here's my advice again: Don't believe those Hawaii detractors. In all probability they just want you to know that they were there on their own money before — before Hawaii was just a freebie on those back-home trips like this one.

In just a short while, I'll be off for the mainland of the U.S.A. From what they've told me about America recently, I hope they were exaggerating about that, too.

# SET YOUR WATCHES BACK

EN ROUTE CLEVELAND, O. — It used to be that if there was anything harder to do than to leave San Francisco, it was to leave San Francisco for Cleveland.

I'm in an especially melancholy mood as I write this, because I've done just that. Leaving Hawaii day before yesterday was tough. But, I was leaving Hawaii for San Francisco. That's quite bearable.

San Francisco hasn't changed much in the time I was away. Oh, there are new buildings and wider streets and more people and things like that. But what I really mean, I guess, is the state of mind I'm in when I'm around San Francisco is what hasn't changed much. But it *has* changed.

I can't tell you just what the origin is of my romance with San Francisco. I've never lived there — only because I've never figured out how to make a living there. I've only visited there on maybe a dozen occasions. And every visit was a business trip.

This, too, was a business trip. Actually, I stayed there less than 24 hours. It's probably just as well. I think if I stayed much longer, the romance may have been in trouble.

Let me explain. For one thing, it was raining. It always rains in San Francisco around this time of year. I know that. But, I was never *there* during this time of year before.

So, this trip for the first time San Francisco turns out to be mortal just like every other town.

Then, there were none of those smiling California-tanned faces to greet us at the airport gate. Anti-hijacking procedures in the States keep visitors back in the main terminal.

One of the things I always loved about San Francisco was the St. Francis Hotel. Long after the rest of America's hotels turned into chrome and Formica, the St. Francis was something out of the storybooks.

Last time thru, it was still that way. The St. Francis always had people — *live* people — operating the elevators.

In the rooms, you could *open* the window. You weren't hermetically sealed in there.

And the St. Francis' telephones: You picked up the receiver and a live female answered! You told her what you wanted and she did it. When she called you in the morning, she remembered your name, too, and added it to the cheery "Good morning!"

Well, this trip we pulled up to the front door in my brother's car (he lives out in Livermore, Cal.). The doorman told us to go around the building to the motor entrance.

I told him I was sorry, I thought it was the St. Francis Hotel. He

154

assured me it *was.*

With a motor entrance?

With a motor entrance!

And with a new lobby. And with push-button telephones — you know the kind: 9 for local, 8 for long distance, 0 for operator, etc. (And "O" doesn't remember your name in the morning.)

Even the bathroom was all new. I didn't ask, but I wouldn't be surprised if Holiday Inn had bought the place since my last visit.

Anyway, it's still a tough job to leave San Francisco and the new chrome and Formica St. Francis for Cleveland.

I'll always remember some years ago, on a similar flight from San Francisco, the captain saying, "Soon, ladies and gentlemen, we will be landing in Cleveland. Will you please be certain that your seat belts are fastened. And, will the passengers from San Francisco please set their watches back 100 years."

All of us who have lived in Cleveland — and some people who have only visited there — get a big kick out of knocking the place.

Even Cleveland radio stations used to run contests that gave as first prize a week's all-expense vacation in Cleveland. Second prize was *two* weeks in Cleveland.

But, how values can change. Like I said in the beginning, I used to think the toughest job was to leave San Francisco for Cleveland.

That was before I left Cleveland for Tokyo.


## HOME SWEET HOME — OFFICE


CLEVELAND, OHIO — It has always seemed to me that, if you have ever experienced for yourself a visit back to the "home office", no explanation of what goes on during such a visit is necessary.

If you *haven't* personally experienced such a "home office" visit, no explanation is possible.

And so, I haven't discussed these visits before. But, things were so different back there this time that I thought I'd better relay — as objectively as possible under the circumstances — the current situation.

If all this serves no other purpose, it may keep you from going back one day soon and walking in as cold as I did.

In the first place, they are all reading too damn much about Japan. As a result — and I can't think of a gentler way to put it — they *know* too much. And, worse than that, too much about all the wrong things.

For instance, The Wall Street Journal recently ran a frontpage story with the headline "Firms Cut Pay Extras of Overseas Managers". The story went on to tell how companies were "slashing foreign-service premiums" and how others are cutting out housing allowances, school tuition payments for children, and general cost-of-living subsidies.

One guy they quoted in the story — a controller-type — said that his company (I'll spare you that name) is going to phase out overseas premiums and "If we didn't have precedent to contend with, there would already be a lot less of these goodies for our overseas people."

Well, take fair warning: They all — and I mean *all* — read that story. The Wall Street Journal clipping was on top of at least 73% of the desks I visited.

It turns out I didn't bring near enough copies of the supermarket ads where they are bragging about having Borden's ice cream on sale for only $3.30 a quart. Or a "special" on roast beef at just under $10 a pound.

And I was so sorry I didn't bring my last two gas bills to show how the cost of cooking that roast beef went up 40% last month.

After all, I hate to have them wondering what I spend those "goodies" on back in Tokyo.

Another favorite clipping back here is a story filed from Tokyo telling about how land prices have gone up in recent years.

This particular story tells how a man bought a piece of property in Tokyo some time ago, for about $250. He was away for a few years, came back, and found an offer of a half-million dollars for the little piece of property.

The writer could have left things right there. But no. He had to go on and tell how many of the foreign businessmen stationed in Tokyo made similar killings.

As home office people recounted this story, the inference was unmistakable. I let it pass.

Even the World Almanac is a problem. It was quoted as the source of information that indicates we foreigners cause our own money problems by not eating as the natives do.

"Listen to this," our Almanac man said. "The average American eats about 200 pounds a meat a year. The average Japanese eats only about 23 pounds of meat a year! If you simply dropped your average to the Japanese level, meat prices in Tokyo would be no problem."

That did it. I suffered in silence no longer. Don't misunderstand. The poor guys who bring up things like money and meat prices are not the head men in any company.

It's the poor guy in the accounting department to whom falls the task of writing you a company check for more money for your kid's grammar school that he pays out of his own pocket for his kid's college.

It's the guy who writes you a company check for one year's rent on your Tokyo house or apartment that matches the *purchase* price of his house.

I realize all this, and so I was as calm as could be expected when I said — ever so slowly:

"Let me, George, clarify the meat situation. We *do* eat only the Japanese average of 23 pounds of meat each year. What annoys me, George, is that I pay more for those 23 pounds than any American pays for his 200 pounds."

"Well," advised George, "you had better find some way to cut down your personal spending over there."

"Oh, I will, George," I assured him, "and I thank you for helping,"

"Thank me?" asked George. "How did I help?"

"Thanks to you, George, I'm cancelling my subscription to the Wall Street Journal."


## RETURN TO THE WOMB


Most Gaijin businessmen assigned to Japan, I've found, consider the "Home Leave" as the nicest goody in the overseas benefit package. Many, these days, get to enjoy this company-picks-up-the-fare sojourn with their families every year. The less-benefited only get the free ride back to the womb every two years.

For most husbands, Home Leave doesn't present any special reverse-cultural-shock problems. Most of us make a few solo crisis trips back to the home office in between benefit trips. For the wives and the kids, however, Home Leave can cause some uncomfortable moments. I know I've had a few on some of those crisis trips.

Last time back, for instance, the home office man who was talking to our crisis meeting suddenly stopped and said, "Maloney, cut that out, please."

"Cut *what* out?" I asked.

"Cut out punctuating every sentence I utter by nodding your head and mumbling 'Eh,' 'Ah ha,' 'So So' — or whatever it is your mumbling. What does all that mean, anyway?"

Now I tried to explain to him that nodding your head and saying "Eh," "Ah ha", "So So" and the like in Japan only means "Eh," "Ah ha" and "So So." It doesn't really mean anything else special.

He acknowledged my explanation with one of those "You've been in Japan too long" looks and went on with his discussion. I really concentrated and didn't nod once or give one more "Eh." It wasn't easy.

That nodding habit is only one of the Japanese habits I've carried back home on occasion. Others — like pushing the "Door Close" button on the elevator, bowing to everyone I'm introduced to, and standing and sitting with my arms folded — draw some very strange looks, too.

Anyway, this upcoming Summer of '74 is our Home Leave time. As soon as Daughter Barbara graduates from Sacred Heart International in Tokyo and Son Donald Junior gets the word about whether he's made eighth grade out at St. Mary's, we're off for the land of cooked fish.

Because I wanted the cultural re-entry to be as easy as possible for the Maloneys, I decided to have an orientation meeting — or was it a *dis*orientation meeting ? — the other night on how to behave back home.

Just in case you are among this year's Home Leave crop, I've decided, for what it may be worth, to pass on here some of the things I counseled them about. Unfortunately, I'm certain only that this advice is good for Americans. I'm not sure what its application might be in other non-Japanese countries.

First off — and this was aimed directly at the kids — *don't* slurp the soup like it was just another bowl of Japanese Soba. Cleveland people will frown on that sort of sound effect.

And, while we were on the subject of eating, I reminded them that you have to call a waiter "Waiter" if you want to get his attention. "Anone" or "Sumimasen" won't do the trick. If you *really* want an American waiter's attention, of course, act like you're still in Japan and don't tip him. American waiters react to that somewhat more obviously than fellow diners will react to the soup-slurping. And take the restaurant's bread — they don't have any rice.

For heaven's sake, *don't* wait for the taxi driver to open the door for you. And don't wait for him to thank you for his tip, either.

Neither Wife Sarah nor the kids is to say anything to home office wives or kids about the maid or the fact that the company pays the school tuition or anything like that. It can't make anybody back there feel any better.

I did instruct them all, however, to remind everybody at home — even people not even remotely connected with the home office — about the high cost of everything in Tokyo. I have some of my own carefully laid-out plans along these lines.

For example, the first time we're with an influential home office group, I'm going to ask one of the wives — next time she goes to the supermarket — to pick up a couple of melons and a bunch of grapes for us to munch on back at the hotel. Then, I'm going to give her five $10 bills.

She'll say, "What's the $50 for?"

And I'll say, "For the melons and grapes."

And she'll say, "You're kidding," and give me back four of the five $10 bills.

Then I'll say, "That's right, I forgot we were in Cleveland, and by habit I gave you enough to buy them at Tokyo prices." She — and everybody else in the room, I hope — will get the message.

In case they don't, however, I plan another part of a one-two punch on Tokyo prices. I'll say to another home office couple some evening, "Wife Sarah and I would like to take you out for a modest dinner tonight, but I didn't get to the bank today and I only have $116 on me."

If they don't pick up the inference, Wife Sarah is all primed to say, "Now, Don, you're not in Tokyo now and $116 here is good for five or six dinners." I'll just smile and say something appropriate.

And don't forget, if you decide to watch some of the baseball games on television, that it's OK to turn on the sound. Chances are, you'll understand every word. Don't plan to watch the movies on TV, however. I'm sure they'll be showing the same ones that will be on at the American Club and the Press Club when you come back to Japan and so you'll spoil next year's social season.

Please don't bring up Watergate when you're back there. They can only have two reactions if you do. One, they'll just jump on you and tell you they're sick of talking about it.Or, two, they'll figure you've never heard about it over in Japan and tell you the whole story. Either way, you lose.

One last bit of advice — one that may upset all your plans and dreams: Don't bring your slides and picture albums of Japan. Nobody back there, painful as it may be to you, gives a damn. Oh, they'll ask you, "What's it like living over there?" And, if this is Home Leave Number One, you might think they really expect an answer. They don't. Most are probably not even certain where "over there" is. All they know is that you've been away for awhile.

And, please, don't think that just because you meet everybody who comes to Japan at Haneda Airport, don't think that means those same somebodies are going to meet you over there. Never happens.

Anyway, have a good trip. Close cover before striking; rub, don't blot; count your change before leaving; fasten seat belts; keep to the right — and all sorts of American things like that. And, when you come back to Japan, *don't* forget to fill out that "Declaration of Unaccompanied Goods!.

## STRANGER IN PARADISE

Home Leave 1974 is over. And I'm glad.

Unbelievable as it sounds—even to me—I'm happy to be back in the land where I almost never understand anything. But, here at least I *understand* that I'll never understand.

Over there — in Ford country — I *used* to understand. I *expected* to

159

understand this time. But, for some ununderstandable reason, I didn't this time. Practically nothing seemed to go right.

Hawaii, of course, was an exception. A fair amount of things there always go right. We spent some time there on both the way over *and* on the way back. Such Hawaiian delays-en-route in both directions are —I believe — mandatory.

For one thing, Hawaii is more expensive generally than the mainland. But, it's no way as costly as Tokyo. So, it gives you a chance to ease down from the $25 steak dinners in Tokyo to the $12 steak dinners in San Francisco by passing through Honolulu's $15 steaks. And the easing-up is just as effective on the way back.

Also, in Honolulu, you get used to the idea of seeing more and more overfed foreigners on the streets. But there are still enough Oriental faces to make you feel comfortable.

At least one person in every store in Waikiki speaks Japanese. Not pure Naganuma, of course, but they understand a "Kore wa hon desu"(This is a book) if you give it to them slowly. Unfortunately, they understand "ikura?" (How much is this?), too.

And the prices they answer with are really no more understandable to me in English than they would be in Japanese. Prices in America have *really* gone up. And, for some unknown reason, I still feel spending most when it's real green dollars I'm paying with. Equal or not, ¥3,000 still goes through my fingers easier than $10. Buying anything for yen still affects me much like buying Park Place with Monopoly money.

Naturally, we were all really into buying non-Kobe steaks at non-Tokyo prices the first couple of days. Sure it was cheaper than in Japan, but every meal for the six of us ended up with a $50 or $60 tab — plus that aggravating tip. On the third night, I did a little arithmetic and decided — at that rate — the supper tab of $60 a day times the 30 days of Home Leave was certain financial disaster.

So, I announced that next evening that — like it or not — we were having our supper at good old McDonald's. We did, and it was great — not the Big Macs, but the bill. I only had to get up $6.15 for everybody.

As we were backing out of the McDonald parking lot, I was commending everybody for the cheerful way in which they accepted this gastronomic sacrifice. Then, there was a loud crunch. I'd backed into another car and severely wrinkled his fender. Unwrinkling that fender cost me $57.20.

That's what I mean about nothing going right. The McDonald's meal — including the fender — was $3.35 more expensive than any of the steak dinners. But, as Wife Sarah later pointed out, I didn't have to tip at either McDonald's or at the body shop.

We even succumbed this time to all the Pacific Ocean hoppers who've always told us: "Don't just stay in Honolulu — get out to the other Hawaiian Islands. Get away from it all. See the *real* Hawaii." So, we went to Hilo.

Well, it's real, all right. And, it's away from it all. In fact, I don't think it's possible to get *further* away from it all. Including the sunshine and the beaches and thousand places to go and things to do that Waikiki offers. I'm even sure the people in Hilo speak English. We didn't see anybody.

On the second day, we headed back to Honolulu and the good old Kahala Hilton. Because it's on the other side of Diamond Head, we can "get away from it all" there as far as we care to go. And, when the sun goes down, Waikiki and all the action are within easy reach. And, don't kid youself — Waikiki is the "real Hawaii."

But, I digress.

Things — from the cultural shock standpoint — did begin to pick up on the mainland. As we went through San Francisco, Dallas and Dayton, I found it easier and easier to remember to tip, to remember that I had to open my own taxi door and to forget to push the "door close" button on the elevators. After eating five melons just because they were only thirty cents each, I admitted to myself that it was foolish to fret about Tokyo's $10 melons. I never liked them anyway.

The worst part was Cleveland. There, on the way back to our motel from a day in the home-office barrel, I sailed through a stop sign. A policeman was right there and he pulled me over and gave me a ticket. I had to pay $19, including court costs. There was no way out.

The Cleveland cops, you see, speak English.


## PLEASE PASS THE SUSHI


They like to say in the ads that "Home Leave" begins the moment you board your outbound jet.

It could happen, I guess, but it certainly wasn't true in our case some weeks ago when we left on our every-two-year, some-but-not-much-of-the-expenses-paid, trip back to Cleveland.

In the first place, the girls on our Northwest Jumbo made those your-life-vest-is-under-your-seat announcements in both Japanese and English.

At least, I *assume* they told the Japanese where the life vests were and how to use them. Just as I assume that Japan Air Lines is giving *me* the straight story about the emergency exits when I'm flying up to Hokkaido or down to Kyushu.

Then, just before the movies, we were served some Japanese raw fish on rice — sushi — definitely not what I would have chosen as my first home

161

leave meal. But, as it later turned out, it was probably the perfect choice. I'll explain why:

We'd decided — as we always do — to stop over in Hawaii for a few days. Two years ago, when the Maloney clan was off on a similar voyage, memory tells me that we spent the whole plane trip talking about what we would eat once we were safely back in the mother country. So, as we were dipping our sushi in the soy sauce, I decided to start a 1974 version of the same conversation. I picked on Son Donald for a starter. "I suppose, Donald," I announced, "that you're going to head for the nearest McDonald's and a Big Mac and French Fries."

"No," Son Donald scoffed. "I had two Big Macs last week over on the Ginza. Besides, I'm off French Fries for life, I think. I'm a rice boy now."

"Rice?" I'm sure the absolute disbelief showed through in what I meant to be a question.

"Yes, rice," he assured me. "And what's bothering me right now is the remembering that American rice comes only in those separate pieces that are always falling off the fork and not that big sticky blob like Japanese rice."

I could tell by the way he was fondling the gummy ball of rice under his Northwest sushi that he was serious.

Turning to Daughter Barbara, I said, "Surely, Barb, *you*'re going to run to some pizza place and down a giant one with the works."

"No way," she assured me. "I had pizza over at Shakey's in Tokyo with the gang last night. In fact, I don't think I've missed a pizza a week for the past six months."

I couldn't believe my ears.

Just then, Daughter Frances chimed in with "I know what they're saying, Dad. Two years ago, I was dreaming on the plane of a banana split and trying to figure out which flavors I'd choose for each of the three scoops of ice cream included with any self-respecting banana split."

"And now?"

"Now, I'm thinking about this sushi and how it must be impossible to find anything like this in Cleveland."

"You mean you don't care what flavors the ice cream will be in your opening banana split?"

"There won't even *be* a banana split — of that I'm certain."

Since she sounded so positive about that, I had to ask her why.

"Because," she said, "when Baskin-Robbins Ice Cream Stores came to Tokyo some time back, I was almost a daily visitor — and, a chooser of exotic flavors. I'm up to here in things like chocolate chip mint, lemon marshmallow, peach mame — whatever a "mame" is — and fudge ripple. The most I could possibly come around to when we get back home is maybe a vanilla cone."

162

"Do you *hear* them?" I asked Son Sean. "Can they be for real?"

"They are as far as I'm concerned," he admitted. "The only thing I might have longed for is a tall, ice-cold A & W Root Beer or a one-of-each bag of Dunkin' Donuts."

"So?"

"So? So I've had *both* in Shibuya in Tokyo in the last 48 hours."

Hopefully, I decided, Wife Sarah would have something to say that would serve to cushion the shock. "Are you listening?" I asked her. "Better than that, do you *understand* what your children are saying?"

"I understand *everything*," she answered, "everything, that is, except why you're so taken back by all this."

"But Sarah," I protested, "I've always looked on myself as the father of All-American family. And All-American families are supposed to want to rush from Home Leave airplanes to pizza parlors, hamburger stands, root beer fountains and frozen custard stands. Those are Gaijin rules and our very own kids are going to break them. Right in front of our eyes."

"Yes," Wife Sarah agreed. "I think they are."

I gave her a wide-eyed, "My God, is that *all* you have to say?"

She thought a minute, then said, "No, there is one more thing."

"Thank heaven," I sighed. "Let's hear it."

"When the stewardess comes by again," she whispered, "ask her if I can have a couple more pieces of sushi."

# VIII.   THE HOLIDAYS

One of the toughest things to adjust to in Japan is the Holidays. I mean, the Japanese Holidays don't mean anything to you, so you have a real problem trying to get into the Holiday mood when they roll around.

And, since the Japanese don't give a damn about your foreign Holidays and carry on with "business as usual" on those days, it's even more difficult for you to find the Holiday spirit on those days. But, you keep trying. That's what I feel gives every Holiday a whole new dimension in Japan.

And, while you're trying, some strange things happen. Read on . . .

# CHRISTMAS, IT WASN'T

I don't know about you and yours — but for me, last week just didn't seem like Christmas. Not that it wasn't exactly as I suspected. After all, it *was* our third December 25 in Tokyo. It just wasn't like Christmas ought to be.

Funny part of it is — and probably because we've been here three years — I can't even tell you any more what Christmas ought to be like. Christmas is not something you can describe, anyway. It's something you feel inside. And, you either feel it or you don't. What I'm moaning about is that I didn't.

Now don't get me wrong. I'm not talking about the religious side of the Holiday. That's a different matter entirely. What I'm talking about is that other side of Christmas, that — you know, the *feeling*, the spirit of Christmas.

The hell of it is, everyone tried so hard. But every try seemed to miss the mark so badly.

For instance, there were lots of Christmas parties. The other night Wife Sarah and I took off for one by car from Kamikitazawa. I was up to here in determination to capture the spirit of the season when we left the driveway.

About half-way downtown, Wife Sarah realized that she grabbed the wrong map and the wrong invitation. We had to go back because you need a map when they don't name any streets. When we did get the right map, it turned out to be an old one that left out a couple of traffic lights and identified some landmarks that were no more.

We got hopelessly lost. The "spirit" slipped away with each wrong turn. A trip that should have taken forty minutes took more than two hours. When we finally got there, and our host greeted us with a "Merry Christmas", I really had a time suppressing my un-Christmas desire to shove his map down his throat.

And the shopping. The traditional crowds were in the stores, all right. But, hell, those crowds are in the Tokyo stores *every* day of *every* season. But, were there candy canes to put on the tree? No. And have you ever tried to explain to that girl who wipes the handrail on the escalator in Takashimaya Department Store that you want a string of Christmas Tree Lights that *don't* blink? Forget it.

When I finally found what I wanted for Wife Sarah, I asked the girl to please wrap it up for me as a "Kurisumasu Presento". Hai, hai, she understood. Then back it came in purple and yellow paper with a pink ribbon on it. Christmas? Hardly. More like Easter.

And, walking back home Christmas Eve, it was all wrong. Oh, there were plenty of open fires. But, they weren't roasting chestnuts; they were cooking sweet potatoes. And that wasn't Jack Frost nipping at my nose, it was the open air Tokyo sewer system. Even those "tiny tots with their eyes all aglow" who, the song says, are supposed "to find it hard to sleep that night" were out of it. They were already asleep strapped to their mothers' backs.

Even the Christmas cards from home had a tendency to turn things off. While we were riding out our cyclone the other night in Tokyo, I opened cards that told of the snow storm back home — the way it ought to be.

And how about the notes people scrawl on the bottom of their cards telling you how much they envy our opportunity to experience Christmas in the Orient? Surely they can't mean that they envy the fact that our College kids will be 10,000 miles away from the Orient on Christmas morning.

Like I said earlier, don't get me wrong. If I sound bitter, I don't mean to. I just mean that Christmas in Tokyo is not Christmas. It's just one more of those things that we forget to send over as unaccompanied goods.

And I like sweet potatoes better than chestnuts, anyway. And I like getting the escalator handrail wiped off for me. And I like getting waited on in a department store instead of ignored. And I like the excitement of going anywhere by car in Tokyo. The lousy maps open up new vistas for me everytime I venture out.

I especially like the absolute chaos that is Tokyo. It keeps me feeling alive and never, never offers a dull moment. Life *is* a banquet here — even if the banquet is spiced with raw fish.

Maybe the big appeal of Christmas back home is, after all, the fact that it offers a once-a-year opportunity to get out of the humdrum of everyday living. You certainly need no such excuse as a foreigner in Japan. There isn't even a Japanese word for humdrum.

The way I feel right now, I wouldn't trade any part of it for a truckload of candy canes or a mile-long string of tree lights that didn't blink.

Maybe I'm crazy. Maybe, like we all tell each other, we *have* to be crazy to live and work here. But, to a large extent *because* I am living and working here, I'm going to have a Happy New Year. Oh, it will have its aggravations and frustrations — that's for sure. And it won't be like New Years back home. And I'll wish a thousand times during 1973 that I was back in Cleveland. But, I *will* have a Happy New Year.

I hope you all have a Happy New Year, too.


## THE SIPPING O' THE GREEN

There aren't many days around here when I feel low. I mean anytime I get an idea that boredom is setting in, there's plenty to get my mind busy

167

again.

For instance, if it's just a mild case of the blahs, I can solve that right at home by turning on the TV. I turn off the sound completely and make up my own stories about what's going on. I make them real exciting stories, of course, so there's no chance of staying bored for long.

If that doesn't work, I just go out in the kitchen and try to open a Japanese milk bottle without using that little pick. You *can't* stand there unmoved while you're doing *that*.

Or, I can pick up the latest gas or electric bill and try to figure out how they decided I owe them that much. Sometimes, however, the sight of either of those bills *over*excites me and that's more dangerous than boredom.

If the boredom seems to be a more serious case, I walk down to the local police box to ask them, in English, the directions to someplace — *anyplace*. That's good for a hour of mind-blowing, anyway.

Once in a while, I go over to the supermarkets and look through the glass on the meat counter. Not to select a certain piece of meat; just to convert the price in yen per 100 grams to the price in dollars per pound.

That's touchy, though, because I always face that danger of overexcitement again.

Today, I know none of those cures will work. I'm going to feel so far down later on, I know, that I've got to come up with some great — make that terrific — medicine.

You see, today is Saint Patrick's Day. And I know from the previous March 17ths spent here in Tokyo, that it's nothing like Costello's Bar on Third Avenue in New York on that day of days.

I was discussing this very subject the other day with a Gaijin group, each of whom claims to have similar Emerald Isle roots.

"We could," one of them suggested, "take a ride on a train someplace and sit in the first-class *Green* Car."

I had to agree that might just work. After all, besides calling the first class coach a "Green Car," the Japanese National Railroads paint a four-leaf Shamrock next to every door.

"Forget it," ruled another. "We'd be riding in a Green Car, alright, but the only thing they serve on the trains is Japanese Whiskey or Sake, and you can't properly toast the good Saint with *that* sort of thing."

I reminded them all that *green* tea is certainly available on all trains with *Green* Cars and *that* — if only because of the color — could be considered appropriate.

"Wait a minute," interrupted another. "March 17 is a Sunday this year. And you *know* that sixty million people are going traveling around in this country — just like every other Sunday."

"But if we call early," I decided, "we might be able to get a seat reservation on some Green Car going somewhere. It's worth a try, anyhow.''

"Count me out," the originator of the Green Car idea announced. "We might get Green Car seats, but there's no hope that, with Sunday crowds, the green tea supply will last all day."

"Hey, I got an idea," I volunteered. "How about we just go out to one of the local golf courses, bring a picnic lunch of corned beef and cabbage and sit around one of the *'greens'* and spend the day."

Everybody jumped on me at once. For one thing, they said, the only place they know of where they can get corned beef in Tokyo is over at Anne Dinken's Kosher place in Roppongi. And most of the cabbage around here, they pointed out, is Chinese.

What they were driving at is that we'd probably be struck by lightning if we sat there celebrating St. Patrick's Day while eating Kosher corned beef and Chinese cabbage.

"Even if we *didn't* get struck by lightning," one lamented, "half of those sixty million people riding the trains are heading for a golf course someplace and we'd be bombarded with golf balls."

"Maybe," I thought, "The Japanese will televise the parade from New York. We can watch that."

"Are you nuts?" I was asked.

"Why not?" the Green Car man wanted to know. "They televised the Princess' wedding and the St. Patrick's Day Parade is more important than that."

That gave me an idea. "Hold on," I told them, "I've got a great idea."

"What?"

"I've got a cousin who is on the New York City police force. Certainly, he'll have parade duty along Fifth Avenue somewhere. And, if I know him, he'll be right in front of St. Patrick's Cathedral."

"So?"

"So? So we'll call him up at home tonight, tell him to call us back from someplace where he's watching the parade on Sunday and tell us all about it. He can describe the whole thing over the telephone."

"What will *that* get us?" they asked.

"*Green* with envy," I told them "*That's* what."


## MERRY CHRISTMAS

With only two days left to shop, I still haven't really figured out what to get Wife Sarah for Christmas. As I look around the house, it seems to me that she has just about everything a normal Gaijin woman could want.

169

I mean she has *two*, not just one, of those Japanese dolls in the glass cabinets. And, she has two or three of those little spears you use to pop the cap off a milk bottle — each with a different color plastic handle.

Plus, she has all the standard crockery — you know, the Imari dishes (certified as "very old" by the Oriental Bazaar), the Kutani vases (in what else can you properly put the fruits of eight Thursdays of Ikebana classes?), and a platter from Mashiko (that somehow survived the bus trip back to Tokyo).

There are as many woodblock prints in our house as there are different kinds of Soba noodles in the window of the shop down the corner. And, Wife Sarah maintains with ease the normal accepted percentage of wall coverage by old scrolls and those folding screens.

She has at least a year's supply of those little name cards with maps on the back that help all those Tokyo legions of "most intimate friends" find our house. And our "spacious garden" is 50% occupied by a little stone lantern. I don't dare buy another — even though 50% of the garden is vacant — because the company will die at the freight charges for the single one we have when pack-up day comes.

Last week, for a fleeting moment, I thought she might settle for an autographed copy of Sumo wrestler Jesse Takamiyama's new book. But I ruled that out as not personal enough. Besides, I notice that a lot of Jesse's Gaijin women fans have cooled on him since he announced his engagement to a local girl last month.

Then, I decided that maybe a gift of an airline ticket to Hong Kong would be appropriate. But, I didn't even come close to winning one at any of the Tokyo school bingos or church raffles. So, I scratched that idea. Because I'm not even sure foreigners in Tokyo are allowed to *buy* a ticket to Hong Kong. I think you *have* to win it.

I don't dare buy her a box of grapefruit like I did a couple of years ago. Now that they are liberated by Japanese customs, grapefruits have lost their snob appeal altogether. There's still grapes of course, but I don't really know whether she'd like the green ones or the purple ones and I'd die if I chose the wrong color.

A trip I made to some of the local department stores confused me even more. Surely you've noticed the displays of gift boxes they put together this time of year. I think the idea is great, but the combinations throw me.

For instance, she likes American-made beauty soap. The one box I saw also included a Japanese Salami; the other paired the soap with a can of corn from the People's Republic of China. I know Wife Sarah well enough to be certain she'd just as soon do without the corn and salami, even if it means goodbye forever to washing up with Ivory.

Another thing she likes is canned ham, but they were boxed with either STP oil additive or pickled eels. Neither combination would put her in the real Christmas spirit, I'm afraid. Especially since it's all packed in that green cellophane grass Wife Sarah would associate with Easter Baskets.

I could, I suppose, turn real egomaniac and give her a picture of me. But, I can't help but notice that, although I only need three little pictures for my Alien Registration card and those clever coin photo machines give me four, she's never seemed especially interested in the extra one even though I leave it right on her bureau.

Actually, I leave it on her ''tansu''. She doesn't need another one of those, either.

There are two things — maybe three — that she *really* wants, I know, but I can't find them anywhere. One is a box of laundry soap and the other is a three-week course on sorting garbage. At least, if I even half-understand the new garbage rules. Plastic garbage, for instance, is being collected only on second and fourth Tuesdays in months of more than 30 days, and only if the sun is out and the wind from the west. Paper, bottles and cans only on the days when plastic and old Yakiimo skins are *not* collected. Or, maybe it's the other way around.

Whatever it is, I imagine the sorting course would take three weeks. Anyway, there's *no* laundry soap and I can't find the College Women's Association or anyone else willing to undertake a real public service course on garbage sorting.

The third thing I'm not sure about is toilet paper. Oh, it would be a personal enough gift, all right. But, I notice our home inventory is almost up to normal again — even if it's all just plain white.

There really is no excuse for me not having this Christmas problem solved by now. I guess it's just because I'm having my annual difficulty in getting into the spirit of the Holidays in Tokyo.

Just the other day, for instance, I ran over to the International Arcade to see if I could get an idea there. On the way, duty called and I ducked into the lobby of the Imperial Hotel to use the men's room in the lobby.

Now I'm not sure whether it's a result of the now-concluded water shortage or because of the current toilet paper scarcity — or maybe some ominous calamity I'm not even yet aware of. But the fact is that the Imperial has boarded up both the men's room and the ladies' room in the lobby. No ''gomen nasai'' sign or anything — just boarded up to look like they never existed.

So, I ran across the street to one of those restaurants to use their sanitary facilities. Now, you can't do that without ordering *something*. And, everytime I pay the check for *anything* in a Tokyo restaurant, I lose my Christmas spirit. Even in the middle of July.

As a result, I came home empty handed.

Now, with less than 48 hours to go, I really should decide on what to give Wife Sarah for Christmas. As I write this, I've been thinking. Maybe

171

the most sensible thing to do is to simply tell her how much I really love her. And, how happy I am that our whole family will be together this holiday season.

Maybe we *won't* have enough laundry soap or toilet paper or gasoline or whatever. But, at least in our little company rented patch of it, we will have peace on earth.

Isn't that, after all, what a Merry Christmas is all about?

That's what I wish for you and yours, too, when I say "Merry Christmas To All".


## 'TWAS THE PLIGHT BEFORE CHRISTMAS

(with apologies to Mr. Moore)


'Twas the plight before Christmas and all through Japan,
Not a Gaijin was stirring; they were in Guam or Saipan.
They had all rushed away, by ship and by air.
Cause they know that St. Nicholas never comes here.
But the natives were futoned all snug on tatami mats,
While visions of sushi danced in their hats.
Wife Sarah was in her nightgown and I turned off the hi-fi.
And we gave to each other an "Oyasumi nasai."
When from out on the street I heard a loudspeaker,
And I sprang from my bed because it wasn't getting weaker.
Away to the window I flew like a vapor
Tore open the shoji and also tore the paper.
The moon thru the smog over Tokyo Tower
Pointed out the effects of GNP power.
When, what to my irritated eyes should appear
But a little old man yelling "Yaki imo here."
So it wasn't plum pudding, I thought as I sighed
But neither was it squid — raw or deep fried.
More rapid than Bullet trains the Kodomos they came
And the sweet potato man called each one by name.
"Now, Akichan! Now, Bochan! Now Hirochan and Takeko!
For ¥ 30 each you can split this potato.
Don't throw the peel in the middle of the street."
And he wrapped it in newspaper, ever so neat.
In the background, the radio played a Christmas song
And the FEN announcer pronounced "Christmas" wrong.
And then in a twinkling I heard from the kitchen,

172

The noise that the cockroaches make when they're twitchin'.
As I grabbed the DDT can and was spraying around,
Up the chimney they ran with our osembe (about a pound)
As I stared at the fireplace, my memory was jarred
Back to Christmas in Cleveland, with snow in the yard.
And to the toys under the tree, all wrapped by hand
And all of them, of course, labelled ''Made in Japan.''
But now here in Tokyo — with no snow — *or* no yard,
Christmas seemed like something just pictured on a card.
I felt like a snack, but there was no turkey
With prices what they are, there wasn't even beef jerky.
I went back upstairs feeling lower than lira,
And on the bed room door, caught my image in the mirror.
There was my broad face and a big old round belly,
That shook when I whimpered like a bowl full of jelly.
I was chubby and plump, a right saddened old elf.
But suddenly I laughed at the sight of myself.
So we can't have a tree with lights that don't blink,
And we won't have a feast that includes the kitchen sink.
But we *can* have some Soba, hot sake and rice,
Where in Cleveland can you celebrate so nice?
Besides, Christmas is within us, not served on a plate
And spending it in Japan ain't such a bad fate.
And I sure like the length of the holidays here.
They start up on Christmas and last till next year.
So my wish for you all, however troubled with your plight,
Merry Christmas, Happy Oshogatsu and to all a good night


## SLOW BURN

Just about the time that President Ford's Air Force One was touching
down for refueling in Alaska on the way to his historical Japan visit, my
Northwest 747 was touching down in Honolulu — heading in the opposite
direction. I was on my way back to Cleveland for some refueling at the Home
Office.

Whenever I head back to the U.S. — for whatever reason — I always
make the Oahu stop. I used to come up with excuses for that delay en route
like ''necessary to fight jet lag'' or ''to help cushion the reverse cultural
shock'', or something creative like that. These days it's easier than ever to
justify because Daughter Barbara is now a Freshman at the University of
Hawaii and it's refreshing to drop in on her occasionally and hear firsthand

173

why she insists her monthly allowance must be increased.

Listening to her gives me some insight as to how the Home Office feels when I make my regular pitches there on essentially the same subject. (Both Daughter Barbara and I, by the way, get the same results.)

During my 24-hour stay with her this time, I was looking for some advice as to what I should pick up on the mainland as an appropriate Christmas gift for Wife Sarah. Well, Daughter Barbara wasn't much help.

After all, she pointed out, this past summer was home leave time for us. She was certain that Wife Sarah stocked up on all the clothes and shoes she needs until next home leave. I had to agree that was probably true and remembered that I had the American Express and Bank Americard bills to prove it.

On other business-related stopovers in Los Angeles, San Francisco, and Chicago — I won't go into the details of justifying those — I spent much of my spare time window shopping in an effort to come up with some unique gift idea. No soap.

Then, in Cleveland, it hit me. Why not, I thought, bring back something special for Christmas dinner instead of some ordinary present? And, I recalled, there's little my family likes better than an old-fashioned baked ham.

There's a place in Cleveland that sells baked hams that have been cured in honey, spiral sliced right around the bone, then slow, slow baked. We often ate them back home on holidays and the family loved them.

So, just before I left Cleveland for New York, where I had Thanksgiving Dinner with Wife Sarah's mother, I picked up a 17 pound ham. As soon as I got to my mother-in-law's, I popped it in her freezer. I reasoned that, frozen solid, I probably could get it back to Tokyo without it spoiling.

Forty-eight hours later, I wrapped the frozen ham in aluminum foil, packed it in newspapers to insulate it, and headed for Kennedy Airport. I had already decided to make a straight run back to Japan — no stopovers that might risk the safe arrival of the ham.

The airline was kind enough to give me one of those shoulder-strapped flight bags to carry it in and, aboard the plane, the stewardess even volunteered to stow it in one of the coolers. When we landed in Fairbanks, the temperature was eight below zero. So, I put the bag with ham over my shoulder and walked around outside the terminal building as added ham insurance rather than sit in the nice warm waiting room.

When my flight was called, I reboarded the plane and restowed the ham in the cooler. Oh, I thought, how well all this is going and how pleased Wife Sarah will be. Maybe even, I was hoping, she'll make some pea soup from the bone for New Year's.

Once at Haneda, I collected my two suitcases, my attache case, the box

174

of duty-free goodies, and the flight bag with the ham and piled them all on the customs counter. Through the side of the bag, I could feel that the ham was still frozen. I knew I had it made since nothing could happen on the short trip from the airport to our Shiroganedai house.

"Anything to declare?" the Customs man asked.

Only this carton of cigarettes and my three bottles of Old Grandad," I assured him with a smile.

"What's in this flight bag?" he wanted to know.

"A Christmas surprise for my wife," I smiled.

"What kind of surprise?" he pursued.

"A ham," I proudly announced. I thought of sharing with him my ingenious method of getting it from Cleveland to Tokyo, but he stiffened.

"A ham? A *meat* ham?"

"Why, sure, a *meat* ham," I assured him.

"Chotto matte," he said and signalled for another inspector.

Now I can't say for sure what he told this other guy, but he headed right for the flight bag. "Open, please."

And I did — ever so proudly.

"You have health certificate for this?" he asked.

"I have this receipt," I offered with my smile faltering.

"No receipt necessary. Just health certificate. Animal quarantine law."

I assured him that this animal in the bag was very dead, very cooked, very frozen and in no way unhealthy.

"Sorry," he said, "but cannot bring into Japan."

Why, considering the look on his face, I said, "You're joking." I don't know. He obviously wasn't. And nothing I said changed his mind. "If I can't bring it into Japan," I asked, "What will you do with it?"

"We'll burn it," he said.

"Burn it?"

"Burn it. In a fire. Sorry." And, he walked away with my Christmas surprise under his arm.

I tried to recover my smile for Wife Sarah who was waiting outside. I told her my story and ended it with the news that they were going to burn it.

She shrugged. "At 350 degrees for three hours, I hope."


## OVER THE RIVER AND THROUGH THE WOODS

It's that time again. The Holiday Season is coming and — with it — that annual feeling of we've "got to do something or go somewhere." Even if you don't think of that all by yourself, you'll soon hear Gaijin friends —

175

the more affluent ones, anyway — reciting their plans to duck out for the Holidays to Hawaii, Okinawa, Guam, Saipan or some other exotic sounding place.

And, more likely than not, you'll get the fever. Especially if the coming Holidays are to be your first since arriving in Japan. I certainly remember our first a couple of years ago.

A casual glance at our bank balance snuffed out any hope of joining the off-to-the-South-Pacific crowd. We decided to have a domestic celebration — and, furthermore, we decided it would be Thanksgiving up in Nikko and Christmas right at home in Kamikitazawa.

It was already mid-October by the time all the Maloneys agreed to this rather austere plan so I asked my secretary to be super polite when she telephoned the Lakeside Hotel up in Nikko. I was sure, at this late date, that all the rooms would be gone.

Fortunately, they had space for us. We set everything for a Wednesday morning departure from Tokyo and a return on Sunday afternoon. And we waited for the day with the highest levels of anticipation I'd seen in our family since we packed up in Cleveland for our Oriental journey.

The last hurdle — seat reservations for our Thanksgiving Eve hour and a half train ride — turned out to be no hurdle at all and we were off without a hitch.

When we arrived at Nikko station, we somehow miraculously managed to get all the Maloneys and our luggage into a single taxi. Now the Lakeside Hotel — for those of you who have yet to do Nikko — is up on the top of a fairly high mountain. And I want to tell you that the pilgrim forefathers could not possibly have been half as terrified of the local Massachusetts Indians as I was while that overloaded taxi was winding its way around the 48 — or 480, for all I know — hairpin turns on the road that leads up the side of that mountain to the hotel.

I remember remarking to Wife Sarah as we entered the empty lobby at the hotel how smart I was to arrange for the morning train. We'd obviously avoided the holiday crowds that were sure to descend upon Nikko before sunset.

Well, sunset came right on schedule. But the crowds didn't. At dinner in the main dining room that night, there were seven people — five Maloneys, one waiter, and the maitre d'. The maitre d' spoke some English, so I struck up a holiday conversation by asking him what they had planned for Thanksgiving Dinner the next day. He excused himself out to the kitchen and returned shortly with the great news that tomorrow's special would be beef curry. He must have noticed my wince, because he hurriedly added that — in case we didn't like curry — mixed sandwiches were always available.

I wasn't able to put a smile on the kids' faces with a promise that — not to worry — we'd go out to dinner tomorrow, but I did quiet the groans. On the way back to our rooms after dinner, I stopped by the front desk to ask the man how many people they expected at the hotel over the weekend.

"Are you staying?" he asked.

I assured him we were.

"Then, five."

Next morning holiday style, we all slept late. Shortly after noon, we were all decked out and ready for Thanksgiving Dinner — our first in Japan. Just down the street about 50 yards from the hotel entrance, there's a main sort of street with a lot of shops and restaurants, and that's where we headed.

All but one was closed up tight. With the help of Wife Sarah's phrase book, we found out that the only open restaurant on the mountain was up on the second floor and that it was serving a pork-chop-and-egg-on-rice thing called "Katsu Don".

With a couple of more instant Japanese phrases, Wife Sarah established that the only other gourmet hopes were in downtown Nikko. But none of us — especially me — was willing to risk a round trip over the hairpin turns on the chance downtown *might* offer an alternative to the Katsu Don, curry or mixed sandwiches.

We took a vote, and Katsu Don won, 4-1. (I never did understand Son Sean's love for curry.) At ¥150 a serving, our ¥900 tab (despite Son Sean's earlier vote, he had two helpings) had to be our cheapest Thanksgiving Dinner ever.

It now became a matter of honor to salvage something out of all this, so I dragged everyone back to the hotel and confronted the man at the desk with a "What is there to do up here?"

We could, he said, walk a few blocks down and see the big falls — only they were turned off for the winter. We could get a taxi out to see some of the shrines — only all the taxis were probably down in town. Or, we could take a bus — there was one every hour — over to the other side of the mountain top and see the bubbling hot sulfur springs.

We did the bus. Unfortunately, you could smell the sulfur springs as well as see them and we just did survive until the return bus showed up.

While I hated to leave that nice front desk man alone for the weekend with the waiter and the maitre d', we checked out Friday morning.

"I'm sorry," the man said, "that it's so quiet in Nikko now. But Fall is over, so nobody's here to see the leaves. And winter isn't here yet, so the ski crowds haven't arrived. Our only busy time in-between was last week when we celebrated Japanese Thanksgiving."

On the train back to Tokyo, it was Daughter Barbara who first broke the silence. "Well, Dad, if you had it all to do over, would you do it differently?"

177

Before I could answer, Son Sean came in with, "I don't know about him, but I'd have the beef curry."


## JUST MENTION MY NAME IN HOSOYA

It wasn't like I didn't have any warning. For weeks, the newspapers had been saying that more than 30,000,000 Japanese would be traveling around these islands during Golden Week — the name given the Holidays during the last week in April and first week in May every year.

Because experience had told me that things were bad enough on the trains and the roads during non-Golden Weeks when only 10 or 20 million Japanese were moving around, I decided to stay very close to home.

With one small — I thought "small", anyway — exception: I had agreed to participate in a weekend meeting, called a "Cursillo," sponsored by the Franciscan Chapel Center of Roppongi.

The Cursillo is held up in Gunma Prefecture in a little town called Kiryu where there's a Franciscan Monastery. I'd been to Kiryu before and remembered it as an easy two-hour ride on an all-seats-reserved express train on the Tobu Railroad out of Asakusa Station.

Things were more than somewhat different than what I remembered when I made the trip on the Saturday holiday that wound up Golden Week.

I tried to get a seat reservation on the express train a couple of weeks before my trip. No such thing, said our travel man. No reservations are sold until a week before the date of departure.

So, I waited until just under a week before that Saturday and tried again for a reservation. No such thing, said our travel man again. What made me think I could wait until a week before departure during Golden Week and still get a reservation?

Even if I did have enough of a handle on the Japanese language to cordially remind him that *he* was what made me think I could wait, my experience in Japan told me that I might very well win any argument I started, but I certainly would *not* wind up with the reserved seat.

Anyhow, I established with my travel expert that there were local trains to Kiryu that did not require reservations and he suggested a 9:03 a.m. train "direct to Kiryu."

I arrived at Asakusa station about 8:30 that morning and tried again for a reserved seat. The agent spoke no English, but the hissing sound of air rushing through his gold teeth was eloquently unmistakable.

There were NO reserved seats.

When I got up to the 9:03 platform, I suddenly realized that the 30,000,000 Japanese who were traveling during Golden Week all intended

178

to do that traveling on that very train. Most of them, anyway.

They all looked — and acted, unfortunately — like the same group I meet girded for battle at Shinjuku station in the mornings.

The only difference on that Golden Saturday was that they had the kids with them. And, more than the usual supply of shopping bags.

Just before our train pulled in, I noticed a couple of large groups of Gaijins on the next platform boarding the train for Nikko. There they were, huddled together, Kodak Instamatics in hand, following the tour girl with the flag.

I couldn't help but think back to those first days in Japan when I wouldn't have thought of going *anywhere* unless some little girl with a flag was leading the way.

How beautiful it was, I remembered. Not only do all those Gaijins have a reserved seat for sure, but that little girl with the flag will see to it that a cup of coffee and a roll is delivered to their seat.

More than that, in a couple of hours they'll *really* be at Nikko — *exactly* where they want to go.

But, you know how it is. You're here awhile and you decide you don't *need* the tour guide anymore. To hell with the little girl and her flag. I'd rather do it myself.

Well, the doors of the 9:03 opened and I was swept into the train — horizontally. When the car was filled to 200% of capacity, about 63 more adults, 133 more kids and 119 more shopping bags — plus 37 furoshikis — were pried in.

The amazing part of it was that, at every station we stopped at during the next two hours, more adults, kids and shopping bags (no more furoshikis) were stuffed in. And, oh, did we stop.

Finally, after the two hours, people began to trickle off — shopping bags and all.

When we reached a station called Ota, almost everybody got off. There were only three of us left in the car where millions had stood closer than the top and bottom half of a McDonald's hamburger bun only moments before.

I had that uneasy feeling you get in Japan when you're not doing what everybody else is doing. But then, I thought, only Christians would be going to the Monastery town of Kiryu, anyway. And three out of millions is about the Christian ratio in Japan.

Just to be safe, I asked the man at the end of the last car — you know, the one who blows the whistle and opens and closes the doors — if I was OK for Kiryu.

That unmistakable hissing sound again. I should have changed at Ota like everybody else. So, they put me off at the next stop, Hosoya, to wait for a train back to Ota to change for a train to Kiryu.

I had twenty minutes wait in Hosoya.

179

My first impression of Hosoya was that if the Japanese radio had a local version of the old "Our Gal Sunday" soap opera, Hosoya would be the town where Sunday was left on some old miners' front cabin steps.

Maybe the kids in Hosoya had seen Gaijins before. I doubt it. At least not one my size. The whole Hosoya population turned out (43, I estimated) to see the Golden Week visitor from afar.

I tried to be nonchalant and walked into *the* store in Hosoya and ordered a Pepsi. I even bought a bag of those Japanese crackers dipped in salty shellac.

I walked up and down Main Street — almost five yards long — with the kids following. The train back to Ota came. We all waved goodbye to each other, and I finally found my way to Kiryu. It only took four and a half hours for the two-hour ride.

Coming back to Tokyo that night was a breeze. I *had* a returning reservation.

All the way back I kept thinking: Imagine, 30,000,000 moved around Japan during Golden Week and only one person — a Gaijin, yet — went to Hosoya.

I can't understand that, either. Hosoya is so easy to get to. You don't even have to change trains at Ota.


## SWEET AND SOUR CHRISTMAS


If on New Year's Day 1970 back in Cleveland anybody told us Maloneys that we would spend the next three Christmases in Japan, we would have classed him in with the other holiday nutty fruit cakes.

But, we *did* spend all three of them here.

And, when I walked in our house one night just before this past Christmas and announced to these same Maloneys that they'd better get packing because we were spending the 1973 edition of the Holiday in China, I got those same fruit cake looks.

But, that's where we did spend this Christmas — in Taipei.

There's no chance I can tell you exactly *why* I decided to stand under the mistletoe in the Republic of China. I don't know myself.

Maybe it was just to hang on to some of my self-respect. I can remember, you see, that in the weeks just before and after our last three Tokyo Christmases, there would be all kinds of parties thrown for all kinds of most intimate friends all over Roppongi.

And, in the days and weeks following the season, hosts of these intimate friends would start conversations with "How come I didn't see you and Wife Sarah at so-and-so's big Christmas Party?"

Now I suppose I could simply say that so-and-so obviously considers us non-intimates.

But this year, at least, I can say, "We couldn't possibly have made it, you see, we were off to China. It *was* China, wasn't it Sarah? Or was it Bali? One paradise in the Pacific is becoming so like every other to me these days, I'm never really sure."

Anyway, we went. And, I'm glad. And, although I haven't checked with them in real depth, I think Wife Sarah and the kids are glad, too.

We left Tokyo on Friday before Christmas on Northwest's early morning flight. I'll digress here for just a moment to tell you that I *always* go Northwest on early morning flights. Mainly because I've found out over the years that other airlines on early morning flights always offer you coffee or tea and then give you a sort of "Oh, you're one of *them*" looks when you refuse both and ask for a Bloody Mary. Northwest, on the other hand — or so it seems to *me* — asks you what you want to *drink* and appears genuinely disappointed if you say coffee or tea.

Anyway, because Taiwan is a four-Bloody-Mary trip from Tokyo, I was really in a Holiday Mood when we arrived. And, I'm really glad that the Taipei Hilton meets you at the Airport with a minibus. I don't see how I could have laid down in one of those small Taipei taxis.

Altogether, we spent eight days there at the Hilton. I probably should spell that "ate" days. Because, with the exception of a couple of big steak — you remember steak — dinners in the Hotel, we really filled ourselves with choices from both column A and column B from almost every menu in town. We had sweet and sour everything except sushi.

When we weren't eating, we were shopping. Both, because of the really cheap prices in Taipei, were a pleasure. Even taking a taxi — or in the case of six Maloneys, *two* taxis — to a store or restaurant in Taipei is a pleasure.

For one thing, the Taipei taxis seem to be happy to have passengers and stop for you anywhere, anytime. For another, when you get in and the driver starts the meter, it reads only *six* New Taiwan Dollars which is about fifteen cents in Old American Dollars. The longest ride we had from the Hilton was only 50 cents U.S.

Like I said, *everything* is cheap there. In addition to the usual Chinese things like Jade, Brass, genuine imitation Ming vases, etc., we even bought an Oriental Rug and a Grandfather Clock. The kids bought a bunch of records — albums are only 50 cents there — and some clothes that come in real people sizes.

In fact, we saved so much money shopping in Taiwan that I think I'm bankrupt. The only thing we *didn't* ship back to our Tokyo home, it seems, was toilet paper. The Japanese tourists had bought it all.

If I filled out my "Declaration of Unaccompanied Goods" correctly, we should receive all the goodies by boat this month without having to write a single "Gomen Nasai" letter.

Of course, Taipei isn't *all* shopping. You couldn't go wrong, for instance, just checking in the Hilton and staying inside. If you don't like shopping, there's the National Palace Museum which this time was showing treasures from 2000 B.C. Now that, you Oriental Bazaar fans will agree, is "very, VERY old" indeed.

Just one last thing, so our Japanese friends don't think this trip was a complete Chinese sell-out: Northwest did get us home in time to go to Meiji Shrine on New Year's Day and buy our arrow.

Now, do me this small favor, please. If you're planning to have a Christmas Party next year and can see your way to count us among your most intimates, kindly send your invitation early.

Otherwise, I'm going back to China.


## 'TIS THE SEASON TO GOMENNASAI

As the Christmas season approaches — however quietly here in the Orient — the holiday spirit is welling up within me and I want to make some public apologies so I can enjoy the season without even a trace of a guilty Gaijin conscience.

I've done some pretty nasty things and said some pretty nasty words during the past year while caught up in occasional fits of frustration, and I won't feel right unless I make things right.

For instance, I remember distinctly complaining openly last month about the new and higher cost of living around here just because the train fares went up 23.2 per cent, the subway fares went up 28.6 per cent, the bus fares went up 50 per cent, and the taxi fares went up 33.9 per cent. I probably even griped when my gasoline bill went up 58 per cent. But now that I look back, all those increases have made it practically impossible for me to leave my house to travel over to my favorite Gaijin-type supermarket. And, after all, any time I can save a trip over there, it's worth ¥50,000, at least.

So, gomennasai for complaining about transportation costs in Tokyo.

And, I also remember getting annoyed at some of the foreigners who said I had no right to complain about beef, melon, or grape prices. "He's in Japan," they said, "Let him eat rice."

I didn't get mad at them at the time for saying that — not until the rice went up 32 per cent. Then, I did show a little annoyance (about 32 per cent more than usual).

Gomennasai for that, too.

I also must make amends for cursing at and laughing at some Tokyo taxi drivers, too. Not both reactions at the same time, of course. Earlier in the year, I cursed them every time I came back to Tokyo Station late at night from an Osaka trip and joined the long line of people waiting for taxis that weren't there.

Then, after Nov. 1 when the taxi fare went up to ¥ 280 for openers, I laughed at the long lines of taxis at Tokyo Station waiting for people who weren't there.

I *am* sorry for that. After all, the taxi drivers' rice went up 32 per cent, too.

An apology is in order also to one of my Japanese friends who I falsely accused of being too Western just because he took the plastic off the seats and the doors inside his car and did away with the box of Kleenex on the window ledge behind the rear seat. It's not so much for that outburst that I feel bad, but because he's the same one who asked me if I thought Evel Knievel could *really* jump over Mt. Fuji and I snapped "Who gives a damn?" at him.

I hope he'll forgive me. (My Japanese friend, that is — not Evel Knievel.)

And why did I deliberately spear a hole through that old lady's shopping bag on the subway last July just because she crushed my left leg with her furoshiki? After all, she couldn't have seen me with my brief case in her face. I pray that she realizes I'm remorseful.

One more apology has to go to the policeman who nailed me in Ginza for making a U-turn. I got away without a ticket because I convinced him I understood no Japanese words like "U-turn." He was only doing his job and I should have taken my medicine.

For knowingly sneaking those little plastic containers that my 35mm film comes in into the garbage on non-plastic garbage days, I apologize to the garbage man. And the same for the mailman and the milk lady for what I was thinking when the squeaky brakes on their bicycles woke me up on Saturday mornings.

Not all of my apologies are "gomennasai," either. Some have to be plain "I'm sorry" because they are directed at other Gaijins — mainly the people at FEN and the 20th Weather Squadron. I can't understand, as I look back, why I get so upset just because I don't always understand what whose announcers at FEN are saying. After all, I understand them at least 25 per cent better than I understand the ones on NHK.

And can the 20th Weather Squadron help it just because the weather never turns out like they forecast? The 21st — when it comes — probably won't be any better.

The airlines deserve a little group of kind words, too. I don't know why it bothered me so much all year that they told me the plane was "on time" over the telephone and then break the "one hour late" news to me when I get to the airport. It could have been worse — they could have told me "one hour late" on the phone and then told me when I got to the airport that I missed it because it was "on time."

The people at the home office get a forgive me request, too. After all they're just doing my job.

It looks as though the only people in Japan to whom I don't owe a "gomennasai" are the ones at Customs out at Haneda. And why should they expect one from me? After all, I've "gomennasaied" to them in writing at least a dozen times already.


## FUN CITY — FOR FIVE DAYS

I waited until now to write about our New Year Holiday because what I have to say is directed to those of you who may just now be returning from Guam, Saipan, Hawaii, Hong Kong or wherever you went to escape Tokyo for a few days.

If you did travel to these places over the Holiday, I think you might have made a mistake. Oh, I know why you left. You wanted to get away — even if just for a week or two — from the crowds, the smog, the chaos that's called Tokyo.

But that's the whole point:  The crowds, the smog and the chaos left Tokyo for New Year's, too. It was fabulous here from December 31 right thru January 4. At least, my whole family had a great time.

No, I'm not kidding. And no, I didn't drink too much of that New Year Sake that flowed so freely. It *was* really great here. Honto.

The last loudspeaker went by our house late on December 30. Not even one call for a week after that. And the mailman put away his squealing bicycle. Nobody came to the door.

On New Year's day, we took the train into Shinjuku and the subway from there to Ginza.

And — are you ready for this? — we *sat down* both ways on *both trains and subways.* Not only that, we got on and off on our own power. Not one elbow in the back. Or in the front.

For all five days, we noticed only one single cab driver stop his taxi to relieve himself at the curb. Besides that, while we were standing on the corner at Ginza on the night of January 2, a taxi driver actually stopped and *asked me* if we wanted a taxi.

Now it turns out that we really didn't want a taxi then, but I was so shocked that I packed the family in anyway and we went over to Tokyo station. We were there in four minutes. Usually, it takes us that long to drive around the garbage at Yurakucho. .

By Thursday — after all the Japanese smoke stacks had been shut down for five straight days and the exhaust belching cars were off the road for an equal amount of time — there was Mt. Fuji! I saw it with my own eyes. It's really out there. We were driving out the number three Expressway toward Shibuya. At first, I thought it was fog on my windshield but it was really Mt. Fuji. Just like on the posters.

I couldn't wait to get home and tell our maid, Machiko, that we'd actually seen Mt. Fuji. She wouldn't believe me. She thought MacArthur took it with him when he left.

And when we were walking thru Azabu and Roppongi on Monday, not once did a shopkeeper throw a pail of water out to clean the sidewalk in front of us. They were all gone, too.

There was no dodging of motorcycles or bikes lugging Soba or sushi deliveries. In fact, nobody was cooking anything. All you could smell was honest-to-God fresh air. Probably the best day was Tuesday, January 2. There wasn't a single newspaper published. Not one word of bad news.

I don't want to get too carried away, however. It wasn't all peaches and liberated grapefruit here over New Year's. For one thing, Wife Sarah had quite a problem figuring out how to stow four days' supply of milk in the refrigerator.

And, of course, the garbage man who shows up all too seldom normally didn't show at all for more than a week. It wasn't noticeably worse than usual, garbagewise, because the people who make the garbage were gone, too.

But, so what? A refrigerator full of milk and a few extra piles of garbage are a small price indeed to pay for once-a-year dividends like a seat on the subway and an honest-to-God view of Mt. Fuji.

About the only native Japanese we saw for the whole five days was the man on our street in Kamikitazawa who works for the Japan Travel Bureau. I was telling him how great we foreigners thought it was here in Tokyo during the New Year holiday. (He knew about Mt. Fuji. My maid had told him.) I mentioned how good it was to see all the Japanese girls wearing Kimonos like in the travel ads.

And, since he is with JTB, I asked him if it was true that the five million Japanese who left Tokyo really go back to Kyushu or wherever they came from for the New Year.

"Some of them do go back to their hometowns around the country," he said. "But," he continued — and this is what made me feel that those of you foreigners who skipped Tokyo surely had made a mistake — "most of the Japanese who left Tokyo went to Guam, Saipan, Hawaii or Hong Kong."

# SLOW TRAIN TO AKITA

Because business commitments took me out of town on two separate trips over both holiday weekends last month, Wife Sarah and I had a couple of some-of-the-expenses-paid, in-Japan, semi-vacations.

And, because the first trip over ''Respect for the Aged Day'' weekend was to a place called Kurashiki, about six hours south — or is that west?; I'm never sure — of Tokyo and the second trip over the ''Coming of Autumn'' weekend was supposed to be eight or nine hours North to Akita, we *did* get to see a lot of Japan. Both the ''Real'' and that other variety.

With the cooperation of the railroad unions and their slowdown, we got a long, *long* look at all of it, too.

Even if the business trips didn't provide a logical excuse — and even if the business part didn't help defer the cost — we probably would have gone out of Tokyo at those times anyway. Surely, you've noticed in Japan that all vital services continue to operate on holidays. The zoo is open and so are the department stores and sushi shops. Only the garbage men, it seems, take holidays off. And, since things are bad enough when they're working, these holiday get-away trips are damn near mandatory.

I want to tell you some things about these two weekends, but I don't want you to get your hopes up. What I have to say is not going to be one of those pieces, so much in vogue these days, about the foreign couple who decided to see Japan like ''the people'' do.

Understand right now, please, that we *didn't* travel by rickshaw or walk in wooden getas with furoshikis and shopping bags strapped on our back. And we *didn't* stay in youth hostels, guest caves or porous tents supplied to tourists by one be-with-the-people-association or other.

We stuck strictly to first class ''Green Car'' — with a disastrous exception I'll talk about later — and slept only in hotels that provided a place where we could each take a bath or shower all alone. And take the soap right into the tub with us if we wanted.

The trip down to Kurashiki was uneventful enough. We took the ''Bullet Train'' to the end of the line at Okayama where we changed for a non-bullet to Kurashiki.

About the most exciting thing that happened after we got there happened because we couldn't get a taxi from the station to the hotel. The line of people waiting that Friday night stretched half-way back to Okayama so we decided to walk the 10 or 12 blocks.

Since Wife Sarah is not Japanese, I was carrying our luggage. The weight of all of it — plus the built-in tonnage I carry around my middle *all* the time — was just too much for one patch of Kurashiki sidewalk and it

186

collapsed under me. Fortunately, only my pride was seriously injured and I was able to climb out. Wife Sarah, hysterical as she was at the sight of me standing knee-deep in a hole in the concrete, was no help at all.

I spent the rest of my time in Kurashiki off the sidewalks and on the streets since my personal bulk more closely resembles that of a Toyota than it does that of the little men who build them.

Kurashiki, even viewed from the middle of the street, is worth the trip. Parts of the town have been carefully restored to resemble the way this country was one day. There are some interesting museums there and a very comfortable hotel. I was dying to have my picture taken on one of the camel-back bridges that span the brook running through the reconstructed part of town, but fresh memories of my encounter with the sidewalk ruled that out.

Because the later trains were all sold out, we had to return to Tokyo early Sunday morning. I couldn't help but notice, while changing trains at Okayama, that probably one of the reasons I went through the sidewalk was that we Westerners carry too damn much baggage. Look around you the next time you take a long trip here. The Japanese seem to make it for just overnight or for a week with only a little black zipper bag no bigger than a bread box. Even if you count the shopping bag and the furoshiki, they tote around nowhere near the volume we consider necessary for survival on the road. I'd love to know how they do it.

Anyway, the trip the following week to Akita was another matter. There are no "Bullet Trains" heading north. And so, we took a sleeper out of Ueno. Now *that's* how you *really* get to see the people. In fact, you see almost every personal part of them while they're changing clothes in the aisle in the morning.

Japanese trains have two kinds of sleepers, "A Class" and "B Class." There are two main differences. One is that "A" sleepers have only upper and lower berths; "B" sleepers have uppers, lowers, and another one in the middle. And, because they're piled this three-high in "B" class, you get to see more of more people in the morning.

Because it was slow-down time again on the railroad that week — like most weeks — Wife Sarah and I got to spend 13 hours in our upper and lower instead of the advertised eight. That doesn't mean we caught up on our sleep, however. Although the conductor was thoughtful enough not to broadcast each stop during the night over the public address system, the engineer announced every arrival and departure by violently jerking the whole train each time.

We did, by the way, choose the "A" sleeper. In addition to being three-high, the beds in "B" class are only wide enough to hold one normal version of a Japanese adult and his box lunch — hardly enough space for either Maloney.

Akita itself, by Japanese standards, is an ecological masterpiece. The air *and* the river running through the city were crystal clear. I don't know if the garbage men up there work on holidays or if everybody saves it in their kitchens, but there was none around.

On Tuesday morning, we rushed down to catch the 6:10 a.m. train back to Ueno. No such thing. The slowdown turned into a stop-altogether for the 6:10 and it was cancelled. A Japanese co-worker of mine was in Akita with us, thank God, or we would never have managed to, A — know that there was no 6:10 that morning, or B — get a seat as we did (non-Green Car) on the 8:25.

The only trouble was that *everybody* in Akita got the 8:25 and each of them brought two crying kids with them. That helped to make the slowdown seem even slower.

In case you're wondering, public construction in Akita is much sounder and I didn't go through a single sidewalk.

But, thanks to the railroad unions' idea of how to get back at management, I almost went through the ceiling.

One thing sure — at least until you've finished reading this book — the Japan you expect to find when you arrive here for the first time doesn't exist. And, for all I know, it never did.

At least that was true in my case. I kept looking for the "Real Japan" I read about in all those books back in the Cleveland Public Library.

I don't look for it anymore. Not since the day sometime back when it finally dawned on me that the "Real Japan" isn't just the crowded city of Tokyo, or the rice fields and the farms out on the countryside, or the factories, or the temples, or the old people who still wear wooden getas on their feet, or the long-haired boys who wear blue jeans. Japan is all of these things crowded into the smallest package possible.

You couldn't describe the "Real Japan" — or find it — anymore than you could describe or find the "Real" New Jersey, or Ohio, or England or Germany.

Even the lies people tell about Japan are true. And so are the "Real Japan" stories that close this book.

# THE INN THING TO DO

I'm sure you've noticed that there are two distinct main schools of thought among foreigners concerning exactly how foreigners should behave in Japan.

One group believes that things and people Japanese ought to be avoided at all cost. And the cost of trying to pull that off in Tokyo can be quite steep.

Nevertheless, this group carries on the most studied avoidance of things like sushi, Soba and other Japanese food, subways and shrines, sake and sumo.

The other group carries on quite the opposite. They are led by the ''Real Japan'' people who believe you have to get with it all the way or get out. You've met some of them, too, I'm sure.

I mean they sit on the floor, never touch a knife or fork, climb Mt. Fuji three or four times every August and go to see Kabuki or Noh theater every Saturday night. They say ''Ah so desu ka'' a lot, too.

Myself, I'm not an active registered member of either group, but more of a middle-of-the-Ginza man. Like some days I want sushi, but I want to sit in a chair to eat it. With a fork, yet.

And on New Year's, I like to join the crush at Meiji Shrine, throw my ¥100 to the gods, but stop at the Press Club on my way home for a Bourbon Manhattan.

I've climbed half-way up Mt. Fuji once, but it was in a tour bus. Plus, I enjoy roaming through the Japanese countryside — looking out the window of a first class Green Car on the Bullet Train.

Oh, there are times when I go all the way in one direction or the other. I remember days, for instance, when I've started with a sausage and sunnyside-up egg breakfast at the Hilton (with home fries), lunched at McDonald's and topped off the day at the American Club with a roast beef sandwich and a Walt Disney movie. While travelling from one of these places to the other, I listened only to FEN (the U.S. Forces radio station).

There have also been times when I've turned 180° from that sort of performance and joined up entirely with the ''Real Japan'' persons.

One such instance that really sticks out in my Oriental memory corner is the time we stayed overnight at an honest-to-God Japanese Inn — a Ryokan.

Understand first, please, that you cannot even be considered for membership in the ''Real Japan'' set unless you've spent at least one whole night in such a Ryokan. It truly makes no difference how much raw octopus you've eaten or how many Imari dishes you've collected, or whether or not you've managed to master a Japanese-style toilet. If you haven't spent a whole night at a Ryokan, you might as well have never left downtown Roppongi.

The night we Maloneys qualified, we were down in Kyoto. That, by the way, carries triple the points that, say, staying at a Ryokan in Osaka or Tokyo counts for.

Anyway, we checked in around four in the afternoon and gave up our shoes at the door. In exchange, we each got a pair of hallway slippers. I say hallway slippers, because there's another set you have to wear in the bathroom and you can't wear any at all in your room.

Our room measured about 10×18 feet and was lavishly furnished with a table on six-inch high legs, six pillows — each about 18'' square — and a ten-inch black and white TV. In one corner of the room were piled some bureau drawers but no bureau. In the opposite corner was an alcove filled with rocks and a flower arrangement executed by someone who obviously took a few more lessons at that sort of thing than Wife Sarah had with the American Club Women's Group.

Hanging on the wall in that alcove was a scroll with some writing that for all I knew was an ad for another Ryokan.

About five-thirty, a young man slid open our door without warning — you can't very well knock on a paper door — and announced it was bath time down the hall. It took a little while and a lot of sign language, but he made it clear we would bathe in pairs. First, Son Sean and I. Then, Wife Sarah and Daughter Barbara. Last, Daughter Frances and Son Donald Jr.

Neither Frances nor Donald Jr. bought that pairing, but Ryokan rules are Ryokan rules.

Then came dinner — in the room. Some kind of cloudy soup with pretty flowers in it, raw fish, very hard soft-shell crabs, and a big drum of rice. I ate the soup. Wife Sarah ate the fish and the flowers. We set the crabs free in the garden and the kids existed on rice alone with a lot of soy sauce.

I ordered Pepsi for the kids, beer for me and whiskey for Wife Sarah. The kids each got a whole bottle of Pepsi. I got a whole bottle of beer and Wife Sarah got a whole bottle of Suntory Red.

After dinner, we had to leave the building for a walk in our Ryokan-furnished robes while the beds were made. Well, they're not *really* beds, but sort of long pillows rolled out taking up every inch of floor space in the room.

That's the *beds* that are made of pillows, by the way. The pillows themselves are sacks of marbles.

In the morning, breakfast was brought to our room. I'd tell you what it was except I'm certain that describing it will make me as ill as looking at it did that morning before we fed it to the crabs.

After breakfast, we payed our bill (the only thing about a Ryokan that resembles the Waldorf Astoria), got our ''Real Japan'' cards punched and headed back to Tokyo.

Only one thing really bothered me about the whole experience. In a genuine attempt to "get with the people," we wound up eating and sleeping in a room all by ourselves.

If that's "Real Japan," I'll take the Green Car.

## SAKURA, SAKURA — OUR VERY OWN SAKURA

There were a lot of reasons that made me resist for so long the idea of moving out of suburban Kamikitazawa into downtown Tokyo. Not the least of which were the Sakura — or Cherry Trees — that lined both sides of the street for a couple of blocks between the railroad station and our house.

There were other reasons, of course. For instance, riding in on the train every morning to Shinjuku and changing there to the subway, gave me daily opportunities to "be with the people." In fact, with *millions* of the people. Complete with lethal shopping bags.

Anyway, I reasoned, if we leave Kamikitazawa, we leave those Sakura trees and the absolute assurance their blossoms give every year of Spring's arrival and the wonderful feeling of no more heating oil bills for awhile.

If we moved into Tokyo, I worried, we'd have to go to Ueno Park or Yasukuni Shrine to view the Sakura. And from what I understood, *everybody* in Tokyo goes to those places during Sakura time and it would be like some sort of outdoor Shinjuku Station.

Besides — according to what I'd read in the know-your-Japan books back in the Cleveland Public Library — viewing Cherry Blossoms, Japanese-Style, is a complicated process.

Like in Kamikitazawa, all I had to do to see the Cherry Blossoms was to walk under the trees every morning and night and look up. On Sundays, I could look up four or five times if I wanted.

But, according to those books, formal Japanese Sakura viewing, such as goes on at Ueno and Yasukuni, requires that you sit down under the Sakura trees, sip plenty of sake, and write some of your own "Haiku" — those three-line Japanese poems.

So, that's what bothered me. I prefer to watch my Sakura while walking, drink my sake anchored firmly in a padded chair, and avoid Japanese poetry under any circumstances.

But, alas, I've sacrificed before in the interest of Maloney family harmony, and we moved into town last summer.

Now what all this is leading up to is the fact that, when I came home the other night, Wife Sarah — who usually reports immediately on the children's escapades of the day — greeted me with, "That big tree outside the living room door; it's a Sakura."

I dropped my briefcase and ran to the window. It was pitch black out there and I couldn't see a thing. I turned to Wife Sarah, "How can you be so *sure* it's a Sakura? Maybe it's one of those lesser-status trees like a plum or something."

She was indignant at the suggestion.

"Why do you doubt my word?" she asked. "Are you insinuating that I don't know my plums from my Sakuras?"

"Perish the thought," I assured her. "It's just that the real estate man never mentioned that that tree was a Sakura when we looked at the house."

"Why would he?" Wife Sarah asked.

"Why *would* he? Sarah, you know that Sakura is second only to Mt. Fuji and Sushi as a Japanese conversation opener. If that tree *was* a Sakura, he would have *said* so."

"So he *didn't*," Wife Sarah recalled. "Does *that* make it a plum tree?"

"No," I said, "but you must admit that he mentioned the 'close to Sacred Heart School' thing and the fact that the house had 'central heating' and a 'spacious garden' and other relatively unimportant matters. If it *is* a Sakura out there, doesn't it strike you as strange that he didn't even *mention* what could have been the number one drawing card of this place?"

"Maybe," Wife Sarah observed, "just *maybe,* he didn't *know* it was a Sakura. After all, who moves in Spring when the Cherry Blossoms are out? And, if nobody is moving, the real estate man never comes. So, he probably just never *saw* the Cherry Blossoms and so he doesn't know."

I decided to drop the whole thing and ask about the kids. Next morning, I looked at the tree myself. They *were* Cherry Blossoms. Thousands of them. I woke Wife Sarah to confirm her findings.

"I told you so," she said, in the same tone she'd spoken those very words so many times before in our twenty-five year relationship.

It was Sunday, so I told Wife Sarah to, "Break out the sake, get me a pad and pencil. I'm going to sit under that tree and do my thing."

"You're *not* serious," she wondered.

"Am I *ever,*" I answered. "I'll meet you under our very own Sakura as soon as I brush up on the Haiku poems."

And I did brush up. The book said that the Haiku could have only three lines. The first line had to have *exactly* five syllables, the second *exactly* seven syllables, and the third *exactly* five — seventeen syllables in all. Otherwise, it counts only as an ordinary poem.

So, I donned my kimono, rolled back the living room door-window combination, and took up my position on the chair under the confirmed Sakura.

195

After two or three sake sips, I was inspired. I sneaked one more look at the Cherry Blossoms and then wrote — for posterity:

"It could never be
That I could possibly write
Anything this short."

## THE *REAL* REAL JAPAN

The first time I went down to Kyoto on the Bullet Train, I remember my Japanese friend who met me on the other end asked whether I rode in the first-class "Green Car" or in the regular coaches.

When I answered, "Green Car," he gave me a sad look.

"Why do you foreigners come all the way over here to see Japan and then ride the "Green Cars" instead of in the second-class coaches where you could *really* meet the Japanese people?" he wanted to know.

"Were those all Orientals in the Green Car Chinese?" I asked.

"You know what I mean," he insisted. "Those aren't the *real* Japanese people up there in the Green Car. The *real* people are in second-class."

I hated to make an issue out of something like this, but I had to tell him that, "No, I *don't* know what you mean. They sure looked like *real* Japanese people that go on the Green Car with me in Tokyo."

"That's another thing," he snapped. "Do you *really* think Tokyo is the *real* Japan?"

"O.K. Then where *is* this *real* Japan?" I asked.

"It's in the country right around here where my family comes from."

"And what makes it *real*?"

"Well, for one thing, there's no American Club there. Or American school. Or Hilton Hotel."

"So," I pointed out, "there's no American Club or American School or Hilton Hotel in Siberia, either. Does that make Siberia the *real* Japan?"

I could see now that his Japanese temper was very near the Oriental boiling point. So was my Irish. I resented the whole point of the discussion — if there was one. Anyway, I decided on another tack.

"What's Japan famous for around the world? Do you know?" I fired at him.

"Certainly, I know," he assured me. "We are famous for Cherry Blossoms, for Sukiyaki, for the Emperor — things like that."

"Well," I answered, "most Americans think Japanese Cherry Blossoms come only from the trees down in Washington, D.C. 'Sukiyaki' was the name of a song popular in the U.S. some time back. And the Emperor lives in Tokyo — where, by the way, we have Sukiyaki *and* Cherry Blossoms.''

He started to say something, but I wasn't quite finished.

"What Japan is *really* famous for around the world these days are automobiles, cameras, transistor radios, televisions. And they don't come from that little town of yours up in the hills."

"How about food. Do you think they have *real* Japanese food in Tokyo?'' He wasn't giving up.

"Look, I've had *real* Japanese hamburgers — you know, the ones with peppers, onions, squid, ginger and corn meal mixed in with a trace of beef — in Tokyo and in *real* Japan country towns all over the map."

"Hamburgers," he rejected, "are *not real* Japanese food."

"They are when they fix them like Japanese do. They're certainly *not* American.''

"And, how about . . . ''

I interrupted with,. "Look, friend, I don't want to be impolite or anything that even smells of impoliteness. But, I *know* what your're up to."

"But, . . . ''

"But, nothing. Just because you live out in the country someplace, you feel that you have to lord it over us city-folk who live in Tokyo.

"I never know whether that's because you're jealous and really want to live in Tokyo yourself or whether you honestly think we're not in Japan.

"I know, because when I moved here I chose Kamikitazawa — quite a ways outside of Tokyo. I felt much more Japanese than my Gaijin friends who were, as I fancied it, 'holed up' down in the Gaijin paradise of Roppongi.

"Well, it just *isn't* true. Japan is Japan like Italy is Italy. Whether you live in Tokyo or Nara doesn't make a particle of difference anymore than it does whether you live in Rome or Florence.

"Oh, the countryside may be prettier and you may have more hardships and less smog in the country than in Tokyo. But, we're all, unmistakably, in Japan.

"So, why should you deserve some special medal for surviving in the country anymore than I should for making it in Kamikitazawa.

"This is 1973. Sure, there may be a difference between 'Old' Japan and 'New' Japan. But *not* between Tokyo and *real* Japan. So, in the country, you're sewage goes from a wood-frame, thatch-roof into a septic tank. In Tokyo, mine goes from a concrete house into a septic tank. So what?''

He stood there, ever so quietly.

"Don't misunderstand, friend," I pleaded. "It's just that I resent being separated from real and un-real because I see things differently from

197

my roost than you see them from yours. I can't possibly be Japanese and you can't possibly be American.

"But, don't you think we'd both have more fun if we'd laugh at all the differences between us and our backgrounds and, laughing, *enjoy* those differences together instead of letting them get us down? I do, and that's why I enjoy this country so much.

"Now don't try to take it away by telling me I don't even live here."

He smiled. "You're right, I guess. Forget I even mentioned it. C'mon, let's go over and have a Pepsi and some Kentucky Fried Chicken."

I couldn't resist. "Pepsi and Kentucky Fried Chicken? Here? In the *real* Japan?"


# THESE INSCRUTABLE ORIENTALS

From the time I was a little boy back in Bergen County, New Jersey, right up until the day we left Cleveland a couple of years ago for Japan, I don't think I ever heard anybody use the noun "Oriental" without modifying it with the adjective "inscrutable."

"You can never tell by looking at them," Asian experts used to warn me, "what they have on their minds. It's always the same deadpan, serious expression." And, I must admit, my first-ever live contact with really Oriental Orientals at Haneda Airport backed up the inscrutable warnings.

I didn't know when the health man looked at my vaccination book whether everything was OK or whether I was going to be forcibly carried away for another smallpox shot. And right up until he gave me back my passport, I was certain the immigration man was going to deport me forever. The customs man's stern stare almost made me confess about the little liverwurst sausage I had wrapped up in my underwear.

Now that I've been here a while, I can own up to the fact that I was indeed terrified at those stone-faced looks every native sent my way. That "inscrutable" adjective, I quickly decided, should have a capital "I." Even people in restaurants who were saying "Welcome" to me in Japanese when I entered looked like they were really saying "Get out."

All this bothered me to the point where I mentioned it one day to an exceptionally scrutable Japanese friend. "Maloney San," he said — stone-faced, of course, "you foreigners fail to realize that you terrify us, too. That's why we look so serious. We're wondering if *we* are going to understand what you say and if *you* are going to understand what we say."

"Surely, you've noticed Japanese when they're together," he went on. "You've cetainly seen them laughing together. You've probably seen

198

young Japanese lovers holding hands and looking lovingly at each other. And you've seen mothers scolding their children. There's no scrutability gap there. It's only when we're up against you inscrutable Occidentals. If we could figure out a way to make everybody relax with each other as you and I are right now, everybody would soon forget how to spell inscrutable.''

I decided to start my own anti-inscrutable campaign that very day. It worked, and so I'm going to tell you about it.

Now, whenever I come face to face with a stone-faced Japanese, I don't stone-face back. Instead I smile and say ''Konichiwa'' — even if I never saw him before. I have seldom been refused a smile and a ''Konichiwa'' in return. In fact, the ''Konichiwa'' acceptance ratio is higher than ''Good afternoon'' would get in Cleveland, I'm sure.

In my first days here, the blank but constant stares of the little school kids used to really annoy me for some reason or other. Particularly the ones that pointed and said, ''Gaijin!'' Now, I bend over and ask them, in the best Japanese I can muster, if *they* are Japanese. It breaks them down every time. Or, I smile and say ''Harro'' — that's ''Hello'' in school kid Japanese — and they usually answer in kind.

Watch the next time you go into a restaurant not normally visited by Gaijins. Chances are, the waiters and waitresses will have a quick meeting to decide who gets the short straw and has to wait on you. When that happens to me, and the loser comes over and asks in English. ''May I helpu you?'' I always say — in *Japanese* — ''Your English is *really* good! Congratulations!'' That's an ice *and* inscrutable breaker more times than not.

My biggest failures at stone-face chipping always came in the same place — our local Ward office — with the same girl — one of the group who issues Alien Registrations we foreigners in Japan must carry at all times. Time and time again, I gave her a ''Konichiwa'' an assortment of ''Harro's,'' and even a ''How are you this fine day?''

Nothing. All she wanted — politely, of course, but inscrutably — was my passport, the filled-in form, and the three pictures.

But, just last week, I finally got her.

You see, recently I had to make a fast trip to Hong Kong. And, of course, I had to turn in my Alien Registration at Haneda as I left. When I returned, I went over to one of those machines you sit in, insert ¥ 200 I think, and get four pictures. Now it's always bothered me that I have to buy *four* pictures in that machine when the Alien Registration girl wants only three. There is zero market for that fourth one.

That get-four-but-need-three thing was bothering me again last time, too. But then, it struck me. With that photo machine, I decided, is how I'm going to break the stone face at the Ward office.

For the first three pictures, I sat very still and straight like you're

199

supposed to. For the fourth, I messed up my hair, crossed my eyes, screwed up my face, and stuck out my tongue. Next day, I went to the Ward office and gave Miss Inscrutable my passport, filled-in form and the strip of four pictures. I didn't say a word.

Her only words were the usual, "Wait fifteen minutes, please." I sat down and watched. She picked up the strip of photos and her scissors. Then, she spotted it. Her recoil was ever so slight. In a few seconds, she began to shudder all over and then, finally, it happened. She burst into laughter before she could even get her hand up to cover her mouth.

Now it was my turn for stone-face. She gave me back the fourth picture and my new Alien Registration. And, she smiled. And when she did, so did I, because the last of the inscrutable Orientals had bit the dust.

So, if you think nobody around here is smiling at you — give them a smile first. Or, a "Konichiwa." If neither works, go get your picture taken.

Best ¥ 200 I ever spent.


## TV OR NOT TV...


On our way back here from Home Leave last month, we passed through Hawaii — much too quickly as always. And, while basting my hulk on the Kahala Hilton's beach with the last of the Coppertone and wishing that everything could go like that forever, a headline in the Honolulu paper caught my squinted eye.

It topped a story about one of those kid hero-vs-monster TV programs (In this one, the hero is "Rainbowman") imported to the islands from Japan. And, it seems — according to the story — Rainbowman did his daily thing on an all-Japanese language TV channel. The local non-Japanese-speaking kids and their parents (contrary to some tales you hear, there *are* some Americans still in Hawaii) put all kinds of pressure on the TV station and finally persuaded them to add English subtitles. Now all know exactly what the magic word is that changes the mild-mannered college student into the anti-monster Rainbow Man. (I never did watch the program, so you'll have to ask Son Donald for the word.)

Now all this set me to thinking about a campaign that was going on back here in Tokyo just as we were leaving earlier this summer. A group of well-meaning non-natives were circulating a petition designed to coax Japanese TV stations into broadcasting the news and other programs in a thing called Multiplex. Multiplex would allow anybody to hear English soundtracks to Japanese TV programs with the help of a little black box you hook up to your set.

Now that might not be an accurate summary of the movement's aims, but the fact is that a group of local Gaijins want to know what was said that makes that shaved-head Samurai lop the head off the guy in the blue kimono with a single stroke of his sword.

In any event, the point I'm trying to get at is that I'm against almost anything that could get me back to watching TV again.

Of course, I didn't always feel this way. And so, I can understand what motivates the black box people. One of the first things I bought when we landed here four years ago was a TV set. And, why not? Back in Cleveland, I spent at least as many hours in front of our Sony as I did in the office. And the second thing I did was to lay out about fifty bucks — fifty 360-yen bucks, at that — for one of the little magic boxes.

With that box, as promised, I could get an English commentary — a *very* English commentary — with the seven o'clock news. I say "with" the seven o'clock news, but actually the commentary from the box was invariably two or three pictures behind what was flashing on the picture tube. I wound up knowing less about what was happening than I do listening to the loudspeakers from the top of those panel trucks parked over near Yurakucho Station.

The TV stations used the black box with some all-time great movies, too. But, it turned out, the ones I *really* wanted to see were some foreign films. And, for those, the TV spouted the usual Japanese and the black box sounded off in French or German or Russian or some other language in which I couldn't even say "This is a book."

If they were old American movies, chances are they were ones I could see any Sunday or Wednesday at the American Club. For the old English movies, I'd have to go over to some Australian friend's house for a translation.

I did enjoy a couple of episodes of Peter Falk as "Columbo" — who was either a detective or a cigar commercial, I was never sure which.

Finally — not because I told them — the TV station apparently decided the whole thing was a total loss and gave up the little black box. And it's OK with me if it never comes back.

It wasn't easy, but I've broken the TV habit now. I've learned again how to carry on social conversations not based on whatever it was that Archie Bunker said to the Puerto Rican who wanted to buy the house next door. I couldn't even get with watching stateside TV again during our Home Leave. After our stay in Tokyo, I can't even relate to "The Price is Right" anymore.

In rare moments here, I still get the occasional urge to turn on the tube. For awhile there, I was watching the Sumo wrestling tournaments because the U.S. military radio station was kind enough to broadcast on radio over the weekends what sort of clever throw Takami-what's-his-name was using in vain against Kuni-whoever. But soon, I found out I could see all the

201

pushing I wanted to see any morning at Shinjuku Station. The ring there is bigger, too, and no explanation is necessary. And besides, I don't always understand the announcers on military radio, and no black box will help *that* situation.

And, I can still get my kicks turning on the picture during those Japanese soap operas and samurai dramas and turning off the sound. This allows me to make up my own dialogue and stories — in English — that have the real advantage of turning out exactly as I want them to.

Practice at that picture-and-no-sound game can be money in your pocket, too. For one thing, on our recent across-the-Pacific plane rides, I didn't have to spend the money for a headset to enjoy the movie. I made up my own plot. Wife Sarah *did* buy the earphones and, when it was all over, we compared stories and she liked mine better.

But, don't let all this talk you out of signing the petition or buying a little black box of your own. In fact, I wish somebody would buy my slightly-used one.

The Price is Right.


## CRIME IN THE STREETS

Just because I was born, brought up, and lived my first thirty-some years in and around New York City doesn't mean I'm an expert on crime in the streets. But, as you might imagine, I do know something about it.

If I interpret the statistics properly, the fact that no street crime was ever committed against me during those thirty-odd years should be preciously savoured as some sort of an against-the-odds achievement.

Not that I didn't frequently ask for it. Our favorite night places in New York were on the lower East Side, in the Chinatown-Little Italy area, and up in Harlem. And, we hit them all as often as financially possible.

Still, nary a mugging. Maybe the fact that I'm physically twice the size of an average New York mugger — or anybody else, for that matter — had something to do with it.

Certainly I know that nasty things go on in New York. Just this past summer, my own daughter Frances was a victim. She graduated from the University of Dayton last spring. Because her degree was Criminal Justice, she headed for New York where the criminals are badly in need of justice.

She found an apartment on West 10th Street in Manhattan and got a job. On her first payday, she and a group of friends headed for a bistro where she celebrated the receipt of her first check ever that came from somebody other than Dad. (I celebrated, too.)

Frances spent about 10% of that pay check on the celebration. On the way back to her apartment, a purse snatcher grabbed the other 90%. I no longer explain away crime in New York as "overstated by the news media" like I used to.

All this is leading up to the fact that I want to comment on the White Paper on crime published recently by the Ministry of Justice in Japan. This White Paper confirms what every foreigner living here for any length of time must have aleady discovered: The crime rate in Japan is among the lowest, if not *the* lowest, of any major country in the world.

For instance, there are only three crimes committed in Japan for every 100,000 people. In the U.S., that rate is 667 per 100,000. In Great Britain, 540. Crimes in the United States, West Germany, France and Great Britain were increasing at the rate of one and a half to three times over a ten-year period. The rate in Japan is going down.

Now I read somthing about this before I ever came here. But that doesn't mean I didn't arrive in Japan somewhat terrified. After all, I'd seen the movies. I knew this was the land of Samurais, Kamikazes, and Fu Man Chu. I'd seen pictures of masked gangs with helmets and sharpened bamboo poles.

My first trip here was in 1969. I stayed at the Hilton in Tokyo. One night, I had dinner in Akasaka (a robbery that isn't considered in the White Paper statistics). After eating, I went out front to hail a taxi. There were plenty of empty cabs. But, the automatic rear doors weren't working. The drivers just sat there, holding up three or four or five fingers and mumbling something that I didn't understand any more than the fingers.

The total message they had for me, however, was quite clear: They weren't going to drive me anywhere (another unconsidered Tokyo crime).

So, I started walking back to the Hilton. And, I'll admit it now, I was slightly nervous. The road from Akasaka up to the Hilton is spooky, indeed. At its darkest point, I spotted two men coming the opposite way. I knew that this was it. There was no point in running; they were obviously smaller and faster than I. And, what would I yell? How do you scream "Help" in Japanese, I thought?

They came closer and closer. My Occidental heart was pounding. But, they walked on by. I wanted to run for the safety of the Hilton. But, uphill? Just then, they turned and came back at me. I froze. We'll see, I thought, if my college wrestling is any match for their Judo or Karate or whatever they're going to do.

They pulled up alongside me — one on either side — and I waited. The obviously older one asked, "American?"

"Yes," I squeaked.

"Congratulations for getting men to moon. Goodnight." They turned and headed back down the hill. I still had my money, wallet and watch — and my sweaty palms.

A couple of days later, in Osaka, a group of teenagers came charging across a street, right at me. Again, I was too chicken to run. Hell, there were dozens of them and in seconds they had me surrounded. The biggest one reached into his pocket — for some secret Oriental weapon, I supposed.

Instead, out came a ball pen and a little pad. "Can we have your autograph?" For the next twenty minutes, I signed. And I knew how Elvis Presley and Rock Hudson felt.

The next frightening occasion I remember was a double header right after we moved here in 1970. I was working very late at the office (Cleveland, please note). I had dinner in one of those Soba noodle shops near Tokyo station. Every Japanese man in that place looked like an Asian Godfather to me that night. I quickly slurped down my Soba and headed for the subway. (I had to take the subway; I still didn't understand the taxi's three-finger, four-finger routine.)

As I reached the curb, the most dangerous looking guy in the Soba shop burst out the door and chased after me, waving in the dark what I was sure was a Samurai sword. I had to stand where I was; the traffic had me nailed to the sidewalk.

When he got to me, "You left your umbrella in the restaurant," he said — handing me the "Samurai sword."

Not ten minutes after that, on the subway, I noticed this woman staring at me. Bonnie (without Clyde) in a kimono, I was sure. Her piercing eyes spelled trouble. And she came at me.

Now, don't misunderstand. I'm a big boy and wasn't afraid really of what she might do to me. But, I was terrified at the thought of what all the Japanese men on the train might have done to me if I raised a finger to defend myself against this moll. They'd kill me, I knew, Fu Man Chu style.

She sidled up to me, nose to elbow. Here it comes, I knew. She spoke. "May I practice my English conversation?"

She did. And I did. It was delightful.

Now, after living here for years, I just don't get nervous when I'm out at night (except when I'm back on home leave). In fact, I'm rather aggressive.

Just the other night, on the Subway platform at Shinjuku, I spotted this especially attractive native lady. Beautiful kimono; no shopping bag. I eased over next to her, elbow to nose. And, I asked, "May I practice my Japanese conversation?"

She took off running up the platform. For all I know, she's still running.

I guess she knew I was from New York.

# IT JUST AIN'T FAIR

A couple of weeks ago, the United States Department of Agriculture sponsored what they called the "1974 American Food Festival" out near Haneda Airport in the Tokyo Ryutsu Center. The general idea was to have American food suppliers show their wares to the Japanese market.

Only representatives of the Japanese Food Industry were invited, not the public. But, thanks to the America-Japan Society, Wife Sarah and I got to go.

Nothing was for sale, but there were plenty of samples. And, Japan Food Industry representative or not, I tried them all.

Most of the food was quite familiar and I remembered it lovingly from our Cleveland supermarket days. A lot, however, was quite new to me. Like the successor to TV Dinners could very well be little like milk containers of omelet-mix that has everything already in it — including the eggs — and you just pour it in the frying pan and cook it.

There were health foods like Granola, Kosher meat, all kinds of beef and plenty of bologna and liverwurst. There was one guy selling horsemeat-and-pork breakfast sausage. And the Jolly Green Giant was there, too.

Like I said, I tried them all. Well, almost all. I passed up the horsemeat-and-pork breakfast sausage. I also said "No thanks" to a thing labeled "Powdered Chicken Skin".

But, bite-size samples only. No matter how Wife Sarah and I smiled at all those visiting Gaijin food salesmen, they all obeyed the rules and sold us nothing.

After we left the Festival, I was dying to eat something American — something more than a bite-size sample. Fortunately, Wife Sarah remembered that she read that my favorite Gaijin-type supermarket was holding an "American Food Fair" the same week.

"It won't be exactly the same," Wife Sarah pointed out, "but I'm sure of two things: They'll sell you *anything* and give *no* samples." So, we went over.

Sure enough, the banners were waving from the building proclaiming the "American Food Fair." People coming out of the store had special shopping bags in red, white and blue. We grabbed a shopping cart and took off.

First nostalgia attack came when I spotted some Sunkist oranges. Not only from America, but flown over here by Pan American. And the first one (that's *one* orange, *not* one *bag* of oranges) I picked up was only a little more than a dollar. I was torn between that and an apple that — in honor of America — was being sacrificed for only $1.14.

Don't let me lead you to believe that only fruit was for sale at cut prices during the American Fair (although grapes were slashed to around $3 a pound and melons were going for only slightly over $22 apiece).

One of the big stars of the Fair was beef from America. Minute sandwich steaks were marked down to six bucks a pound. And hamburger meat was a low $3 something a pound.

Of course, there was tenderloin steak for you Green Car people at a mere $32 a pound. I asked Wife Sarah if she thought we ought to get a few pounds for the kids' supper on Children's Day.

At those prices?'' she gasped. "Let them eat bologna."

As a matter of fact, I checked the bologna — American bologna — and it was cheap. It was only $3.50 a pound.

While Wife Sarah was checking out (we bought — to prove we were at the American Fair — some Campbell's Vegetable Soup that somehow got priced at only 32 cents a can), I did some fast figuring. It turns out that the samples we ate at the Fair would have been worth about $363.54 at local supermarket prices.

It looks like the only bargains in American food in Japan might be the horsemeat-and-pork sausage or the powdered chicken skin I scoffed at earlier. But, somehow, American food sales to Japan are climbing every year. In fact, an American Embassy man out at the Food Festival told me that last year alone, 20 per cent of the U.S. food exports came to Japan. In case you're wondering, the total amount of U.S. food exports to Japan last year came to three billion dollars.

In any event, what worries me about all this is that I can't imagine how the Japanese government is ever going to balance their food trade with the U.S. To even off the $3 billion, they'd have to send over about 20 billion bowls of Soba noodles.

Or, come to think of it, one tugboat load of melons.


## WHEN IN ROME

If you're not already aware of it, you're bound to find out one of these days. There is a fair-sized group of Gaijins around here that get more than somewhat upset if you even casually mention that Japanese food prices may be sukoshi high.

They will attack—either orally or in writing—your right to complain about anything under your status as a tax-paying "guest." And, they'll tell you to stop griping, get with it, and act like a native. Sooner or later, they include the advice, "When in Rome, do as the Romans do." (Once, when we were actually in Rome, I said that myself — but Wife Sarah wouldn't let me.)

Anyway, the fact that the natives themselves seem not to be overjoyed at the current cost of food, and say so in large organized groups around town, doesn't seem to indicate to these stop-your-complaining people that the local Romans, too, might be upset. In spite of that, they constantly tell you to live like the Japanese do, shop where the Japanese shop, and eat where the Japanese eat.

Under a mountain-high barrage of that sort of wrist slapping a while back, Wife Sarah convinced me that we ought to try just a little harder. Why not, she asked, start with eating where the Japanese eat?

Why not, indeed, I thought.

The first problem I ran into while trying to comply with the advice was the fact that what Japanese restaurants serve is generally spelled out on a little blue or white cloth hung over the restaurant's front door. If you can't read the characters on the cloth (and I couldn't), you don't know what the restaurant serves.

Some, of course, have little show windows by the doors with plastic models of their specialties. But, since what you see outside is almost never exactly what you get inside in color or in quantity — although some Japanese food does taste like plastic — I decided I'd better learn the Japanese characters on the curtains.

During my curtain studies, Wife Sarah and I had to stick with no-curtain spots like McDonalds and Kentucky Fried Chicken. But, finally, I was sure I had the curtains down pat and we were ready to do that Roman thing.

At the time, we were living out in the Tokyo suburb of Kamikitazawa and we walked out along the Koshukaido Highway. "What would you like for your first native lunch?" I asked Wife Sarah.

"Why don't we go about this sensibly," she suggested, "And start with some kind of meat?"

"How about chicken?"

"I thought the whole idea was to get away from chicken and hamburgers."

Carefully, I explained that the kind of chicken I was talking about — yakitori — was nothing like the variety I bring home in the bucket. "In the first place, there are no bones. Each piece is cut rather small, and they put about four or five of the small pieces on an oversized toothpick, add an onion here or there, paint it with some sort of sauce — three guesses what sort — and cook it all over charcoal."

"Is it cheap?"

"It must be;   it's native."

"OK, let's try."

207

About 30 seconds after that exchange, I spotted a blue drape on a store front across the highway. "That's it," I proudly announced. "A yakitori place."

Wife Sarah asked a dozen times, "Are you sure?"

"Of course, I'm *sure*."

"You were sure that time in Shinjuku, too, when you told me the Japanese characters on that door said *Ladies Room* and I walked in on all those men."

"Well, this time, I'm really sure. I've been studying pictures of those curtains for weeks."

As I was sliding back the restaurant door, Wife Sarah mumbled, "I still would feel better if there was a window outside with some plastic chicken."

There was a long counter with a glass case. In the case were frosted pipes and little pieces of all kinds of things in various shades of pink and red.

"Maybe it's that sauce they put on it," Wife Sarah observed, "but the chicken smells like fish."

It *was* fish. It was a sushi shop. We both figured *that* out at the same instant. "Let's go," she said.

We couldn't; we were the only ones in the place and the man — towel around the head and all — was standing right in front of us, waiting for our order. He put a pile of something in front of each of us that looked just like canned tuna fish. Since I couldn't think of anything to say, I popped my pile into my mouth. It was ginger — red, hot ginger.

Fortunately, just then two men came in, sat down beside us, and distracted the counter man. They started ordering their sushi a piece at a time — always something different. That solved the language problem. I just pointed at everything they got and said, "Onaji." (The same, please.) It worked. Thank heaven they ordered beer, too, because that's how I got my sushi down.

Finally, after 10 pieces each, the two men had enough. That was about 9.5 pieces after *I'd* had enough, but the ordeal was ended.

Back out on the Koshukaido heading home, I was waiting for Wife Sarah to blast me. Instead came, "I *like* that sushi. We *have* to find out how to order our own, though. I really wasn't crazy about that one that tasted like a white wall tire."

"I'll study up on it," I volunteered.

"Never mind," she shot back, "We'll just point like we do everywhere else."

"But how," I asked, "Can we be sure we'll find another sushi shop?"

"Simple," Wife Sarah answered. "Just keep looking until you see a curtain that says *Yakitori.*"

# A LAMB IN THE YEAR OF THE TIGER

It's that time of year when any responsible citizen — even, I suppose, if he's nowhere near the land he's a citizen of — sits down and writes a list of New Year's Resolutions. I know I always do, anyway.

Usually, I must confess, they're not worth the paper they're written on. Resolutions, for instance, to quit smoking, go on a diet, quit losing my temper with the family, etc., appear annually on the list. And, also annually, they bite the dust within twenty-four hours.

But this year, I decided to take this resolution thing seriously. And, as a result, I've listed only those resolutions that I'm *certain* I can keep. Furthermore, I'm going to publish them here so all will know what I'm promising to do — or not do — and, therefore, all can help police that I keep them.

Here's my list:

1.-I promise never to ask any of my Japanese friends about the ingredients in new Japanese dishes they introduce me to in Japanese restaurants. I promise this mostly to spare them embarrassment. Nine times out of ten, I get sick when they tell me that the little spheres of multi-colored jelly that I liked so much were eel eyes. Or that what I thought were crispy little stalks of some green vegetable or other were really dried grasshopper legs. During 1974, I've resolved not to care why the soup is half cloudy and half clear. Or, what those little black specks are they've sprinkled over my rice. Or, why parts of my salad are moving. Oh, I'll care all right. But, I *won't* ask.

2.-I'll never curse under my breath at another Tokyo Taxi Driver. After all, I now understand his problems. I understand the strain he goes through driving around Tokyo. Particularly where there are so many other taxis threatening his life at every intersection — and between intersections, for that matter. And I understand the troubles he can have picking up Gaijins who hand him little scraps of paper covered with Kanji characters scrawled there by a helpful hotel clerk, secretary or neighbor. Particularly when the confused Gaijin hands the note to him upside down which gives the Kanji a completely different meaning and causes the cab driver to take him someplace he doesn't want to go. And I also understand how unnerved he can get at the consequences when a Gaijin carries three different such notes — one with the office address, one with the home address and one with the supermarket's address — and, since he can't read any of them, hands the driver his home address when he's just jumped into the cab right in front of his house. Now, I even understand why taxi drivers want three or four thousand yen plus the fare when they pick up people at night after the subways and trains stop running. After all, it's no different than the New York storekeeper who charges $10 for 50 cent batteries and candles when the electricity fails. No more swearing at these wonderful people.

3.-I promise to start taking Japanese lessons again. As difficult a time as I have trying to understand a local native when he talks to me in Japanese, I really have a hell of a time when he talks to me in English. At least I *know* I don't understand the Japanese. I *think* however, I understand the English. I've decided that, after all, it's his country. And, I should try harder to speak *his* language. Then, let *him* think *he* understands what *I* mean.

4.-When I order my soup, entree, salad, dessert and tea all at once in a Tokyo ''Western-Style'' restaurant, I'm not going to complain anymore when they *bring* me the soup, entree, salad, dessert and tea all at once. After all, when the Japanese themselves go to McDonald's for a milk shake, hamburger, french fries and hot apple pie, we do the same thing to them. In a paper bag, yet. I'm simply, during 1974, going to go to a different restaurant for each course. Or, to McDonald's.

5.-I'm not going to act like local Japanese men on the subway or on the Yamanote Line. I'm going, in 1974, to offer my seat to ladies. How the hell I'm ever going to get a seat on the subway or Yamanote Line in 1974, I don't know. But, if I get, I'll offer.

6.-Just because I'm an American, I'm not going to walk around with a shamed look on my face for weeks after Jesse loses in a Sumo tournament. After all, we Americans ought to be proud for just the fact that one of us is willing to dress like that and go on national television — win, lose or draw. Besides, has any Japanese ever won the Heisman Trophy for playing football?

7.-If the situation comes up again in 1974, I promise to believe the Japanese government when they say there is *no* shortage of toilet paper even if I can't buy toilet paper anywhere. It's obviously a case of government over matter and I just have to get with it.

8.-Also, I promise not to get upset in 1974 when people write letters to the Japan Times taking me to task for wrongly assuming that prices are high here, or that living here can be complicated, or that the language can be difficult, or that milk bottles are hard to open, or that — as an American businessman — I'm over-paid, over-fed and over-housed. From now on, the only thing I'm going to read on the back page of the Times is Max Lerner. And, *I'm* going to write letters to the editor about what Mr. Lerner says.

9.-Lastly, I promise that not once in 1974 will I cut an article out of the local papers about the rising cost of living and mail it back to the home office. Mainly because, the way things are going in Tokyo, if I *can* afford the newspaper, I probably won't have the money for the postage.

# THEY'RE GOING TO THROW THE BOOK AT ME

Sometime back, the wire services carried a small story that could eventually — mark my words — signal the end to an important piece of what's left of the "good life" for foreigners in Tokyo.

The story itself had nothing really to do with our Japan, but I'm certain it *will*, someday *very* soon.

It seems, the story went, that policemen in Honolulu were having a hell of a time communicating with the floods of Japanese tourists. So, one do-gooder Honolulu policeman, who happens to be married to a Japanese girl, prepared a little phrase book in Japanese and distributed it to all the Honolulu policemen.

If I understand the whole thing correctly, a policeman can now collar the law-breaking Japanese tourist, break out the little book, and find the English words for what he wants to say. Under that English is the Japanese for the same phrase. He simply points to that Japanese phrase and shoves the book under the tourist's nose. The Japanese tourist, on the same page, has a multiple-choice of answers, one of which he can point to in order to reply to the policeman.

The worst part of this whole thing is that it's working. And *that's* what scares the wits out of me. Sure as hell, one of the Japanese that gets stopped in Honolulu, and has that book pulled on him, will be a vacationing Tokyo policeman. And, he'll rush back home and have a similar, reverse-English book put together for us.

Then, sayonara to another slice of the good life.

I don't know about you, but I *love* the fact that I have never been able to understand one single Tokyo policeman — and they haven't been able to understand me. Glorious. Over my three years here, this communications gap has probably saved me at least ¥300,000 in fines and 90 days in jail somewhere.

Don't misunderstand. It's not that I'm a hardened criminal; it's just that I'm a stupid Gaijin.

For instance, out where we used to live in Kamikitazawa, it was OK to park your car on the street during the day. I had a driveway for *my* car, but — when we expected guests — I'd put my car in the street and leave the driveway to my visitors.

Usually, I parked right across the street; this time it was up the street a ways. When our guests left, I went to retrieve my car. Pasted — with *real* paste — on the windshield was what had to be a parking ticket. For what the irony is worth, parking tickets in Tokyo are red, white and blue.

The maid explained that I would have to go right to the little police box

211

up by Kamikitazawa railroad station and pay up. I went, with what was left of the pasted ticket after I pulled it off the windshield.

Neither the policeman there nor I, of course, could understand a word spoken by the other. With hands flailing all over, I told him it was OK to park on my street. He finally got across to me that, yes, that's true, but not within five meters of a fire hydrant.

I waved that he was nuts; there *were* no fire hydrants on my street. And now that he brought them up, I wanted to complain about their absence.

He insisted a hydrant was there and offered to show it to me. I stormed off behind him trying to keep up with his bicycle, confident of victory. When we got to our street, I asked him: Where is the little red hydrant? And I answered him: *Nowhere.*

As from the beginning, he didn't understand me. Then, he pushed my car about ten feet — I didn't get that at all — and pointed to a metal plate on the street. It was about three feet by two feet, outlined in yellow paint, with yellow Japanese writing all over it.

About this time, the maid came out of the house, pointed at the yellow-bordered plate and said:

"Fire hydrant down there."

The message was getting thru. I hadn't parked *near* the hydrant; I parked *on* it. But, I would have been a fool to admit it then. After all, I didn't park there on purpose. So, I started to tell the policeman how sneaky I thought it was to hide fire hydrants, and how I would take this to the supreme court, and how. . .

But, he threw up his hands in the international signal for despair, tore up what was left of the torn ticket, and pedalled away.

If he had that damn phrase book, I'm sure it would have been a different ending.

And, another time, a motorcycle cop followed me — red light blinking — from Tokyo Station right into the parking lot at our old office in the Time-Life Building. I didn't even know he was after me until I parked. He pulled up alongside, dismounted, removed his gloves, and pulled out his ticket book.

When I got out of the car, he saw I was a Gaijin. His eyes widened, he dropped the ticket book and managed a "Harro." He didn't even bother to put his gloves back on, jumped on his motorcycle and sped away.

Thanks to no phrase book, I'll never know what I did wrong.

I've only mentioned two of a score of similar encounters with Tokyo's finest. All had a similar happy ending — thanks to the absence of such a phrase book.

But now, one day soon — thanks to that meddler in Honolulu — they'll probably throw the book at me. And, at you, too!

# WHAT *DO* CANADIANS EAT?

While going thru the newspapers one day, I spotted an ad announcing that one of our favorite Gaijin-type supermarkets was holding what they chose to call a "Canadian Food Festival".

Now I don't recall seeing any ad in any paper ever that aroused my curiosity like that one did. What, I was asking myself, *do* Canadians eat? And I couldn't for the life of me come up with anything.

Think about it — you non-Canadians, anyway — and I bet you'll be as hard-pressed for an answer to that one as I was.

First, I ran thru my mind the restaurants in Tokyo's Roppongi, Aoyama and Akasaka. I could remember seeing dozens of French restaurants there, a handful of Italian pizza places, three Greek restaurants, a Hungarian eatery, Anne Dinken's Kosher joint, — *all* kinds of different country menus are represented. But a *Canadian* restaurant? *Never.*

I don't remember any Canadian restaurants in Cleveland or New York or Teaneck, New Jersey either. As I was thinking back to business trips I've made to Toronto and Montreal, memory tells me that when I was *in* Canada, I didn't eat at a Canadian restaurant. Canadian friends always took me to a Chinese or French restaurant. I even remember having Sukiyaki once in Montreal.

When I was a little boy in Buffalo, we put in a lot of weekends at a place on the Canadian side of Lake Erie called Crystal Beach. All we ever ate there, I recall, were hot dogs, hamburgers or bags of popcorn. Hardly "Canadian" dishes.

Anyway, I decided that I *had* to get to this Canadian Food Festival and see what it was all about — and to see what I'd been missing in the way of northern North American cuisine. So I did.

You couldn't miss the place. Canadian flags were flying all over the building entrance — next to Japanese flags, of course. Since both are red and white, they fly very well together.

Standing guard on either side of the main doorway were life-size cardboard cut-outs of the Royal Canadian Mounted Police. I was really getting into the Maple Leaf mood.

Seeing the Mountie cut-outs jogged me back to those childhood Saturday matinee days where those fellows in red *always* got their man. But that still didn't give me any gastronomic clues since I don't remember them ever eating anything in those movies.

As I walked inside the store, I turned left and passed the meat counter. Of *course,* it dawned on me — Canadian bacon!

But, they didn't have any.

They had some Tenderloin Steaks at ¥6,500 or $21.66 a pound. However, I don't think they were *from Canada*. Kobe, I'm sure, is right here in Japan.

Opposite the meat counter, there was a big display of Canadian stuff. It included apple juice, apple sauce, apple candy — even apple wine. Just so you won't think apples are all Canadians eat, I hasten to include the fact that there was Canadian honey and Canadian pickles nearby.

Down the first aisle, I mostly passed non-Canadian things like raw fish and frozen pizza. There was a lot of cheese there, too. From every country in the world, it seemed, except Nigeria and Canada.

Then there was the cookies. *All* from Canada. The Canadian dollar — according to the prices on the cookies — must be taking less of a beating than the United States version. The Canadian oatmeal cookie packages were marked "79 cents". The Japanese price was ¥640. If I figure right, that makes one Canadian dollar equal to ¥810. Not bad.

If ¥640 is too high for oatmeal cookies you could get Chocolate Chip ones for only ¥506.

Later on, in the next aisle, I got all mixed up again on currency exchange. Over there, 39 cents Canadian candy was ¥235; the 39 cents throw-away pie pans from the US were ¥240.

Another genuine article from Canada — a bottle of Canadian Club whiskey — was only ¥4,500 a bottle.

Next came a confusing display of canned meatballs, macaroni in cellophane bags and canned ravioli. All were marked "Made in Canada". I've spent many hours in the past trying to nail down in my mind whether Marco Polo brought macaroni from China to Italy or vice-versa — and now it turns out it's a Canadian dish!

The apples at the fruit counter were a sight to see. Not the apples themselves, that is, but the ¥1,000 *each* price tags on some of them. Now ¥1,000 for a single apple seemed a little high to me — *until* I noticed the ¥3,800 melon halves.

As Wife Sarah and I got to the check out counter, I was glad I didn't grab a basket on the way in. We only had to pay for the few things we were able to carry in our hands. As it was, the bill was ¥17,243. They didn't charge us anything though for the little pocket pack of tissue paper marked "Canada".

As we were leaving the store, I finally realized why I'd never seen a Canadian restaurant anywhere.

Their food is too damn expensive.

# FIGURES OF SPEECH

Seems to me — as I'm sure I mentioned before — the Japanese love statistics more than anybody in the world. In fact, I'll bet the average Japanese in his lifetime collects 17.4 times as many statistics as the average anybody else.

Everyday, the newspapers come with a fresh supply. For instance, I just read the other day that the average Japanese adult drank 13.3 bottles of sake, 81.3 bottles of beer and 3.3 bottles of whiskey during last year.

Frightening part of those particular numbers is that it's probably safe to assume that 50% of those "average Japanese adults" are women — most of whom stick to canned orange juice or Pepsi. If that's true, you can double those bottles for the average Japanese adult male.

That, for me anyway, helps explain all that sleeping on the subways.

Anyway, after a short time here, I was amazed at the numbers my average Japanese business counterparts carried in their heads. They all seemed to know this county's GNP to the nearest ¥ 10. *And* the present dollar surplus. And what the yen *would* be worth six months from now — against the dollar, peso, lire or whatever. Plus all kinds of other numbers.

Well, I started to develop a statistical complex. I seldom remembered more than my home and office telephone numbers and how many yen I got for my dollar at the bank that very morning. Those phone numbers, I quickly discovered, were vital when the taxi got lost, and the dollar-yen situation becomes important in correspondence and conversations with the home office.

As a result of all this, I got superinterested in learning some numbers that would let me hold my own in daily confrontations with the locals.

I mean I wanted to know things like: How many train rides does the average Japanese take a year? And, on what percent of those rides does he sit and what percent does he stand? How many kilometers does that average train rider get per box lunch? How many tangerines and hard boiled eggs does he eat?

If he doesn't eat on the train at all, how many of those adult Japanese comic books does he read?

But, I couldn't find that sort of thing out anywhere.

Then, just last week, my whole life changed. Just perchance in the Hilton's bookstore, I spotted a book called "Statistical Handbook of Japan". It's published every year by the Bureau of Statistics of the Office of the Prime Minister. I read it, and now I'm ready to tangle with anyone, anytime.

Like did you know that Tokyo has an average of 1,972 hours of sunshine a year? No, you were probably concentrating on that 1,503 millimeters of rain. And, if you're from Los Angeles, you get five times as much mileage out of your umbrella here because it only rains 321 millimeters back there.

It's all in that little book.

I bet when you look at a map of Japan, you only see those four big islands and don't even give a tumble to the 3,000-plus little ones. And tell the truth, did you know those 3,004-plus islands altogether measured only 377,000 square kilometers versus the 9,976,000 of Canada and the 9,363,000 of the United States?

The facts are right on page 9.

Just wait until some Japanese businessman hits me next time with the GNP. I'll say, "Is that so much for 107,322,281 people — 52,639,000 of which are men and 54,693,000 women?" Then I'll say, "And you'd better forget about GNP and start thinking what you're going to do with 2,054,000 women who have nobody to marry. Those women are going to live an average of 75.58 years, you know."

He *can't* very well argue with the Prime Minister's Office.

And, do you know how you get that feeling once a day (at least) that Tokyo is sukoshi crowded? Well, you're right. Japan — on that "average" again — has 284 people per square kilometer. But "average" Tokyo has 5,386 people in every per square kilometers. While there's no place here to really get away from it *all* , try Hokkaido. The square kilometers up there only entertain 62 people each.

543,000 people in Japan work in the fishing industry and they catch 9,900,000 tons of fish. Peru does better — they catch 12,600,000 tons. But, the Peruvians cook the fish and probably boil away an easy 3,000,000 tons. So, Japan, I bet, is still number one.

Each average Japanese, by the way, eats 84.2 grams of those fish each and every day. And he probably eats it in one of those homes without thinking about the fact that 75% of those homes are wooden.

What that average Japanese does every night after he eats that 84.2 grams of fish, the book doesn't really say. Only hint is that two nights a year, he goes to the movies. Back in 1968, he used to go 12 times. Maybe he just sits home and worries over the obvious problem caused by the fact that 81% of his homes have running water, but only 18% have a sewer to run it into.

Also in that book is statistical proof that the home office doesn't answer our questions. Last year, we sent 2,831,000 telegrams overseas and they only sent 2,605,000 back to us. Tell them about *that* the next time you phone them (you did that 1,350,833 times last year).

And tell them you know it's true because you read it right here — in one of the 55,845,000 newspapers delivered today in Japan.

216

# THINGS HAVE CHANGED

I can't help but notice that everytime I talk for any length of time with any foreigner who has been in Japan even one day longer than I have, he invariably says at some point in the conversation: "Things sure have changed in Japan."

It happened again the other night, and — being in a semi-ornery mood at the moment, I nailed him with a "Exactly what the hell are you talking about 'changed'? I don't notice any difference — unless you're talking about all the construction."

"The buildings are only part of it. A small part," he said. "I'm thinking of the big changes. Not physical changes. Attitude changes."

"For instance?" I asked.

"Well, take this hotel," he pointed out (we were in the coffee shop). "It used to be that you couldn't get in here without hearing at least six 'Irasshaimase's' (Welcome). Or get out without seven or eight 'Domo Arrigato Gozaimashita's' (Thank you). We only got four 'Irasshaimase's' on they way in and I'll settle now for five 'Domo's' on the way out."

"That's a big change?"

"No. But it's part of the big one. Yesterday on the Ginza, I couldn't help but notice that the girl who wipes the handrail on the escalator wasn't really leaning on her white rag."

"Oh, for God's sake," I shrugged. "You're really splitting hairs."

"That's another thing: hair. My barber this morning gave me a half-hearted massage after my shampoo. Hardly fifteen minutes."

I had to tell him that I thought he was imagining things.

"Imagine, hell. Look at the cashier's counter over there. Remember when there used to be a girl who just said 'Arrigato Gozaimashita' and handed your check to the girl with the abacus or whatever they call it? Then, after moving the beads around, the girl used to hand it to the girl who said another 'Domo' and handed it to the girl by the cash register who totaled it again and gave it to the fifth girl who put the check on the little silver tray and told you how much it was?"

"So?"

"So? just look. Now the same girl who gives the first 'Domo' pushes the beads around."

"That's a big change?"

"Not only that. The silver tray is now plastic."

"And that's serious?"

"Go ahead," he said, "give me that knowing grin. Next, you'll deny you saw any significance in that color supplement the Sunday Japan Times carried a couple of weeks ago about the new shrine or temple or whatever they call it."

I had to admit that yes, I did see the color supplement and that no, I didn't see any "special significance".

"You are asleep," he snapped. "That was a *new* Temple — a *new* one — and the Japanese were pushing it. In color, yet. It's not long ago when they pushed only *old* Temples and Shrines. And the older, the better."

He had something there, I agreed.

"Why just yesterday on the Marunouchi Subway Line, I saw three women in a row get on *without* shopping bags. And I even saw one *man* carrying the baby while his wife was empty-handed."

Right about then — at the very height of my friend's concern over all this "change", I had to cut off our discussion to get back to my office for a meeting. "Relax, Bill," I prescribed. "Everything's going to be all right with Japan."

I paid the check and — as Bill predicted — I heard only five "Domo Arrigatos" as I walked out. Maybe, I thought, Bill has something to worry about. Once outside, however, everything seemed right. The smog was still there. Every woman had a shopping bag. The school kids were in those baggy uniforms. Even the first two empty taxis passed me by without stopping.

By the time I reached the office, I dismissed Bill's phobia about change as a figment of his imagination. Once in my office, I rushed into the meeting room. There they were — five of my Japanese business associates — already seated around the table.

I bowed myself into my seat and looked around at each of them. Suddenly, it struck me like a ton of rice: Bill was absolutely right. Here were five Japanese and myself, and I was the *only* one wearing a plain *white* shirt!


## AMERICAN FAIR

"She's nothing like I expected. But, then neither are you. Now I'm more confused than ever about the Americans".

That's a Japanese business associate of mine speaking. He said it in my car the other night while I was driving him to Shinjuku station after dinner at my house. The "she" he was talking about was my wife.

"What do you mean?" I asked. "Is she younger or older than you expected."

"Oh, no. Nothing like that. I mean you two are just not what Americans are supposed to be."

218

My immediate reaction was irritation, "What the hell does that mean, 'not like what Americans are supposed to be'. What are we supposed to be?"

"Now don't get excited — although *that*'s definitely American. I mean that you two don't fill the image we Japanese have been carrying around about Americans."

I *was* excited. "Exactly what is that image?"

It was hard to explain, he said. But generally it came from what they saw and heard on television and in the movies. "You know," he went on, "We get the idea that all American men are cowboys or private eyes — or the Indians and crooks that the cowboy or private eyes are always chasing. The American women in the movies are all painted up, half-dressed glamour girls whether they are running around with the cowboys, the Indians or the private eyes or the crooks;   at least that's what the movies tell us."

"And the television?" I asked.

"That's what's confusing. On TV, Americans are generally a collection of stupid families that are always involved in a very funny situation week after week. But, you and your wife don't fit at all. That's why I'm confused what America — and Americans — are really like."

We pulled up at Shinjuku Station just then and I promised him that, tomorrow afternoon, I'd give him his answer.

The next day, Saturday, I took him down to Seibu Department Store in Shibuya. They were having an "American Fair" and the ads promised the fifth floor would have a real slice of America. Perfect, I thought. I promised my friend an end to his confusion.

Right inside Seibu's front door was a big department, all decked out with American flags selling hundreds of varieties of Max Factor cosmetics.

"See what I mean?" he smiled.

I pulled him toward the escalator. Lining the wall all the way up to the second floor were dozens of pictures of Marilyn Monroe — in among more American flags. She was fully dressed in only one of them. And in that one, the wind was blowing her dress above her navel. He poked my back and pointed.

"See what I mean?"

Finally, we got to the fifth floor and the American Fair. The first counter had a display of Playboy jig-saw puzzles and Playboy playing cards. All picturing naked women.

"See what I mean?"

I steered him — hell, I pushed him — around a pillar, but another counter there was selling replicas of "Wanted" posters out of the wild west era. I knew what was coming and it came.

"See what I mean?"

219

Over near the elevators, I saw some American appliances. I dragged him over to the big G.E. Refrigerator with the automatic ice crusher, freezer, the works. "How about *that*?" I smugged. "*That's* America."

"That's what I mean," he said. "Look at the ¥595,000 price tag. You have to be a crook to afford that much for an ice-box."

I was ready to give up and headed back toward the down escalator.

"Wait a minute," he called. "Don't you want to show me the model guns or the automatic hair curlers or . . . "

"Forget it. I'll explain America some other day."

He knew I was crushed. "I really appreciate this little look at America," he comforted. "Now, let me show you a real *Japanese* salaryman's evening. Follow me."

"Where are we going?" I wanted to know.

"I'll buy you a Pepsi and then take you over to Korakuen Stadium to the baseball game."


## OCCIDENTAL ORIENTATION

Just a few days ago, I read a report that told of how a Gaijin women's association in Tokyo ran a five-week-long course designed to cushion the cultural shock for Japanese women about to join their Japanese husbands who have been transferred abroad.

Most of the gals were headed for the United States. The orientation seemed to be quite thorough — at least according to the newspaper report.

The Japanese wives, it seems, were invited to homes of the association's foreign members to see "Western-style living in action."

And, the Japanese women were led thru some of the Western-style Supermarkets in Aoyama to get them used to American-Style shopping.

One of the Association members even volunteered to demonstrate a Western-style bath in a bathroom at the home of an American member.

They were told, these Japanese, to be experts in the Oriental arts of flower arrangement and tea ceremony so that they could please their American guests when they got to Seattle or New York or wherever.

Now I only read the news story about all this and wasn't with the group while they toured the Aoyama supermarkets or, obviously, while they watched the American lady take a bath.

And, just reading about all this, I'm afraid these Japanese might have the wrong idea about what awaits them.

Like I hope they hid the maid and the driver when the Japanese women visited the Gaijin apartments. I wouldn't want the Japanese women to think for one minute that Cleveland people have such domestic assistance.

And, for another instance, in America you take a bath in your own house, alone. I hope they didn't think because of the demonstration that you go over to somebody else's house and bathe while a group is watching you and taking notes.

And, when the expatriated Japanese see the prices at the Seattle A&P as compared to the Tokyo supermarkets, they are surely going to be afraid to buy anything so cheap. After all, you only get what you pay for — at every place *but* in Aoyama supermarkets.

Also, I have news for the Japanese wives: The first time they have the neighborhood girls in over in the Bronx and tell them to sit on the floor to get ready for a tea ceremony, they'll be all alone again.

Ikebana is great, all right. But, Americans have a tendency to walk around the flower vase and look at *all* sides. You know Ikebana can't take that treatment.

Actually, however, it's the things the report didn't mention that has me worried. For example, did they tell them *not* to wait for the taxi driver to open the back door automatically like it happens in Tokyo? I know a Japanese that waited on the corner of 42nd and Madison for two weeks for a taxi driver to open a door. When the cabs stopped for him and the door didn't open, he offered them — with Tokyo finger sign language — two, three, four times the meter and they *still* wouldn't open the door.

And while green tea just might turn out to be great for afternoon parties in Seattle, did they show the Japanese how to make an extra-dry Martini with a twist?

How about the finer points of American driving versus Tokyo? Did they tell the Japanese wives that, in America, a red light *means* stop and "No Parking" signs *mean* no parking and that telling an American cop that they "don't understand English" will merely triple the fine?

Do they know that when they go into Macy's or Gimbel's that they'll have to wipe their own escalator handrail?

Have they been warned that people in Brooklyn who eat raw fish in public are put away?

I hope somebody told them that when two guys wearing masks come at them on Fifth Avenue that these guys are not suffering from colds.

And I hope nobody forgot to tell them that in America there's no sense in saving your old newspapers. You have to pay cash for your toilet paper.

The whole course will really have been a service if they told the Japanese wives to forget about studying English. Let the kids learn the language and handle the translation just like our kids do in Japan.

There was one thing in the report that really leads me to believe that our local foreign women's association really went all-out to prepare the Japanese wives for what things will really be like in New York. They charged the Japanese 33 bucks each for the course.

221

Anyway, I wish nothing but good luck to the Japanese wives — and their families — during their American stay. I hope they enjoy living there as much as I did.

And — for what precious little it may be worth — I offer my sincere congratulations to that foreign women's association for trying to ease the terror that's inherent when you move to a strange country.

I really wish that there had been a similar project back in Cleveland so that Wife Sarah could have been forewarned about what she was likely to face when I dragged her to Japan. If there was such a project, and if they had done a fairly accurate job of describing the life of an American in Tokyo, it would really have changed our life.

For one thing, we'd have stayed in Cleveland.


## I JUST DON'T KNOW HOW TO TELL HIM

There were two different reports in the papers recently indicating that President Nixon is thinking rather seriously about visiting Japan. One came from the office of the Japanese Foreign Minister and one was credited to the American Ambassador.

Now I don't really know what's running through the Japanese Foreign Minister's mind about Nixon's trip, but I do know how our U.S. Ambassador must feel about it. After all, I've had visits by people from the Home Office myself. I wish him good luck.

But what's really bothering me is the fact that I feel compelled to write President Nixon and give him some advice before he takes off for the land of the rising everything. I just don't know how to go about it.

Please don't get me wrong. It's not that I feel the U.S. Embassy here won't do a good job filling him in with a long list of things to watch out for. It's just that now with Okinawa, parts of Tachikawa and some other awa's back in Japanese hands, it's been a long time since I've seen any people wearing painted helmets and towels wrapped around their faces storming the Embassy or snake-dancing through the streets shouting things that could be construed as non-complimentary to the United States.

And, because I'll apparently be living here for a while to come, I don't want the President's visit to start any trouble that will linger long after he leaves here on Air Force One with Prime Minister Tanaka's "presentos" under his arms.

Another thing occurs to me: There are probably many things the Embassy people *know* they *should* tell President Nixon but can't because of protocol.

So, *that's* why I want to write him myself. But, I don't want my letter to offend him. Good God, wouldn't it be awful to come up an "Ugly American" in the eyes of your own President?

For instance, the first thing I want to tell him is simply this: *Don't* bring Pat.

My guess is that Mrs. Tanaka is still steaming over the fact that the President brought Pat to China where Mao loaded her up with all those goodies to take back for the houses at San Clemente and Key Biscayne.

I'm not even sure that Mrs. Tanaka got to go to Haneda to say Sayonara to her husband, much less make the trip to Peking.

Besides, I know what Wife Sarah and my secretary go through when the wife of one of *my* home office visitors tags along.

If Pat comes, then the Ambassador's wife will have to make another trip — probably the All-Day Tour down to Hakone to show Pat Mt. Fuji. Since Mr. and Mrs. Ambassador have been here almost as long as Wife Sarah and I, she probably needs another All-Day Tour to Hakone like Tokyo needs more $12 melons.

Besides, what the hell can she say to Pat when they get all the way down there — or even up to the fifth station — and they can't even *see* Fuji San through the smog?

And don't forget poor Mrs. Tanaka. She'll probably be expected to take Pat shopping. Sure as hell, Pat will see something in the Imperial Hotel Arcade and say, "I can buy that cheaper in the U.S."

The Japanese press will next day headline the fact that Pat is resurrecting charges of "dumping." I can see them painting the helmets already.

Even if Pat *doesn't* say something like that, Mrs. Tanaka will still have to take her *someplace* while the two husbands are deciding when to liberalize papayas. And how do you think Mrs. T. would like the idea of roaming around the streets of Japan knowing the last poll showed that only 16% of the Japanese thought her husband ought to keep his job?

And another thing: I want to tell the President to come up with a good explanation of Henry Kissinger's actions — or lack of action — on his last trip here.

I'm not talking about the political aspects of Kissinger's visit. For all I know, they might have been just perfect. What I'm talking about is the fact that every time Kissinger goes to Paris or London or someplace in Europe, the papers seem to always print pictures of him going out someplace at night with a local beauty on his arm and a big grin on his face.

Not once during his visit here did he date a Japanese girl. Don't think the locals didn't notice. Come up please, Mr. President, with a good excuse.

And if I know Japanese meetings like I think I do, President Nixon will be here a lot longer than he thinks he will. So I want to warn him not to forget his PX card. I'd hate to see him have to pay local prices for his Bayer

Aspirin. Or, worse than that, set a bad example for the American business community here by having some government or military person pick up aspirin at the PX for him. And he's *definitely* going to need aspirin.

He should also be warned that when Mr. Tanaka takes him out to a Geisha Girl party (another reason, by the way, not to bring Pat) he shouldn't say that he already *knows* how to use chopsticks because he learned how in China. In fact, he shouldn't even *mention* China.

Another warning I want to pass on is to keep quiet when he's riding around Tokyo. If he slipped and called Iceland a "godforsaken place", what might he say when he drives past the garbage piled up under the railroad tracks in Yurakucho?

And I don't want him to learn any Japanese phrases. Sure as hell, he'll say "Ohayo gozaimas" in the evening and "Konbanwa" in the morning.

He should know that no matter what Tanaka San and the Old Japan Hands from the U.S. Embassy do, Mr. Nixon *shouldn't* pick his teeth at the table.

I also want him to know that when he hears a Japanese say "Mizu no mon", Mr. Nixon should cock his head and make a hissing noise thru his teeth.

Because "Mizu no mon" translated to English means "Watergate."


## HE COULDN'T PICK A BETTER TIME

I really hate to bother you, but I need some help. I'm sure you've read, as I have that President Nixon is thinking of coming over here sometime in November.

Because there are some things we need at our house for the holidays, I thought it would be a good idea to drop him a note and ask him if he minds bringing some of these things with him. The problem is that we've been away from Cleveland for three holiday seasons in a row and, so, I'm afraid I'm going to forget something.

Please read over this draft of my letter to him and, if I've left anything out, drop me a line right away. Better send it special delivery because I want to get this in the mail as soon as possible so he'll have time to collect everything. Thanks.

Here goes:

Dear President Nixon:

According to what I read here in the papers, I understand that you're finally going to make your trip to Japan. When the rumor of your visit first circulated here some months back, I know you probably thought me presumptuous to write you as I did about how to conduct yourself while you're in this country.

But, let me say again that I only did that for your own good. Most of us Americans get in trouble here only because nobody every warned us about what we were really in for.

Anyway, all of what I said back then, still goes — even including the part about not bringing Pat.

But that's not why I'm writing you today. Actually, this is probably even *more* presumptuous than that first letter because there are some things I'd like you to bring me. I usually don't ask visitors from home to bring me anything, but then they usually don't have their own airplane to carry the stuff in anyway. You do — a couple of them — so I know you won't mind.

The amazing thing is that you couldn't have picked a better time. Most of these things I want for the holidays and I was really afraid you were going to put off your trip till January.

Most important is the food. Please pick up a couple of turkeys. If each is about 20 pounds, they'd be perfect. Get them frozen, because one I want to save for Christmas dinner.

It's not, Mr. President, that I couldn't buy a frozen turkey here in one of the local supermarkets. But, if I do pick up a 20-pounder over here for Thanksgiving, I won't have any money left to buy any of the kids anything for Christmas.

And bring a couple of bags of that ready-mix stuffing too, please. We tried stuffing the five-pounder we could afford last year with rice and it blew up.

If you can get a frozen Mince Pie, bring that along too, please. The local variety is kind of heavy on the bean paste. That's for Wife Sarah. For me, please ask Mr. Kissinger to pick up a pumpkin pie from Horn and Hardart the next time he goes to New York to meet somebody.

And while we are on those two subjects — Mr. Kissinger and New York — ask him if he'll go over to Coney Island and pick me up a dozen or so hot dogs at Nathans Famous. Better tell him to get a cup of the grease they put on their grill, too. I always thought it was that, and *not* the meat, that makes their hot dogs taste so good.

Perhaps Henry won't mind packing some bagels and bialys, too. A little cream cheese, a little lox wouldn't hurt. He knows where to get them, I'm sure. I don't care if any of Henry's stuff is frozen. We'll eat it all the same day you arrive.

As for Christmas, the only food I can think of we want (besides the Turkey and the stuffing) is some of those red and white striped candy canes. You can't believe how difficult it is to feel like Christmas without those things.

What I really need is three or four strings of those Christmas tree lights that *don't* blink on and off. I *know* they're made here, but they export all of them and save only the blinking ones to sell here. I'll go nuts if we have them on the tree again this year.

Please pick up some games I can give to the kids for Christmas. You know, Monopoly, Life — games like that. The Monopoly games they sell here have all the "Chance" and "Community Chest" cards printed in Japanese. That takes all the fun out of passing 'Go' and collecting the ¥53,000 (That's all $200 is worth here these days, Mr. President.)

I also need a big bottle of cherries, the kind you put in Manhattans. I'll be tipping a few over the holidays for sure, and the local cherries are all made out of some kind of plastic.

Another thing the kids want for Christmas is a Sony color television. Again, I know they're made here, but I read where Congress says they are cheaper in the U.S. So, please dump one on your plane for me.

Getting back to the Manhattans, I just remembered that you and the hundreds of staff and newsmen who will probably come with you are entitled to bring in three bottles of booze each from the duty free shop. Please do. I don't care what you select, but please be certain that out of every three hundred bottles, at least three or four of them are Johnnie Walker Black. Then, I can sell them to pay for all the rest.

Another thing that would be nice is if you can bring a couple of pictures of the Pandas in the Washington Zoo. We've never been able to get near the ones here in Ueno. From what I hear, color pictures of Pandas are a waste of money so black and white will do.

Oh, there are so many other things I'd love — like a sandwich without cucumbers, for instance — but I think that will do for this trip.

If for some reason all this doesn't fit on Air Force One and you have to ship it separately, please don't forget to fill out the "Declaration of Unaccompanied Goods" or we won't get any of it out of Japanese Customs until next Christmas at the earliest.

One more thing, if you come to Tokyo thru Cleveland — don't laugh; I did — please call my office and tell them to stop forwarding my "Book-of-the-Month" mail by sea mail. The books themselves don't get here until after I've seen the movie made from them at the American Club, and the notices get here a months after they had to be back saying "No" if I didn't want the next book.

I don't know how I can ever pay you back for these favors, Mr. President, but I'll try. Maybe next home leave I can bring you some batteries or cassettes for your tape recorders or something.

If, for some reason or other, you *can't* bring all these things with you, just bring me a card that will let me shop in the PX. That would solve all my problems.

Hopefully yours,
Don Maloney

# WHAT EVERY VISITING PRESIDENT SHOULD KNOW

As the day of President Ford's arrival in Japan draws closer, I find myself getting more and more nervous about the whole thing. Not that I'm worrying about what he'll do and say about the great issues of the day. I'm sure he'll handle all that OK. Most home office visitors do. It's how he might address those little everyday issues that concerns me.

After all, a lot of the management people in his Japan branch office are fairly new here. This, plus the fact that his Japan operation is a wholly-owned operation and not involved with any advice-giving joint venture partner, makes me believe that chances are better than even that they might have inadvertently neglected to brief Mr. Ford on some of the finer points of visiting fireman behavior. Especially since Mr. Ford will be the first top executive ever to come here from his home office.

For instance, I hope somebody has warned Mr. Ford about applying early for a visa. He wouldn't be the first home office visitor to arrive here without one and embarrass the local staff. I emphasize "early" application since Mr. Ford is the President and it might take dozens of meetings in the Japanese Embassy in Washington to decide exactly who shall sign the guarantee letter for somebody like that.

Then there's the gifts. How many should a President bring? I mean down to what levels should he give them out? Certainly he has to bring something to Tanaka San. And probably to all the Cabinet ministers too. But he should be warned not to put names on minister's gifts.

What *kind* of gifts to bring I don't know. But he won't bring anything, I hope, that could ordinarily be purchased in a PX. Chances are good that the Prime Minister and his Cabinet ministers have Japanese friends who can pick up any PX item they want right here. Safest thing to do, probably, is to stop over in Hawaii and pick up a few boxes of Papayas.

He should make sure that each Papaya box is stamped "JAPAN" of course, so he doesn't have any trouble with Customs. There are a couple of sound reasons for the Papaya choice. One is that he can decide after he gets here how many people he wants to give gifts to and then hand them out one, two or three to a person — depending on the number of people he decides to give them to.

Second reason is that, loaded down with Papaya boxes, he'll draw the least attention at the airport since everybody else will be carrying Papayas, too.

Airport reminds me that I know first-hand how difficult it can be in Tokyo to spot a home-office guy you've never seen before as he's coming out into the waiting room at the "Arrivals" building. I hope he'll settle with his Tokyo people now, before he leaves Washington, whether he'll wear a red carnation or they will hold a sign that says something like "Mr. Ford — U.S.A." — or maybe an American flag. And because I understand that there may be more than the usual crowds at the airport to greet him when he arrives, I hope someone has sent Mr. Ford a subway map so he can get to the new guest house in Akasaka or Aoyama, or wherever it is, in case he misses his meet.

I can only assume or hope and pray that someone will tell Mr. Ford that the large tiled pool full of water that will certainly be in that guest house is a Japanese bath and not a swimming pool. Not like he won't find out immediately if he dives in it some night.

Just going on past performance of other visitors from lower levels of Mr. Ford's home office, I trust he's been given a list of questions *not* to ask. Like, for instance, "Why did the atomic-powered Mutsu stay out of port so long on a simple test run?"

Or, as he passes under Yurakucho Station, "What made you think of locating a garbage disposal plant in such a convenient downtown location?

Heaven forbid he'd ask, "Any chance of me seeing Mt. Fuji while I'm here?" Or, "Is it true that, in Japan, *people* eat soybeans?" Or, "What do those signs say that all the people along the roads are carrying?" Or, "Where is this Narita Airport I've read about and when will it open?"

On the other hand, I hope he's being briefed on the proper *answers* to some questions the Japanese might ask him.

Chances are, Watergate won't figure much in any conversation he'll have here, but he'd better get ready a reply in case somebody asks him how come President Nixon's secretary transcribed the Watergate tapes on a German machine instead of on a Sony. And he should have a prepared answer for "How come your private plane — Air Force One — is a Boeing but you sent Japan an ambassador who worked for Lockheed?"

How he might be inclined to answer a sure fire question from his hosts like, "How do you like Japanese sushi?" worries me, too. Especially since I read just the other day where England's Prince Charles wrote in his new book that raw Japanese squid tastes like "chopped-up rubber hose."

I don't want any chance of President Ford being influenced by a remark like that.

I want him to taste raw Japanese squid for *himself* — and he surely will have that opportunity — and to decide on his own what it tastes like. And, he should tell the truth.

As long as he adds, "But, *I like* chopped-up rubber hose."

# THE ELECTION'S OVER — I THINK

I waited until now to say anything about the Presidential Election in the United States to be certain that the counting of our absentee ballots didn't materially change the outcome. They didn't.

Besides, even though this column appears some five days after the election, the excitement is still at the same level now as it was then — zero. I still find it hard to believe that the voting really took place at all.

This was the first Presidential Election since I arrived in Tokyo. It certainly was different. Right from the very beginning.

In the first place, I didn't even get to see the conventions on television. I have no idea who had the best floor demonstrations after the names were placed in nomination. Or who had the most balloons. I don't even know who actually made the nominating speeches. Sometimes those people make up my mind for me.

And, when Nixon and McGovern accepted the nominations, how did they sound? Did they bring the whole family with them to the rostrum? Was McGovern holding wife Eleanor's hand? And what, really, is Eleanor really like?

Then, the months after the conventions. Not a single campaign bumper sticker. No buttons. (I did see one that said "McGovern — Shriver," but without my glasses I thought it said "McGovern for Sheriff" and I paid no attention to it.) Not one Tokyo telephone pole sporting a poster with either major candidate. Not even a Dr. Spock poster.

I'd never voted before for a president without knowing whether he *really* ate the pizza or the hot dogs or the potato knishes. If you see them on television, you can tell if they really eat it or if they are just posing. Things like that affect my decision.

And, of course, we saw none of the television commercials for the candidates. How are we to know who has the most charisma? Or who has the best ad agency? Or make-up man? Damn it, all those things count.

The crowds. Were they for the candidate or against him? What were they yelling? Who were they?

The newspapers in Tokyo weren't much help, either. I knew more about the Pandas in Ueno Park — and what they ate all day — than I knew about Watergate or Eagleton. And what about Eagleton? Was he really . . . you know.

And, of course, I couldn't even see whose button my boss back in the States was wearing. Or my mother-in-law's button. They're a factor, absolutely.

The voting process itself was the only controversy I heard. Some of my fellow Americans were solidly against voting because then they would really be Americans and subject, maybe, to some American taxes. I listened to them carefully, measured what I received in every country around the world for the taxes I've paid there, and then cheerfully voted.

But, even the voting was hollow. Instead of closing the curtain, I sealed the envelope. Instead of smiling at my next door neighbor poll-watcher, I raised my right hand to a stranger. And instead of rushing back home to see it counted on TV, I mailed it and waited three weeks for a count.

Then came election day. I turned on the radio only to be reminded that today in Tokyo is really yesterday and that I'd have to wait for tomorrow.

Tomorrow came and still no excitement. First word, as always was from Dixville Notch in New Hampshire. They were 16 to 3 for Nixon. Then CBS gave the election to Nixon. So did NBC and ABC. Before breakfast was over, the election was over. Only the local military radio station here didn't concede, and — as far as I know — they still haven't. That provided the only spark of excitement.

Anyway, it's over. I made my choice without posters, buttons, bumper stickers, conventions, baby kissing, knishes, political jokes, Agnew, sky writing, liquor store and bar closings — nothing. It was really dull. For the first time, I was forced to make my selection based entirely on the candidates' records and their platforms.

And, wherever I am in 1976, I'm going to do the same thing.


# OVER THERE, THE PEOPLE ROB
# THE SUPERMARKETS


He just started up the conversation with one of those semi-exasperated "Well?"

Now I'm seldom sure what an Occidental is getting at with a "Well?" opener, and I've been in Tokyo long enough to realize that I *never* know what a Japanese means to kick-off when *he* says "Well?"

And since at that particular moment I was riding west on the Koshukaido Highway with one of the first native friends I made after coming to Japan, I decided to counter with a zippy "Well, *what?*"

"Certainly," he said, you've read that Prime Minister Tanaka will visit your President Nixon in Washington later this month."

I had to admit that, indeed, I did read about the upcoming trip. "So what?" I asked. "What do you want me to say?"

His semi-exasperation seemed to be rushing headlong toward *total* exasperation as he said, "Well, you took it upon yourself a couple of weeks ago to write a lot of advice to Nixon when you thought he was coming to

Japan. Don't you think you owe the same service to Tanaka San to guide him through his stay in your country."

"I can't even *speak* enough Japanese to give any advice to Mr. Tanaka," I admitted, "much less write him a letter."

"You don't have to," he assured me. "Just tell me what I ought to say and *I'll* write the leter."

"I don't know if I should," I thought out loud.

"What do you mean 'you don't know'?" he steamed. "You've been a guest in this country for almost three years. The least you can do is reciprocate by performing this small service for your host."

I dislike digressing, but I do get a little uptight when somebody — anybody — refers to my status here as that of a "guest." And that was particularly so that day since this "guest" was just twenty-four hours away from offering some of that reciprocation in the form of the first quarterly payment on next year's Japanese Income Tax.

But that wasn't what prompted my "I don't know" anyway. I was merely thinking that I will be going back to the U.S.A. someday and I was wondering if giving advice to Mr. Tanaka on how to approach his Washington visit might get my name on some list in the White House.

Then I decided, what the hell. I've been on people's lists before. How else would I have been sent to Tokyo?

"O.K.," I decided. "Take this down."

He pulled one of those ever-present black Japanese note books from his inside pocket and said, "Go."

First off, I told him, I think Mr. Tanaka should bring his wife this time.

And, bringing Mrs. Tanaka to Washington will give her a chance to size up Pat on her home grounds. Surely Pat will show her around the house — on Pennsylvania Avenue as well as at Key Biscayne, Camp David and San Clemente.

That will give her a good idea of what Pat's like and what sort of furniture and knick-knacks she likes. Then, when Pat comes here, she might be able to skip the shopping trip to the Oriental Bazaar and go right over to Isetan Department Store. Who knows?

Chances are, Julie won't be anywhere around the White House — or the other houses. So I told my friend to tell Mr. Tanaka not to ask about her. If he wants Julie's opinion or anything, he should ask the President's Press Secretary directly.

And, if Mr. Tanaka wants to make an issue out of Nixon's embargo on soybeans and what it's doing to the Tofu industry here, for God's sake take along a sample piece of Tofu. There's no point in his trying to describe it to Nixon.

Since Mr. Tanaka's new ambassador to the U.S. just left Tokyo, I told my friend to tell Mr. Tanaka not to bug the poor man about how things are going. There's nothing worse than a home office bugger. Especially when you're new and spending most of your time at language school anyhow.

I also advised my friend to have Mr. Tanaka ask Nixon to take him to the Washington Zoo to see our Pandas. And, while he's there, to tell Nixon how much healthier and bigger the U.S. Pandas look and how much nicer their zoo home is than the one the Japanese Pandas have up in Ueno. Mr. Nixon needs all the reassurance he can get these days.

Mr. Tanaka should also tell Mr. Nixon about all the Japanese are doing to help reverse the flow of dollars into Japan. But he *shouldn't* mention they're doing it by buying up Hawaii.

The Prime Minister should also be advised that all those "Keep to the Right" signs he'll see along the roads in Washington refer to traffic and are *not* placed there by demonstrators annoyed by what's happening in Japanese politics.

If Mr. Tanaka has to bring a gift to President Nixon — and I'm sure he does — make it a Kutani vase or a Hiroshige print, not any clever Japanese electronic transistorized gadget. Mr. Nixon is extremely sensitive to electronic transistorized gadgets these days.

And, no matter how well the children in Mr. Tanaka's family are doing in school, he should never mention the "Dean's list."

And, I suggested that Mr. Tanaka should keep his cool and not be upset about the contradictions he'll observe between the two cultures. Like, for instance, that in the U.S., the *people* rob the *supermarkets,* not the other way around like it is in Tokyo.

"That's it?" my friend asked after a long pause.

"No, there's one more thing," I added. "On the way in from the Airport to the White House, Mr. Tanaka *shouldn't* ask Mr. Nixon to drive him past Watergate."

"Should I ask Tanaka San to bring back anything for you, Maloney San?" my friend wondered.

"Yes," I dreamed, "ask him to bring back 360 yen for a dollar."


## PLEASE, TANAKA SAN, SEND BACK THE KEY

I don't know about the rest of you Americans here in Japan, but I'm personally relieved to see that Prime Minister Tanaka is safely back in Tokyo after his trip to the U.S.

Come to think of it, though, I guess Tanaka San is not really too safe in Tokyo these days. But you know what I mean. I knew he was going to Washington, but I didn't know that he planned to spend some time in New York and Chicago.

232

When I heard that news, I was afraid he might get mugged in Central Park, or something New Yorky like that, and set back Japan-American relations another row of soybeans.

Actually, it apparently worked out OK. After all, Mayor Lindsay gave Tanaka San the "Key to New York City." That was a very nice gesture, particularly since I've never read that Governor Minobe ever gave Tanaka San the Key to Tokyo. In fact, I'm not even sure Governor Minobe allows the Tokyo sanitation department to pick up the garbage over at the Prime Minister's house.

All, in all — from what I've read between the Watergate lines in the papers — Tanaka San's trip seemed to be a great success.

I am, however, slightly put out that he didn't take my advice and bring his wife. Pat must be muffed, too. She missed as a result, the duck dinner for Tanaka San at the White House.

The stories about why the dinner was duck instead of beef were confusing. One story was that Pat's butcher refused to deliver the beef she ordered because he was mad over President Nixon's Phase Four thing. Another story was that there was no steak in Washington because the Japanese meat packers had bought up all the cattle last week.

We'll probably never know the real reason until they release the tapes of the phone conversation between the butcher and the White House cook.

One of the local newspapers described the Prime Minister as "startled" when he saw duck instead of sirloin steak. I hope that "startled" doesn't mean he's going to send out for Soba noodles when and if Mr. Nixon comes to Japan.

Anyway, if he lets bygones be bygones and serves Mr. Nixon sirloin steak, Tanaka San will be a little more than "startled" when he gets the bill.

Another thing I can't let go without comment is the Prime Minister's Chicago speech. He told Mayor Daley and his group, one paper reported, that the Japanese people like Midwestern beef as much as midwesterners like Japanese cameras.

Now I don't want to take issue with Tanaka San over his remark, but I must say that my fellow Americans are always bugging me to bring them back Japanese cameras when I go over on home leave. I'm still waiting, however, for the first Japanese person to ask me to bring back midwestern beef from the U.S.

Hershey Bars, yes. Johnnie Walker Black Label, yes. Even Papayas. But midwestern beef? *Never.*

Tanaka San also said in the U.S. that he was planning to place the Japanese economy on a more stable basis by limiting the annual growth rate here to about 10 per cent. I do hope he was including the Aoyama supermarket prices' growth rate.

Also, at his San Francisco stop, Tanaka San was quoted as saying that he "felt like he was back in Japan already." Now I never miss a chance to stop in San Francisco myself. And while I'm there, I feel many things. But, feel like I was back in Japan already? Hardly, If he was in Hawaii when he said that, I would have understood.

Anyway, what really concerns me is the visit to New York. Especially the fact that, while handing the City's Key to the Prime Minister, Mayor Lindsay referred to Tokyo as New York's "sister city."

Mayor Lindsay went on, to point out this "sister city" relationship, that New York has "more than 70 Japanese restaurants." For my money, that makes New York a "father city." That's because I don't think Tokyo itself *has* 70 Japanese restaurants. Seventy French restaurants, maybe. Maybe even more than 70 Italian restaurants.

Hell, I think I've counted more than 70 McDonald hamburger stands in Tokyo and certainly there are over 70 Kentucky Fried Chicken places in town.

And, if being a "sister city" of New York means I have to be afraid from now on to walk through Hibiya Park at night, I don't want any part of it.

And, does "sister city" mean that from now on we'll have garbage strikes here at the same time we have slowdowns on the subway and trains the way they do in New York?

Or, does it mean that we are going to have policemen riding all the subways? Where are we going to put them?

Of course, on the other hand, maybe being a "sister city" of New York will be that taxi drivers are going to stop and pick us up at night. But maybe that luxury will be offset by making us open the taxi doors ourselves the way they do in New York.

And maybe it means that we'll get a couple of pro football teams like the Giants and the Jets. That would be terrific.

But it could also mean that our electricity would go off every other day during the summer.

I suppose there are a lot of good things and bad things to say about having Tokyo become a "sister city" of New York. However, after only skimming the surface of the whole idea, I have one thing to say to Prime Minister Tanaka:

Please, send back the key.


## THERE *MUST* BE A WAY

Some time ago — while we were on a trip to Kyushu, I think — we visited an aquarium someplace. Near the aquarium entrance, in the rack where all the pretty pamphlets were, there was one in English. I read it. In there, it mentioned that the Emperor himself was quite a Marine Biologist and really knew what everything under the deep blue seas was all about.

I bring this up because last week, I finally received my January copy of "Audobon" magazine. "Audobon" is the official publication of the National Audobon Society in the United States. That Society is — as you might have guessed — primarily interested in birds. But now, their concern seems to cover all sorts of wildlife, whether on land or sea, and anything connected with the preservation of natural resources.

For instance, in the January issue, they had a cartoon that shows two cavemen. One is smiling and staring at a pile of burning twigs in front of him. Black smoke is rising from those twigs. The second caveman is chipping some prehistoric writing on a big clay tablet. This second caveman is asking, "How should I refer to you in the chronicle, as the discoverer of fire, or as the first man to pollute the atmosphere?"

Now I don't subscribe to "Audobon" because of the birds *or* the cartoons. I subscribe merely to receive copies of what I think is the most beautiful magazine ever published.

There are always plenty of great color pictures of wild animals and gorgeous scenery. And, since it's printed on one of the machines our company manufactures, I find it a great help in demonstrating the printing quality of that machine to the Japanese.

But, so much for the digression and back to the Emperor.

This January edition let off with a thing about birds, all right, but almost all of the rest of the issue was about "Life in a Cold Ocean". And *that* story included pages and pages of some of the greatest color pictures I've ever seen of all kinds of fish — from goldfish to starfish — in their natural habitats.

The first person I thought of was the Emperor. I'll bet, I thought, that he's never *seen* pictures *that* good about part of this world he obviously loves so much.

And, since his trip to the USA has been put off till who-knows-when (the Japanese Ambassador in Washington certainly doesn't know), he may never get to see "Audobon" on the newstands anywhere. Chances are he doesn't subscribe, either.

So, I decided I'd send him my copy of the January issue. That should be, I thought, a fairly simple chore. I just handed it to my secretary and said, "Please, clip my business card on the cover and mail this to the Emperor." Then, I forgot about it.

About an hour later, she brought it back. "I can't find his address," she said.

"Look it up in the phone book," I advised.

"I did. He doesn't have a telephone," she replied.

"Wait a minute," I said. And, I turned to the various directories I keep around the office. Right away, I decided that he didn't belong to the American Club or the Press Club. There was no sense in looking there.

And chances are slim that any of his kids are still young enough to be attending St. Mary's or Sacred Heart or ASIJ or any of those schools, so I skipped their parent directories.

I did look through the big Japan Times Directory, but nothing there either.

"Just put it in an envelope, addressed to him and I'll drop it in his mail box on the way home," I decided.

I should have known better. That afternoon, I circled his palace twice. And, I stopped at every gate. No mailbox.

I tried to leave it at one of the police boxes by the gate on the Yotsuya side, but no go. The policeman never goes in, he says, and he's never seen the Emperor go out. So, he was in no mood to accept responsibility for delivery.

Next, I ran alongside a couple of men jogging around the Palace dressed in red undershirts and white shorts with their headband tied in back. Neither of them, in their daily jogging trips around the moat, remembered seeing a mailbox at any of the gates either.

So, I flagged a taxi. "Did anybody ever," I asked the driver, "hand you a piece of paper or a card with the Emperor's address on it?"

"Of course not," he snapped, "I *know* where the Emperor lives."

"So do I," I told him. "But, I don't know the address."

"*That's* different," he smiled. "Usually you foreigners know the *address* of where you want to go, but you don't know *where* it is."

I explained my problem as best I could. He listened — his smile getting broader every minute.

"Why don't you," he suggested, "wait until his birthday and deliver it in person. They open the Palace, you know, on April 29 and you can go in."

"I've done that before, but you only get to wave as you walk by his window — quite a long way from the window, at that."

A little draw of air through the teeth and he was gone.

And here I am with this beautiful magazine that I know the Emperor would love to see.

Anybody got any ideas?


## THIS TIME NEXT YEAR, YOU COULD BE IN THE U.S.

You know how the Japanese beam all over when they talk about their shrines, temples, Mt. Fuji, sushi, the Bullet Train, and so on.

But don't let this beaming fool you. The first love of every fine, upstanding Japanese is statistics. I mean when I see a Japanese businessman reading some table or chart of statistics, I feel I shouldn't be watching.

Initials like "PPM" and "GNP" are special favorites. Some of these statistics must be real pleasant for them to peruse, like the projected 15.8% growth in their economy I read about the other day.

Others, such as the report I saw that some town around Tokyo with a population of only 15,000 manages to produce 15,000 tons of garbage a day, must be terrifying.

Some — ones that the Japanese look at as neither necessarily reassuring nor frightening, only confusing — cause no end of troubles.

For instance, mark my wards, *somebody* is going to have to resign from someplace over that chart that was put out showing that eating such-and-such number of fish each week is only slightly less effective than shooting one's self in the temple with a howitzer.

I saw one statistic the other day, that really took me back — back to 1950, anyway — and turned on all kinds of wonderment. I'll tell you all about it.

It seems that most Japanese companies hire people only once a year — in April. Since a Japanese worker picks a company when he first gets out of school and stays with it forever, there's nothing here like the rather constant job-hopping that goes on back in the U.S.

Of course, there *are* exceptions in both countries. I know an American (my father) who retired from the same company he joined when he graduated from school. And, I even know a Japanese who claims he knows another Japanese who changed jobs once. That report, however, is unconfirmed.

Anyway, I read someplace that the recruiting of employes for next April is already underway at full steam. Because, the report added, in April there will be 2.1 new jobs for every available new worker.

Now since no Japanese is likely to take more than 1.0 jobs for openers, it's likely 1.1 jobs could go begging.

Seems to me this is quite a switch for Japan. My personal observation since I've been here has given me the impression that there are 2.1 people doing every 1.0 job. Especially in department stores. I *could* be mistaken.

Be that as it may, the companies are concerned. Some students, I read, have already received mailed pleadings from as many as 200 companies. One company alone sent out some 20,000 letters to prospective April employes. Another company, who needs only 300 new employes, mailed letters to 10,000 students.

But one thing about all this recruiting really set me thinking back to my school days. That was a report saying that one company had mailed tape cassettes to graduating students.

On that cassette, the report said, a girl's voice says "I want you to know about my firm. Why don't you apply? You might be in the United States on an overseas assignment for us by this time next year . . . "

As I read that my thoughts raced back to Teaneck, N.J. and to my high school senior year — 1944 — and to a recruiter who approached me and promised that, if I would join his organization, I might be in Japan by that time the following year. Come to think of it, though, "enlist" might be a more accurate word than "join."

I grabbed his offer, but I never did make it to Japan — not until 26 years later, anyway. And *not* with that recruiter's organization.

Anyhow, then I began thinking about the year I finished college. At that time, there were certainly no 2.1 jobs waiting for me. For all I know, the U.S. national average back then *might* have been 2.1 jobs for every applicant.

But, if it was, nobody was offering 2.1 jobs to me. In fact, as I recall the situation, I would have been happy with .5 of a job. Finally, I did take a 1.0 job with the railroad, editing their employee and stockholder magazines. The pay, however, was only .5.

Anyway — back to the report and the cassette tape. After I read it, I began thinking of what my reaction would have been right after college to a promise of being "in Japan on an overseas assignment at this time next year."

After rolling around that thought for awhile, I decided my answer would have been a certain "No." I wasn't really very adventurous in those days.

After all, I was married and the first daughter had already arrived. We had our own car and a nice place to live.

Still, 26 years later, when I was still married, had four kids instead of one, had an even nicer place to live and *two* cars, I jumped at the chance for "an overseas assignment in Japan."

I learned a lot in those 26 years. Almost as much as I've learned during the last three years here in Japan.

The point is, I'm still chuckling about that report. While I haven't personally heard the cassette tape they were talking about in the story, I wouldn't be a bit surprised if the girl who recorded it works for my company back in Cleveland.

That's because they are always telling me that, if everything goes right here in Japan, "by this time next year, you could be *back* in the United States *from* your overseas assignment."

There's only one problem:  Nothing here *ever* goes right.

# GOMEN NASAI — IN TRIPLICATE

If you live and work right downtown and can walk to all the bank openings, visiting firemen cocktail parties and the Wednesday night movies at the American Club, you probably have never run into the local police department's booze blockades.

Or, if you live and work out in the rice paddies and don't give a damn whose bank is opening, save your newly-acquired Oriental charm for only your very own visiting fireman, and can skip another look at the Wednesday movies that you already saw back in Cleveland a couple of years ago on later-night TV, you have probably never made the run for the Four Roses, either.

But, when Wife Sarah and I were "Real Japaning" it out in Kamikitazawa, we jumped in the Toyota and bumper-to-bumpered into Tokyo at the drop of an RSVP. We never cared whose bank was liberalized, where the fireman was visiting from, or how many times we had seen the Walt Disney movie. After all, ignoring such happenings could cancel out 96.8% of Tokyo Gaijins' social life.

Coming into town was always rather uneventful — save for the normal challenge of survival while driving among the Kamikazes.

Because I always had to drive back home when festivities were over, I hit the hors d'oeuvres and vinegared cucumbers pretty heavy and limited my liquid intake to Pepsi-Cola or iced tea. Wife Sarah — in her passenger status — was quite free, of course, to wash everything down with Old Granddad Manhattans.

Now the Tokyo police are quite annoyed with people who drive after they've had something alcoholic to drink. And, I thank them from the bottom of my bucket seat for that. It's exciting enough on the roads around here with *sober* people behind the wheels.

In order to occasionally express their annoyance directly to the imbibers, the police set up roadblocks at night on the streets that lead out of town. I know the routine quite well, since I've been pulled over at least once for every bank opening, fireman party and old movie.

They wave every driver — except taxis — over to the side of the road. I can't imagine why they skip the taxis, unless they agree with my theory that drinking could, at the worst, improve their driving.

Anyway, when the policeman gets you into his net, he very politely asks for your driver's license and casually sticks his head in your window to get a whiff of your breath. At least, I *think* he asks for my driver's license. Whatever it is he says, that's what I give him.

And, just in case a gaze into my baby blue eyes and a look at my non-gold teeth doesn't tip him off, one of the lines on my driver's license tells

239

him I'm a Gaijin. As hard as they might try to keep their cool at such a discovery, I always spot a sukoshi panic setting in at the news.

However, they always recover quickly and long enough to ask for something else. Repeated encounters tell me now that this second request is for my Alien Registration. It doesn't really matter either, because that's what I always give him.

Usually, that's all there is to it. The policeman then gives everything back, bows slightly, and waves me on. Once in awhile, however, I did run into a regular viewer of the TV Educational Channel. In those cases, they usually manage an English question or two before the bow and wave-on. Also in those cases, the most popular question goes something like "You drinku some whis-su-key?"

Like I said before, when driving I always stick to the Pepsi and the iced tea, so I never worry about the breath test. What really worries me, though, is that I might some day forget that Alien Registration at home. Then what, I wondered.

Well, now I know what — second-hand, thank heavens.

The other night, Son Sean was coming home late from a non-bank opening with some of his fellow students at Tokyo's Waseda University. He got off the train at Meguro and started to walk over to the taxi stand.

As he passed the police box, he gave a little bow. The policeman standing in the doorway bowed back, and invited Son Sean into his office. May I, he asked, see your Alien Registration? Instantly, Son Sean remembered he'd left it on his bureau at home. And, with a smile, that's what he told the policeman.

Without a smile, the policeman — now joined by three others — asked a whole lot more questions. After about an hour, they allowed him the traditional one phone call. It was now after midnight, and the ringing got Wife Sarah out of bed. I heard nothing. Wife Sarah got the story and yanked Daughter Barbara out of bed, since she's our resident Japanese language expert, stuffed the forgotten Alien Registration into her purse and took off for Meguro.

Daughter Barbara explained that Wife Sarah really *was* the mother, and turned over the little brown Alien Registration book. But, that wasn't the end. They put Son Sean in a police car — with four policemen — and whisked him off to headquarters.

Wife Sarah was told to follow in her car. Once at headquarters, Wife Sarah had to sign a group of those "Sorry, and I won't do it again" forms on behalf of Son Sean. And, Son Sean got a "We'll let you go this time" — according to Daughter Barbara, anyway.

They finally got back home about 2:30 a.m. That's what I heard, anyhow. I slept through it all. I got the details the next morning at breakfast. Wife Sarah poured my tea and told all.

"There were," she started, "ten million stories in the Naked City last night. I'm going to tell you just one of them . . . ."

## TWO STORIES DOWN, 10,999,998 TO GO

If it's true, as they used to say on that old TV program about New York police, that "there are eight million stories in the Naked City" — then there must be 11 million daily stories in this Naked City of Tokyo.

What's beginning to get to me is that more and more lately, we Maloneys wind up as one or more of those stories and spend all or part of an evening in one or more of the local police boxes.

Now a police box — you *have* to call it a "box"; they're never big enough to be called a "station" — in Japan is usually a place about one-third the size of the local tobacco store. It usually can be spotted by the little blinking red light and "wanted" posters out front and has two or three white bicycles parked out back.

I digress for a moment, but those "wanted" posters remind me of something. I worry that someday I might witness a crime around here and that, later, the police will ask me to describe the man who did it. What could I say? Black hair? Not too tall? Dark brown eyes?

How in the world do they sort out the crooks in Japan?

But, back to the police box.

Anyway, sometimes when we wind up in those police boxes, we are innocent bystanders. Sometimes, innocent doesn't accurately describe our situation. I'll give you a sample of each.

On the innocent bystander side, Daughter Barbara was changing trains in Shinjuku the other night when she spotted this little brown wallet on the platform.

It had all the little goodies that you might expect to find in little brown wallets anywhere:  some pictures, a commutation ticket, enough yen to buy dinner in Shinjuku for someone who was on a very strict diet, a couple of what looked like membership cards, driver's license, credit cards and a calendar.

Since Daughter Barbara couldn't think of any better way to get the little brown wallet to its rightful owner, she decided to simply drop it off at the police box in Shinjuku Station.

Now, assuming that you could do anything like that "simply" was a serious error in judgement. Oh, the policeman took the little brown wallet OK. But, it wasn't going to be "Thank you" and that's that.

Exactly where did she find it? Why did she pick it up? What was *she* doing in Shinjuku if she didn't live or work there? What was her name and where did she live? Can we see your Alien Registration? The questions went on.

And, since fortunately — or unfortunately, depending how you look at it — Daughter Barbara handles Japanese better that the average Gaijin person, she answered them all and finally broke loose.

A couple of days later, a local version of Cleveland's May Company delivered an oversized box of chocolates to the house addressed to Daughter Barbara. The sender was listed as someone she never heard of before. The sender's telephone number was there, too. Curiosity got the best of me and I finally convinced her to call and see why the chocolates.

Turns out they were a sweet "Thanks" from the little girl who lost the little brown wallet.

Our other police box story last week featured Son Sean — a far from innocent bystander. And the story doesn't end with any box of chocolates, either.

We received a phone call the other night about eight o'clock. Son Sean had taken Wife Sarah's car to an evening meeting at school. The caller was a policeman near the school who said the car was parked where it blocks a man's driveway and we'd better get there to move it, like right now.

We couldn't call the villian, Son Sean, so we apologized and took off in the other car. I won't tangle you in the details of why we never found the place where the car was parked. You can fill those in yourself.

Around nine o'clock we called home and, sure enough, Son Sean had returned home.

Yes, he said, he guessed he was blocking somebody where he was parked. Evidence was a colorful slip of paper that was glued to his windshield.

The police box that called earlier left their number and so Son Sean called them. No, it wasn't a ticket — just a warning. *But,* he'd have to come in the morning and apologize to the policeman who would be in the box then, *and* an apology to the man with the blocked driveway was also listed as mandatory.

Next morning, Son Sean set out on his rounds but had no better luck finding the police box than I did the night before. Finally in the afternoon, he did. And, he apologized. Then, he said to the policeman, let's go see the blocked driveway man.

No, said the man in blue, that was no longer mandatory. It seems that the night before — without telling the policemen — that man had removed Wife Sarah's registration and gasoline credit card from the car to insure that Son Sean would return. They knew that to be true, because he delivered them to the box just before Son Sean arrived.

Now, the policemen decided, they *really* had a justice-dispensing problem. Son Sean *shouldn't* have blocked the man's driveway. The man

242

*shouldn't* have removed the stuff from the car. But, Son Sean *shouldn't* have driven the car home the previous night without the registration in the car.

The fact that Son Sean claimed he didn't *know* the registration wasn't there didn't cut any raw fish with the police. He should have looked.

Many alternatives were discussed.

Son Sean's apology was definitely ruled out. After another consensus, an original decision that he should press charges on the man who removed the registration was reversed. And Son Sean was *not* sent to the local substitute for Alcatraz for driving without the registration.

Finally, he was released on a promise never to block or drive registrationless again.

I'd like to end all this by saying that Son Sean drove right down to Ginza and bought a couple of boxes of chocolates to send to that police box and to the blocked driveway man.

But, I'm afraid Wife Sarah won't let him take the car any more.

# X. NO MORE LITTLE WHITE —
## OR YELLOW —LIES

Even without the football games, I can tell we're up to here in Fall. After all, the sweet potato man is back with his loudspeaker and — I assume — his hot sweet potatoes. And, the morning sun is coming up much later than the summer-style 3:45 a.m.

Most unmistakable Fall sign of all, however, is the higher than average number of home office visitors.

It's not really those home office visitors themselves I want to talk about today, but the initial reactions of the first-time-ever-in-Japan variety.

Invariably, one of the first observations they make comes out like "Gee, where are all the girls in Kimonos I expected?" And, before they pack up to return home, they eventually express their disappointment at not seeing rock gardens, Geisha girls, Mt. Fuji, cherry blossoms and rickshaws.

Of course, this newcomer disappointment with the Real Japan of today isn't only limited to the home office crowd. The genuine tourists I talk to — most recently Wife Sarah's sister — felt the same way.

Most of the problem, I fear, stems from the little white lies about Japan that are repeated over and over again in an effort, apparently, to conjure up an image of a Japan that once was but isn't any more. Not for the ordinary visitor to see, anyway. He just normally doesn't get to that other real Japan of Yesteryear. (Under our Oriental circumstances here, I guess you really should call them little 'yellow' lies)

Oh, they come close when they go down to the cities Kyoto and Nara, I guess. They do see the old temples and the expansive gardens and the quaint neighborhoods. But, they go from temple to garden to shrine in a big Diesel bus full of other foreigners. And they sleep in the Holiday Inn and snack at a McDonald's hamburger stand and eat in a French restaurant at night.

They're hell-bent, apparently, to see as much of this assumed Oriental Paradise as they can. But, as they rush from one supposed asset of Japan to the other, I'm afraid they miss Number One. And, unfortunately, so do most of the foreigners who live here for an extended period for one reason or another.

And that Number One "Living National Treasure" of Japan I'm thinking about are the Japanese people themselves. For my money, *they* are what make Japan unique.

Not the Mt. Fuji you seldom see (and it's mantle of beer cans when you *can* see it). And *not* the cherry blossoms that last only a few days. And *not* the gardens that are about as plentiful as Soba noodle shops in Cleveland.

Just the people.

People like the policeman in Shibuya who parked his bicycle and led me by the hand for two blocks the other night to show me the A&W Root Beer shop we were looking for.

People like the school teacher I called by mistake one middle of the night when I meant to call the local automobile club to bring gasoline for my

245

stalled car. Even when we both discovered my dialing error, he insisted he'd get dressed and deliver a can of gas.

People who volunteer to help translate for me when they see my attempts at Nihongo carrying me to certain disaster.

People like the storekeeper in Shinjuku who didn't have the kind of typewriter ribbon I wanted and stopped what he should have been doing to make a least a dozen phone calls until he found a place that *did* have it.

People like the taxi driver who won't give up asking anybody he sees for directions in order to get me where the note I gave him said I wanted to go.

People like the woman I dragged out in front of a Soda shop one day to show her the plastic model in the window representing the dish I wanted to order. It wasn't until we both got back inside that I found out she was a customer, too — not a waitress. But she smiled and ordered for me.

People like the Shinkansen conductor who found me a seat even though my ticket was for a train that left an hour earlier.

All this doesn't mean that these aren't part of the same groups of people who push me on and off subway trains. And try to run me off the road in my car.

But, we have plenty of those aggravating people back in Cleveland, too.

What I'm trying to get around to is to tell you of a small pledge I've made to myself. From now on, to hell with taking my visitors to Meiji Shrine, Mt. Fuji, and Kyoto. I'm not going to participate any longer in promoting the little lies, whatever color they are.

I'm going to make sure that the newcomers somehow get to meet the people here — no matter how hard both sides will probably resist. It's not going to be easy, but I think I've figured it out.

While they are with me, I'm going to run out of gas, get lost, give the taxi driver a bad map, and go into the wrong store.

All of that comes naturally to me in Tokyo, anyway.